D1825829

Badiou and the Political Condition

Critical Connections

A series of edited collections forging new connections between contemporary critical theorists and a wide range of research areas, such as critical and cultural theory, gender studies, film, literature, music, philosophy and politics.

Series Editors
Ian Buchanan, University of Wollongong
James Williams, University of Dundee

Editorial Advisory Board

Nick Hewlett
Gregg Lambert
Todd May
John Mullarkey
Paul Patton
Marc Rölli
Alison Ross
Kathrin Thiele
Frédéric Worms

Titles available in the series

Badiou and Philosophy, edited by Sean Bowden and Simon Duffy
Agamben and Colonialism, edited by Marcelo Svirsky and
     Simone Bignall
Laruelle and Non-Philosophy, edited by John Mullarkey and
     Anthony Paul Smith
Virilio and Visual Culture, edited by John Armitage and Ryan Bishop
Rancière and Film, edited by Paul Bowman
Stiegler and Technics, edited by Christina Howells and Gerald Moore
Badiou and the Political Condition, edited by Marios Constantinou

Forthcoming titles

Butler and Ethics, edited by Moya Lloyd
Nancy and the Political, edited by Sanja Dejanovic

Visit the Critical Connections website at
www.euppublishing.com/series/crcs

Badiou and the Political Condition

Edited by Marios Constantinou

EDINBURGH
University Press

© editorial matter and organisation Marios Constantinou, 2014
© the chapters their several authors, 2014

Edinburgh University Press Ltd
22 George Square, Edinburgh EH8 9LF

www.euppublishing.com

Typeset in 11/13 Adobe Sabon by
Servis Filmsetting Ltd, Stockport, Cheshire,
and printed and bound in Great Britain by
CPI Group (UK) Ltd, Croydon CR0 4YY

A CIP record for this book is available from the British Library

ISBN 978 0 7486 7879 2 (hardback)
ISBN 978 0 7486 7880 8 (paperback)
ISBN 978 0 7486 7881 5 (webready PDF)
ISBN 978 0 7486 7882 2 (epub)

The right of the contributors to be identified as Author of this work has been
asserted in accordance with the Copyright, Designs and Patents Act 1988, and
the Copyright and Related Rights Regulations 2003 (SI No. 2498).

Contents

To Ellipolis, my daughter, for having realised prematurely the distinction between *politico* and *diplomatico*. I hope one day she with her friends will be able to resolve the crisis of witnessing so much stupidity in their lives.

Preface

This book rethinks the singularity of the political condition in the wake of Badiou's philosophical rupture. By way of genealogical investigations, expositions and reactualisations, the present collection of essays retraces the intellectual strands and intensities of thought that weave together the Badiouian *political knot*. These range from Epicurean materialism and Platonic communism to Xenophon's philosophic warriorship as anti-imperial thought in action; from Paulian universalism and Pascalian existentialism to Rousseauean republicanism, Marxian anthropology and Wagner's aristocratic populism; from Althusser's neo-Epicurean materialism and Maoist anti-imperialism to Lacanian psychoanalysis and militant musicology; from the aesthetic vanguards to May '68, and from the Cultural Revolution to the politics of the love-event. This manifold constellation of Badiou's political thought, patiently and incisively examined, casts new light on the singularity of the political condition after the return of the subject as a novel philosophical concept and militant wager.

Moreover, this book assesses the political import of Badiou's philosophical challenge in the light of the current imperial impasse in southern Europe and the contradictory awakening of History in the Middle East and the eastern Mediterranean. A cohort of established scholars and rising theorists of the Badiou-effect engage the critical question of 'how to transmit the exception' politically, at the intersection of contemporary anti-imperial polemics and debates that strike at the heart of the postmodern condition (Lyotard), deconstruction (Derrida), psychoanalysis (Lacan–Žižek), biopolitics (Hardt and Negri) and pedagogy (Rancière).

In terms of its general conceptualisation, the theoretical praxis of this book adheres closely to the political knot that ties being

Socrates: 'Λέγεται γοῦν, ὦ Φαῖδρε, δίκαιον εἶναι καὶ τὸ τοῦ λύκου εἰπεῖν.' (Even the wolf, you know, Phaedrus, has a right to an advocate, as they say.) (*Phaedrus* 272c)

We must conceive of imperialist society not only as a substance but also as a subject. (Badiou 2009b: 42)

Introduction

Forcing Politics: Badiou's Anabasis in the Age of Empire

Marios Constantinou

From the Crisis of Negation to Political Affirmation

For Badiou, politics is an exceptional creation in its own right. It is a self-ruling procedure for which philosophy cannot provide an ethical ground or foundation in advance. Philosophy can only think retroactively in terms of the consequences of politics and its evental structure. It cannot invent politics but can disclose as afterthought the emancipatory truth of its procedure. It can disambiguate this event of politics by unmasking sophistic usurpations that eliminate its singularity and obscure its possibility of becoming a condition of philosophy. In other words, what sustains the philosophical idea of justice are the egalitarian incarnations of politics. Philosophy remains a futile exercise insofar as it refuses to cut across the intellectual quagmire that obscures singular affirmations of politics by superimposing stereotypes and equivocations, and insofar as it does not dare to name the emancipatory stakes of justice in the wake of such politics: 'Sartre and Althusser are very different even opposed. But you can reconcile them on one point, namely, that philosophy is nothing if it is not linked to political commitment' (Badiou 2008g: 647).

And yet, despite Badiou's profound respect for the revolutionary tradition, his acknowledgement of the singular institutional accomplishments and organisational inventions of the communist movement, he critically dismisses the orthodox pillars and grand narratives of Marxism-Leninism. The 'vanguard class party', the 'Socialist state', the 'People's Republic', the 'People's Army', even the trade unions are considered 'saturated and exhausted' (Badiou 2008g: 649). The Anarchist critique of centralisation-hierarchisation, the Trotskyite critique of the bureaucratic Thermidor, the Maoist critique of Revisionism were all alarming premonitions of what Badiou calls the crisis of the negative, pointing in the long term towards a new idea of politics without a party as well as at a distance from the state. The party–state model 'solved the problem of the nineteenth century, but we have to solve those of the twenty-first' (Badiou 2008g: 649). Marxism-Leninism and its master concepts are therefore disqualified from Badiou's reconceptualisation of the political as a constituent condition of contemporary philosophy. Having been the victorious real of the twentieth century, the empirical compensation for the failed proletarian attempts and massacres of June 1848 and the Paris Commune, Marxism-Leninism operated as the political subject of the effective act par excellence, of victory as the transcendental theme that determines even failure itself (Badiou 2007: 58). Badiou epitomises the lesson of the Marxist-Leninist century as follows:

> The consequence of these theses is that politics can be defined therein as an assault against the State, whatever the mode of that assault might be, peaceful or violent. It 'suffices' for such an assault to mobilize the singular multiples against the normal multiples by arguing that excrescence is intolerable. However, if the government and even the material substance of the State apparatus can be overturned or destroyed; even if, in certain circumstances it is politically useful to do so, one must not lose sight of the fact that the State as such – which is to say the re-securing of the one over the multiple of parts (or parties) – cannot be so easily attacked or destroyed. Scarcely five years after the October Revolution, Lenin, ready to die, despaired over the obscene permanence of the State. Mao himself, more phlegmatic and more adventurous, declared – after twenty-five years in power and ten years of the Cultural Revolution's ferocious tumult – that not much had changed after all. This is because even if the route of political change – and I mean the route of the radical dispensation of justice – is always bordered by the State, it cannot in any way let itself be guided by the latter, for the State is precisely non-political, insofar as it cannot change, save hands, and it is well known that there is little strategic signification in such a change. It is not antagonism which lies at the origin of the State because one cannot think the dialectic of the void and excess as antagonism. No doubt politics itself must originate in the very same place as the State: in that dialectic. But this is certainly not in order to seize the State, nor to double the State's effect. On the contrary, politics takes its existence on its capacity to establish a relation to both the void and excess, which is essentially different from

that of the State; it is this difference alone that subtracts politics from the one of statist reinsurance. (2005a: 110)

What Badiou argues above is that the twentieth century's adventurous passion for a radical dispensation of justice failed because it underestimated the resilient, unmanageable and 'shellproof' character of the state, condensed in his cardinal formula of the 'errant excess'. Moreover, for Badiou the state is either a non-political or anti-political force, hence no change worthy of the name of justice can come about under its direction. Steered change under state tutelage bears little strategic significance because of its manipulable and simulated status: it doubles the state's effect. Consequently, politics is subtracted from the range of statist preview, protection, surveillance and so on. What could, then, be the organisational form of emancipatory politics in its post-Leninist, post-military, post-party creative restatement? How is Badiou responding to the failed passion of the last century delineated above, without sliding into the commonplaces of anarcho-pacifism?

The appealing power of the 'subtractive' model of politics at a distance from the State lies in its articulate empirical assumptions and promising prospects. For Badiou, any politics that is true to the name of justice appeals to a logic of destatification. Distance from the state 'protects political practices from being oriented, structured and polarized by the State'. For instance, 'when the State decides to call an election, to intervene in some conflict, declare war on another State. Or when the State claims that an economic crisis makes this or that course of action impossible. These are all examples of what I call convocations by the State, where the State sets the agenda and controls the timing of political events' (Badiou 2008g: 650). Badiou's conceptualisation of subtractive politics is meant to counteract what Louis Althusser had cogently illustrated as interpellative practices of the state. What Badiou calls state convocations are directly implicated in the constitution of a semblant subject, thus repeating creatively the Althusserian problematic of the subject as a recurrent process of disciplinary interpellation. Let us recall that this disciplinary loop of identification with state structures, norms of biopower, the effect of the psychoanalytic mirror stage and so on were not simply the privileged theoretical arcana afforded by individual philosophical figures such as Althusser, Foucault and Lacan, but were literally the cultural politics of French Maoism. Consider, for instance, Badiou's Maoist reading of Lacan which elucidates politically the operation of lack and the structure of interpellation, recast as a neurotic apparatus of 'irrational regulation', with the Superego being 'commandment stripped bare' (2009b: 146). Here anxiety enters catalytically the political formation of the subject:

> anxiety is that which does not deceive . . . As in Lacan's superb expression, anxiety is nothing but the lack of lack. But when lack comes to lack, its metonymic effect is interrupted and a mastery of real loss begins, paid for by the ravaging of all symbolic points of reference. Hence, anxiety never deceives. Destruction must reach the law of lack in order for the lure of deception, semblance and the oblivion of oblivion to be swept away. (2009b: 146)

Indeed, one could argue that if Althusser has added a psychoanalytic supplement to structural Marxism, thus counteracting Marcuse's 'humanist' synthesis of Freud and Marx, Badiou has added an improbable Maoist supplement to psychoanalysis, reinforced also by the late turn of Althusser to the Epicurean materialism of declension that 'eventalised' his structuralism of the earlier period. Althusser's later writings were collected under the telling title *Philosophy of the Encounter* (Althusser 2006). This aleatory materialism of the encounter where Mallarmé's dice throw meets the Epicurean swerve of the atoms randomly declining from the straight line in the void furnishes the philosophical ground for Badiou's recommencement of the dialectical materialism of the event. Consider this late and enlightening Althusserian fragment: 'History here is nothing but the permanent revocation of the accomplished fact by another undecipherable fact to be accomplished, without our knowing in advance, whether, or when, or how the event that revokes it will come about. Simply, one day new hands will have to be dealt out, and the dice thrown again on to the empty table' (Althusser 2006: 174). Epicurus' audacious materialism of the *clinamen* which posits the random swerve, not Reason, Unreason or any other prior meaning as the point of departure of any subjective process, is the driving force of Badiou's philosophical renewal of contemporary materialism as political thought of the event. This may also explain Badiou's sharp refinement of Pascal and the latter's critical relevance for the conceptualisation of the event. Not incidentally, Althusser too had noticed that Pascal in the seventeenth century had repeatedly overtured towards this materialist idea by introducing the void in terms of a theological wager on the existence of God (2006: 175). In the same vein, Badiou's philosophical materialism wagers on the existence of politics.

Yet Badiou attaches an important caveat which could be fateful to the dialectical theory of political negation. He argues that

> just as the party, which was once the victorious form of insurrection, is today outdated, so too is the dialectical theory of negation. It can no longer articulate a living link between philosophy and politics. In trying to clarify the political situation, we also need to search for a new formulation of the problem of critique and negation. I think that it is necessary, above all in the field of political action, to go beyond the concept of a negation taken solely in its destructive and properly negative aspect. Contrary to Hegel, for whom negation of the negation produces a new affirmation, I think we must assert that today negativity, properly speaking, does not create anything new. It destroys the old, of course, but does not give rise to a new creation. (2008g: 652)

Badiou's notion of subtractive politics is meant to be a response to this crisis of the Hegelian category of negation. All the same, when Badiou engages soberly with the development of a new type of contemporary negation, he thinks in terms 'of a new articulation of destruction and subtraction' (2008g: 653), precisely in order to avoid the problem of 'weak negation' which takes the form of biopolitics or what he calls 'democratic materialism'. Indeed, at moments Badiou attaches the subtractive form to the 'prepolitical gesture' of migration and the problem of unionising immigrants (2008g: 658). In other words, he inclines to classify the subtractive gestures addressed to profoundly atomised, destructured masses, the proletarianised poor, immigrants and so on into the category of the 'prepolitical' and the 'predisposition to politics'. For instance, subtraction from conditions of poverty regarding undocumented immigrants living in ghettos and suburbs is met with the complication of a split subjectivity not always willing to affirm the implied risks of politics, hence alternating between submission, corruption and 'doing whatever it takes to remain there', on the one hand, and the depressive melancholia of destructive negation on the other, as it was manifested in the French revolts of November 2005 (Badiou 2008g: 658). In this sense subtraction is a propaedeutic gesture, a prepolitical disposition that may or may not lead to a political sequence.

This is more or less the political measure by which Badiou considers the possibilities and openings exemplified by more structured and armed popular organisations such as Hezbollah in Lebanon, experimenting with the 'theologico-political' at obscure distance from the state, and Hamas in the Gaza Strip, operating halfway between an urban guerilla government and a religious welfare-foundation. Badiou acknowledges that, however experimental in the Zapatista fashion, sectarian, particularistic or localised these examples are, 'including those that might seem a little strange or foreign, strong but limited, they [still] must be taken into consideration' (2008g: 656). This may sound both gracious and condescending, even more so because they are the only existing examples that sustain a dialectical synthesis of subtraction and destruction, however much they depart from the norm. Even the Polish example of the *Solidarnosc* movement that appears closer to Badiou's political norm in the sense that it was non-proletarianised, structured, factory-based, self-organised, anti-party, subtractive from the state and so on, was nonetheless profoundly enmeshed in a strong Catholic and national particularity, patronised by the Pope and Western powers. Is this a symptom of the yet unconfessed fatality of reformist politics at a distance from the state? I think not. Badiou's conceptualisation of politics assumes risk, a heroic mastery of loss, and a militant crossing of lack by way of confrontation with all forms of surrogate politics and facilitative logics of governance. This is uncharacteristic of both the deconstructive deferral of politics as well as of current biopolitics. But it still remains an ambivalent gesture. I suggest that the most promising way of thinking through this question is by considering the trajectory of the concept of *forcing*.

The In-Tensity of Forcing and the Politics of *Im-passe*

Crossing the Leibnizian hypothesis: the errant state and the political subject

It has been remarked that Leibniz's thought was prodigiously modern, despite his stubborn error concerning mechanics, his hostility to Newton, his diplomatic prudence with regard to established powers, his conciliatory volubility in the direction of scholasticism, his taste for 'final causes', his restoration of singular forms or entelechies or his popish theology ... The thesis I propose is that Leibniz is able to demonstrate the most implacable inventive freedom once he has *guaranteed* the surest and most controlled ontological foundation – the one which completely accomplishes down to the last detail, the constructivist orientation ... What Leibniz absolutely rejects is chance – which he calls 'blind chance', exemplified for him, and quite rightly, in Epicurus' *clinamen* – if it means an event whose sense would have to be wagered. For any reason concerning such an event would be, in principle, insufficient ... Leibniz is the principal philosopher for whom God is the language in its supposed completion. (Badiou 2005a: 315, 316, 317)

Badiou's polemical reckoning with the symptomatic tensions of Leibnizian metaphysics, foregrounded as it is by anecdotal detail that illuminates the duplicity and failure of character, encapsulates the stakes and strains of Badiou's conceptualisation of politics as well. Here Badiou makes it lucidly clear that character and perspective are co-implicated. There is no perspective on truth or depth of fidelity or sequence without virtue. The scope of politics embraces unavoidably relentless polemics and extensive use of *ad hominem* arguments, as reflected in the above passage. To the extent that philosophy considers politics as one of its conditions then it is equally subject to this spectre of antagonism.

Badiou comes across duplicity as a political problem where else but in the *Theory of the Subject*. There he takes issue with the disabling implications of the Lacanian concept of lack and the necessity of a *crossing*:

A balancing, in an unclarified half-saying, of gain and loss: such is the outcome of any structural concept of the political subject. If it is possible to say anything more about it, it is only insofar as there is an effective *mastery of loss*. The objection being that it cannot be a question of form of knowledge, much less a recollection. So what is the mastery of loss? Marxism is teaching us that it is destruction. (2009b: 138, emphasis added)

Ever since, Badiou has struggled to balance between a condescending toleration of the sophist, as the incarnation of deflected thought on the one hand, and its constitutional expression on the other, namely, capitalo-parliamentarism, the errant duplicity of the state par excellence. The crossing of this limit, of this lack of being, is, in fact, the task of politics (and of the politics of destruction in particular) which Badiou occasionally feels the need to balance, or soften up equivocally, with his notion of subtraction. But this remains a strenuous gesture insofar as he maintains against all odds that there exists a constructivist continuum of corruption between the parliamentary apparatus and 'the *singleton*' summoned in elections (Badiou 2005a: 323). We should thus never lose sight of the political import and philosophical significance of Badiou's *ad hominem* meditations.

For Badiou, the Leibnizian metaphysics of God is the cardinal metaphor of this impasse of politics. The Leibnizian God 'is in reality, the complete language, he cannot tolerate this unnameable extra' (Badiou 2005a: 318). God is the global reason of this panlinguistic seriality that engulfs everything completely, in a causal chain of local approximations, thus excluding the event from its syntax. The subject implied by this constructivist enterprise is ultimately a grammatical subject that 'meets its limit in being unable to exceed it . . . a subject required by the absence of the event, by the impossibility of intervention' (Badiou 2005a: 323). All the same, what Badiou appears to be opposing to this Leibnizian figure of egoistic monadology is an equivocal subject. The Leibnizian subject 'whose concept is proposed in the end, is not the subject, *evasive and split*, which is capable of wagering the truth. All it can know is the form of its own Ego' (Badiou 2005a: 323, emphasis added). Badiou ends Meditation 30 on Leibniz with a wagering but evasive figure that reflects the aleatory structure of the postmodern condition. It turns out that this is not an entirely apolitical condition.

Interestingly, during the same year 1988 when Badiou was publishing in French his Meditations in *Being and Event*, a cardinal figure of the postmodern condition, Jean-François Lyotard, was publishing *The Inhuman*, engaging in concurrent and converging polemics against the 'Leibnizian hypothesis'. In this improbable doubling, the Leibnizian hypothesis appears as a Heideggerian *Gestell* that accomplishes metaphysics by explaining the world in terms of cause and effect and hence neutralising the event by rationalising the present (Lyotard 1993: 69).

A special tribute is certainly owed to this 'uncelebrated' political affinity between Badiou's thought and Lyotard's. This affinity is not simply eclectic but profound at moments, bearing in mind the 'extreme consequences' of an encounter between an ex-Trotskyite and an ex-Maoist, who not only worked through seminal breaks with their own traditions but, moreover, were separated by what Badiou called 'a political gulf' (2009d: 109). Despite Lyotard's attunement to Heidegger's hostility to the 'techno-scientific system', and despite Badiou's antipodean affirmation of science as one of the four cardinal conditions of philosophy – restricted so far only to the singular contributions of mathematics – this chasm could also be a political opening for thought. Both come to share considerable ground in their critical refutation of the 'Leibnizian hypothesis'.[1] The political implications of this refutation are pivotal for understanding the scope of Badiou's conceptualisation of politics under the aegis of *forcing* the *im-passe*.

Lyotard argues that the long-term normalising effect of the Leibnizian apparatus of rationalisation on the procedure of thought is that it denies the latter's passibility to the event. It forecloses the event by regulating or scanning its passibility and whatever subject happens from time to time to testify to its recurrent alterity (Lyotard 1993: 59). The fundamental metaphysical intuition that sustains this hypothesis, according to Lyotard, is the following. A virtual communication apparatus, the Leibnizian God, as 'the absolute monad in complete retention of the totality of information constituting the world', comes to embody the ideal of Western rationalism, an overwhelming monad of completeness, of saturated memory that subordinates the present to a predetermined future (Lyotard 1993: 60, 65). For Lyotard, the topological mind of the Leibnizian God is like a *Mathesis Universalis*, a monstrous encyclopaedic Babel in which no more learning or truth is possible insofar as complete information and foreknowledge precondition the future and neutralise the event. Within the structure of this grand monad only simulacra of events are possible. Lyotard argues that the passibility to the event as something unthought and emancipated from the mental hold of this speculative sovereign is impossible for Leibniz. Nothing can exceed its organisation. Nothing can shock, seize or strike the doubling power of this 'consummate archivist' and information genius whose vocation, Lyotard claims, conforms to the 'metaphysics of capital' (1993: 107). What, then, is the political stake in this metaphysical structure of retention? What is the political orientation of this theological positivism of capital which Badiou calls 'constructivist thought'? How does it double up any interventional pass to the nomination of the event?

Drawing on this critical background, Badiou salutes the following in 'complete agreement':

> Lyotard advanced the powerful thesis that what had destroyed revolutionary parties and groups was 'the primacy given to transformative action.' Or as I would put it today: politics is not the realm of power, it is the realm of thought. Its goal is not transformation: its goal is the creation of possibilities that could not previously be formulated. It is not deduced from situations, because it must prescribe them. (2009d: 97–8)

For Badiou, then, politics is an exceptional procedure equally marked by its passibility to the event. Hence it contradicts the received wisdom of all the twentieth-century metaphysics of success that enfolds the state–capital logic of efficiency. Politics takes place at the point of this apparent *im-possibility*: 'the norm of politics does not lie in its *objective* possibility' (Badiou 2008e: 151, original emphasis). The real of politics 'lies in its very *impossibility*' (Badiou 2008e: 151, emphasis added).

The far-reaching encyclopaedic implications of the Leibnizian hypothesis are consistent with the empirical operations of what Badiou calls 'the errant State'. This is how he defines the structural orientation that underpins the positivist epistemology and computational politics of the errant state: 'And since the State is the master of language, one must recognize that for the constructivist, change and diversity do not depend upon presentational primordiality, but upon representative functions. The key to mutations and differences resides in the State' (2005a: 291). It is apparent that, for Badiou, not only 'the representative function' of reformist politics, but equally the multicultural logics of extra-parliamentary diversity, including its more advanced biopolitical mutations, are simply flattened simulacra, surveyed and run through by this errant state fold. Hence the significance of prudential, programmatic party platforms entwined with governance projects within what Badiou calls the *metastructural field of the state*:

> The programmatic vision occupies the necessary role, in the field of politics, of reformist moderation. It is a mediation of the State, in that it attempts to formulate, in an accepted language, what the State is

capable of. It thus, protects people, in times of order, from having to recognize that what the State is capable of exceeds the very resources of that language; and that it would be more worthwhile to examine – yet it is an arid and complex demand – what they, the people, are capable of in the matter of politics and with respect to the surplus-capacity of the State. In fact, the programmatic vision shelters the citizen from politics. (2005a: 293)

What Badiou describes as metastructural operations of the state are, therefore, capable of pre-emptive biopower. This functional programmaticism of the biopolitical order of the day, sustained and simulated by the errant folding of the Möbian state, explains the demanding, courageous and rare character of politics. But, above all, it explains why the errant state as a global Leibnizian archive articulates politics of the non-governmental type too: 'We must conceive of imperialist society not only as a substance but also as subject' (Badiou 2009b: 42). It is precisely these hustling biopolitical loops knotted around the Möbian state-subject that make necessary the misrecognised impasse of politics. In this sense we should read *Being and Event* as an affirmative recapitulation of the insightful lessons of *The Theory of the Subject* rather than as its negation.

The exceptional difficulties in achieving subjective mastery due to the massive operations of pre-emptive biopower is, I think, a critical point that may also elucidate Badiou's intriguing polemics with Slavoj Žižek. Bruno Bosteels has encapsulated compellingly the dramatic hermeneutics of this comradely confrontation. Through a psychotic breakdown scenario, Žižek identifies the instantaneous strike of the real with the political act of truth. Badiou instead forces the real through an 'actively produced step-by-step intervention'. Bosteels thus foregrounds emphatically Badiou's warning that truth is a post-evental, laborious procedure of fidelity and not simply an act of mystical illumination (Bosteels 2011a: 167–8). The event as a sudden punctual irruption of novelty is not self-sufficient. Only a supplementary intervention sustained by a procedure of fidelity and the strenuous recompositions of a political work-force can generate retroactively the truth of the event. Bosteels is the savvy and official 'hermeneut' of the Badiou–Žižek controversy and, no doubt, the demanding challenger and interrogator of every act of speculative leftism 'no matter how heroic'.[2] This is all well taken and, indeed, it sums up the distilled wisdom of the global '68 sequence balancing vicariously against the reigning philosophical Thermidor. Placing inordinate emphasis on Žižek's presumably voluntaristic nihilism implicated in the leftist deviationism of the political 'act' on the one hand, and the 'impolitical radicalism' of tactical non-action on the other,[3] as opposed to 'emancipatory politics' proper, runs the risk of assuming too much. For one thing, it appears over-confident regarding the implicit 'golden rule' that balances force with prudence outside law. In my eyes, any pre-emptive critique of speculative leftism that does not foreground the disciplines, heroic virtues, mental and physical strengths at work in Badiouian notions of 'courage', 'fidelity', 'perseverance', 'immortality' and so on remains impotent. On the other hand, it is not certain if even Žižek himself is fully self-conscious of this heroic dialectic of virtues at work in the politics of emancipation and the kind of subjective mastery they call into being, whether Lacano-Leninist or otherwise. Žižek's attempt to introduce the 'death drive' as an apocalyptic present-absent mediator between Being and Event is equally insufficient to account for Badiou's 'Greek' ethic of com-munist virtue. This is precisely what is at stake in the 'three claims to greatness, three moments of real existence, three figures of pos-sible universalism: the Paris Commune in 1871, the Resistance between 1941 and 1945, and the uprising of youths and workers in May–June 1968', not to mention the Cultural Revolution and the anti-imperialist movements in the colonies (Badiou 2009b: xl).

All the same, in defence of the 'algebraic side of the real', Bosteels counters that 'if Badiou occasionally seems to fall prey to the temptation to present the event as such an absolute break or caesura, as dogmatic in its radicalism as it is blinding in its instantaneity, then this is because he too does not always resist the siren's song of antiphilosophy' (Bosteels 2011a: 168). What I surmise, however, is that if Badiou forsakes entirely his psycho-analytic or any other bewitching temptation, including his fascina-tion with Wagner and opera-singing, there will be nothing left for the political wager of supplementation to stake its duration.

Anti-imperial paradigms of recommencing emancipatory politics

Thus we come to realise what a pivotal and intricate idea is this painstaking procedure of *subjective forcing*. It designates the passage of the subject, a procedure which unavoidably invokes the redemptive suffering, the courage not to let go of justice in the face of utmost adversity. Not least, the passage of the subject convokes the unshakable discipline of the Eastern Passover, the Jewish *Pesach*, commemorating the Exodus from the state of bondage in Egypt. If we follow Bosteels on this point, this constitutes yet another 'antiphilosophical' punctuation of the subjective procedure, yet another 'temptation'. Indeed, regardless of how much we may try to de-purify or de-emphasise the prophetic overtones of the Passover as a subjective procedure of fidelity to the Exodus sequence, it does persist as the antiphilosophical real of a haphazard, collective truth. Is not the Passover a retroactive founding act that recommences Judaism? Is not, ultimately, the recommencement of politics an unconfessed but resonant tribute to the courage of forcing or repeating the Passover as the abiding consequence of the act of coming out of 'Egypt'?

Badiou provides some initial but vague ground for this kind of investigation in his lecture titled 'Action, Manor of the Subject', dated 14 January 1975 and published in his *Theory of the Subject*. This attempt remained incomplete and overly schematic. In *Saint Paul*, Badiou remains equally cautious and excessively anxious to avoid Hegel's dialectical traps, set up around 'the theme of a Calvary of the Absolute . . . which, it has to be said, corresponds to a Christian imagery that has been omnipresent for centuries' (2003b: 65). Instead, Badiou focuses on the more 'undialectical' formula of Paul for whom '[t]here is Calvary, but no ascent to Calvary. Energetic and urgent, Paul's preaching includes no masochistic propaganda extolling the virtues of suffering, no pathos of the crown of thorns . . .' (2003b: 67–8)· In this case, Badiou, unfortunately, historicises excessively, giving away too much, while subtracting too little, almost nothing from the anabasis to the Calvary. Consider this alternative scenario that may attest to the political possibilities of the anabasis and its retrieval on Badiouian terms.

Christ breaks with the legalistic inertia of the Jewish tradition, inaugurating the illegal truth of the new Passover, proclaiming in the middle of the disciples' confusion and distress a new testament. I cannot resist invoking by reverse analogy the same sequence, with Lenin arriving mysteriously from exile in the 'sealed train', addressing his notorious *April Theses* to a confused, disoriented and hostile party, attuned as it were to the legality of the situation and prone to support the provisional Kerensky government. Isn't this the Leninist moment par excellence which tips the balance of party power and calls against all odds for the takeover of state power? Moreover, Christ is the knot at the crossing point of the old and the new testament, the crossway of a new master procedure of subjectivation marked by a) the vitalistic intensity of the vanishing force in Matt. 26: 18, 'My time is near'; b) the almost conspiratorial organisation of the Passover assembly, canonised as the 'last supper'; c) the calling, from those premises, to 'armed defence' right before the final departure for the Mount of Olives: 'purse, bag and sword' (Luke 22: 36); d) the *caesura* of the subject in Gethsemane, which means the *crossing* of doubt and anxiety (about the prospect of attesting to the universal, inevitably anti-imperial possibilities of immortality) with the courage and resolve to witness its consequences within finitude. Gethsemane in this sense is the forcing point of what Heidegger called *anticipatory resoluteness* (1996: passages 302–10, 385).

   Turning to Badiou's logic of forcing, it is apparent that the obscure status of what happened in Gethsemane will be decided later by a retroactive sequence. Subtracted from the ideological schema of Hegelian theodicy, Gethsemane designates terms which will have been presented in a new situation. That is a condition 'which results from the addition to the situation of a truth (an indiscernible) of that situation' (Badiou 2005a: 398). With the resources of the situation, 'with its multiples, its language', Christ generates speech-acts and names 'whose referent is in the future anterior: this is what supports belief' (Badiou 2005a: 398). A comic, almost Žižekian real of this trajectory of the anabasis to Gethsemane is precisely the critical moment recounted by Luke (22: 36–8). Christ ends his forceful address to the disciples at the last and recollectable Passover meal by calling them, this time, to sell their cloaks and buy knives; however, the disciples think he is asking for table service! Here, the evental site is a comic subset that effects a division within the situation. The speech-act is both less and absolutely other to the situation with respect to its far consequences. Badiou says that such statements '"will have been" assigned a referent or signification, when the situation will have appeared in which the indiscernible – which is only represented or included – is finally presented as a truth of the first situation' (2005a: 398). Such statements or names 'are suspended, with respect to their signification, from the "to-come" of a truth ...

Their local usage is ... an approximation of a new situation, in which the truth of the current situation will have been presented' (2005a: 398).

And yet Badiou dismisses not only the trajectory but also the language of anabasis prior to the resurrection. I mean precisely 'the language which is internal to the situation, but whose referent – multiples are subject to the *condition* of *an as yet incomplete generic part*' (Badiou, 2005a: 398, emphasis added). Paul in my reading is the prospective hero of the truth of Christ's anabasis which enacts the supposition of reference to come. Christ's anabasis to Gethsemane appears now as a finite inquiry into 'the future anterior of a generic infinity'. Christ is the supporting name of the future anterior, of the trialectical truth knotted by his crucifixion, resurrection and, let us not forget, ascension. The shocked, wavering and occasionally unbelieving community of disciples will ultimately fail to live up to this anticipation, until Paul's coming *which will have reforced* the unfinishable hypothesis of the 'second coming' in terms of a stronger, anti-imperial supplementation. Let me recapitulate the logic of this synoptic investigation into sites and sub-situations of Christ's anabasis which exemplify forcing as the fundamental norm of the subject.

What appears in Gethsemane is a paradoxical site; it approximates what Badiou calls an 'abnormal multiple' whose evental site is not represented, although it is already at work in the situation in question. Even if part of the situation, the singularity of the evental site is not and cannot be represented within the situation. It is senseless, autistic, self-referential. The question it bears cannot be answered within a situation of irresoluteness, betrayal, lack of discipline and a sleeping chorus of lotus-eaters cum disciples. Why? Because 'the spirit indeed is willing, but the flesh is weak' (Mark 14: 38). Isn't this the way Badiou envisions the future of philosophy?

> We must endure our thoughts all night forever ... When we feel that a truth-event interrupts the continuity of ordinary life, we have to say to others: 'Wake-up! The time of new thinking and acting is here!' But for that, we ourselves must be awake. We, philosophers, are not allowed to sleep. A philosopher is a poor night watchman. (n.d.: 3)

Badiou 'repeats' Christ and the possibilities that are concealed but also attested in Gethsemane. Only the 'infirmity of flesh', of sheer facticity, counteracts against the possibilities open to the situation. Christ's forewarning 'keep awake' is repeated three times and three times the disciples are taken to task: 'Are you still sleeping and taking your rest? Enough! The hour has come; . . . Get up, let us be going. See, my betrayer is at hand' (Mark 14: 41–2). They cannot go far. Why? Because, Badiou argues, a subject only 'measures the newness of the situation to come, even though it cannot measure its own being' (2005a: 406). Even Christ appears as a split force: 'Father, if you are willing, remove this cup from me' (Luke 22: 42). Indeed, Badiou continues, the subject grasped in its being 'is solely the finitude of the generic procedure, the local effect of an eventual fidelity. What it produces is the truth itself, an indiscernible part of the situation, but the infinity of this truth transcends it. It is abusive to say that truth is a subjective production. A subject is much rather *taken up* in fidelity to the event, and *suspended from truth*' (2005a: 406, original emphasis). Truth splits the situation, the subject is suspended. Yet the 'angel' intervenes, Jesus recovers his courage, recomposes his 'divine' and 'human' nature, withdraws from the factical thrownness of the situation and becomes an 'anticipatory subject'. Only as 'anticipatory subject' can Christ cross anxiety and lack, that is, by a courageous act of consistency.

The *impasse* of being is in truth, Badiou argues, the *pass* of the subject: 'the impasse of being is the point at which a subject convokes itself to a decision . . . the possibility of a decision without a concept . . . it is not impossible to decide – without having to account for it' (2005a: 429). As was suggested above, Badiou radicalises Heidegger's existential concept of anticipatory resoluteness. Every subject forces decision and passes in force. Badiou's emphasis on decision opens the facticity of the situation to anticipatory resolve. Badiou, however, departs boldly from Heidegger's projection of anticipatory resolve on to the capital possibility of being-towards-death, being guilt and so forth. Unlike Heidegger, Badiou does not accept being-towards-death as a master possibility in the light of which all possibilities are evaluated. Rather he repeats it as a formal principle of political forcing that crosses over the factical impasse of irresoluteness, lack of coherence, paralysing comfort and safe speculation on opportunistic possibilities lurking on the near horizon or made immediately available by the situation. Badiou emphasises affirmative forcing against the mood of 'being lost' within the self-covering over of the situation. Political forcing thus discloses both the forgotten possibilities of the past reduced to the *fait accompli* of a finished transaction and the blocked or obscured possibilities of the future. Hence Badiou's equal emphasis on disciplined invention, that is, the concrete manifestation of the declared fidelity to the event by a wagering subject. Discipline is more or less the 'sacrament' of a fidelity procedure oriented to the redemption of the universal possibilities of the event and not a Foucauldian aesthetic of the neoliberal self. Neither does it approximate the organisational norms of the party apparatus or state administration.

Badiou provides some clues about this unresolved problem between event and organisation through his rethinking of Xenophon's *Anabasis*, which he duly exalts in *The Century* as 'the arduous construction of novelty, an exiled experience of beginning' (2007: 81). What has inspired Badiou's interest in Xenophon's *Anabasis* is not necessarily the Platonic connotation of 'reascent towards the source'. After all, the concept of anabasis is equally inflected with materialist significations of swerving, sloping up, inclining. What then is the measure of this negativity? What is Badiou affirming under the name of anabasis? Why is Xenophon a reference point for Badiou's assessment of the polymorphous creativity of the twentieth century? What is it that is thought, promised or organised under this name?

On the face of it, what focuses Badiou's passion for the *Anabasis* is the heroic achievement of the Greek exodus to the sea. Its driving force, however, is discipline:

> a discipline of thought, the compact force of certainty, a political patriotism ultimately concentrated in military cohesion. Similarly, when Lenin wants an 'iron discipline' to rule within the proletariat party, it is because he knows that the proletarians, deprived of everything, will not have the slightest chance of prevailing, unless they can impose upon themselves – as a consequence and material figure of their political consistency – an unparalleled organizational discipline. (2007: 81)

But the issue of discipline as a norm of fidelity is not sufficient on its own to explain Badiou's philosophical *nostos* for a new figure of politics. Anabasis is an ultra metaphor that folds Badiou's rethinking of *force* and *im-passe*. It serves as the master signifier of the political condition par excellence. Badiou literally seizes the analogical force of a major classical work that combines the genres of autobiography, biography and imperial ethnography, in order to outstrip at a single stroke both the disorienting logic of empire and the Leibnizian metaphysics of the state. In the first place, anabasis is the *nom de guerre* of a 'homeward movement' through imperial terrain, 'of lost men, out of place and outside the law . . . the Greeks find themselves brutally deprived of any reason for being where they are. They are nothing now but foreigners in a hostile country. At the root of *anabasis* lies something like a *principle of lostness*' (Badiou 2007: 82, emphasis added). Here Badiou restates the Heideggerian rationale of existential moods: lostness, despair, disorientation, confusion and *im-passe*. The Greek expeditionary force is called to repeat Ulysses' disciplined invention and pass through the monstrous, impassable situation of Scylla and Charybdis. Certainly, subtracted from any historical reference, anabasis may signify, depending on preference, an aleatory Epicurean swerve with Althusserian punctuation; a neo-Heideggerian re-ascension to a 'being-together that still harbors alterity' (Badiou 2007: 96); or a new *Apocalypse Now* with missing marines, lost in some jungle or desert, abandoned by politicians, having to fend for themselves, becoming taskmasters and inventors of destiny.

If, however, anabasis is a principle of the political condition, which is what I suggest it is, then we ought consider supplementary verifications of Badiou's hypothesis. If anabasis is 'the free invention of a wandering that *will have been* a return, a return that did not exist as a return-route prior to the wandering' (Badiou 2007: 82, original emphasis), then it is important to qualify what this wandering in the imperial wilderness might have been. If the concept of anabasis provides not only 'a possible support for a meditation on our century' (Badiou 2007: 82), but also a subtracted form of the epic resonances of the political condition in itself, then we need to retrieve the principles that sustain the epic subject of *anavanein* 'that constantly embarks and re-turns' (Badiou 2007: 83).

The truth is that, of Xenophon's two masterpieces, *Cyropaedia* was destined to become the best-seller of imperial Rome. It provided the necessary Socratic lustre to the moral training and sophistic tactics of imperial statesmanship. The Persian prince Cyrus is in this sense an imaginary Greek. Unable to anticipate a future for polis and politics or to suppose the liberation of the Greek cities of Asia Minor, Xenophon stages an ideal compromise with the Persian Empire under the condition that it will be edu-

cated by Greece. *Cyropaedia* conjectures a spectacular transplantation of Athens and Sparta to Persepolis, envisioning an empire
cum constitutional monarchy. At variance with *Cyropaedia*,
Xenophon's *Anabasis* is more or less a detached third-person narrative, which, despite its obsession with leadership, is transfigured
by the egalitarian becoming of collective greatness. This is the saga
of the Odyssean *re-turn* of a 10,000 strong Greek army, forcing its
way through the encircling imperial army of Persia and painstak-
ingly inventing its way back to the Euxine sea by crossing Central
Anatolia. For Badiou, this epic anabasis provides a glimpse into
the procedure of what it could possibly mean to force a passage
into the collective condition of affirmative excess. The critical
epitome, however, of this subtractive insight is the following.
Already in the preface to *Cyropaedia*, Xenophon does not fail to
exhibit his admiration for Cyrus and his successful manipulation
of the arcanum of imperial power, affirmed as an alternative to the
Greek problem. What is the Greek problem to which *Cyropaedia*
is the answer? Xenophon is fully aware that the Greeks 'conspire
against none sooner than against those whom they see attempting
to rule over them' (Xenophon 1914: I.i.2). What is played out in
Anabasis is precisely this tension between the real of politics and
the appearances of empire. Xenophon's *Anabasis* is about this
fierce, unspoken dialectic between event and empire. It is caught
up in an obscure movement of collaboration with and resistance
to imperial power in the following sense.

The 'Ten Thousand' Greek mercenaries join forces with the ren-
egade prince Cyrus, aspiring to the destabilisation of the Persian
Empire, a constant threat to Greece. This also explains why at
the end of Xenophon's narration the remnants of this force that
survived the *anabasis* and *katabasis* rejoin the Spartan army under
the banner of restoring freedom to the Greek cities of Asia Minor
(see Brownson 1998: 24–5). Hence, the ambiguous position of the
Greek force operating at the heart of empire, between apparent
collaboration dictated by necessity and the freedom of political
exodus to the coast. Without this idea of a Greek fidelity to the
event of *eleutheria* – which originates from the verb *eleuthō*, the
be-coming of freedom – *Anabasis* remains a simple adventure
story. Anabasis as an evental signifier of the egalitarian becoming
of freedom proceeds by forcing itself against the imperial logic
of sheer necessity. Anabasis is this egalitarian commitment to
the anti-imperial becoming of freedom, affirmed and reaffirmed

constantly against the necessity of corruption and the persistent temptation of empire. That is the measure of the Greek critique of empire, but it is also a measure taken against its own possible hubris.

The materialist Democritus had already contemplated this condition, arguing in fragment 251 that the hardship of poverty under democracy is a more worthy choice than 'so-called happiness' under imperial dynasty. For Democritus, democracy is a site of choice between freedom and bondage. Likewise, in *Anabasis* III.2.25–6, Xenophon contrasts the 'homeward way' with the imperial way of idleness, luxury and lotus-eating, arguing that 'it is just and proper that our first endeavour should be to return to our kindred and friends in Greece, and to point out to the Greeks that it is by their own choice that they are poor'. What happens, however, when Athens turns the anti-imperial league formed against Persia into a hometown treasury, aspiring to an empire over all Hellas? Thucydides attributes this big mouth inegalitarianism to the arch-sophist Alcibiades: '*it is not possible* for us to exercise a careful stewardship of the limits we should set to our empire; since we are placed in this position, *it is necessary* to plot against some and not let go our hold upon others, because there is a danger of coming ourselves under the empire of others, should we not ourselves hold empire over other peoples' (Thucydides 1921: Book VI.XVIII.3, emphasis added).[61] Thus, Athens repeats Persia against Hellas: 'it is not possible', 'we are not at liberty' and so on. Alcibiades recapitulates the syndrome of measureless power cum necessity. Turning the anti-imperial block into empire first corrupted the Athenians and then crushed them. Alcibiades here simply duplicates Persian wisdom. Herodotus reports the same sophistic watchwords, delivered by a Persian 'guest' invited to a banquet that was organised by Greek collaborationists on the eve of the battle of Plataea, attended also by the Persian commander Mardonius! 'What I have said is known to many of us Persians; but we follow in the bonds of necessity. And it is the hatefullest of all human sorrows to have much knowledge and no power' (Herodotus 1925: Book IX.16). Empire is driven by necessity, anabasis by the egalitarian anticipation of freedom. The freedom of wagering on what 'will have been a return' that did not exist in advance as a return-route (Badiou 2007: 82).

Interestingly, and quite cynically, the termination of the egalitarian sequence of anabasis was followed by all the symptoms that Badiou designates as 'thermidorian corruption', namely lack of discipline and virtue, plundering, preoccupation with wealth and the eruption of divisive regional particularisms, elbowing for proportional representation and vying for leadership (Xenophon 1998: V.7.14–16, VI.2.9–10). Having run through this unprecedented course, the sequence, according to Badiou, undergoes a shift of the centre of gravity from the 'situation' to the 'state of the situation', from the 'aleatory trajectory of truth' to 'the interest one has in a statified order' (2005c: 133). The formal features of the terminal loot-state (namely calculable interest, search for territorial spoils, race for property and accumulation of wealth) are consistent traits and classified symptoms of any thermidorian condition and its coextensive imperial impasse. Structural corruption, compulsive deception, confusion and disorientation are all attendant on this regressive territorialisation of anabasis too. This is the primary mood by which the imperial impasse appears as ineluctable necessity.

Synoptically: *impasse* is not only an analytical situation but the *imperial condition* to be crossed by the forcing of consequences regarding this break; politics is the way, the pass, by which the egalitarian truth of this break with necessity is manifested, if we anticipate it; that is, without complying in advance with any pre-existing norm of evaluation or principle of objectivity: 'the trajectory involved is a hazardous one, lacking in concept' (Badiou 2008e: 123).

Aporias of the Anticipatory Condition of Politics in the Age of Simulation

Substitutionism and fidelity to the simulacrum

Let's say that the forcing, which represents the infinite genericity of a truth in the future perfect, is most radically tested in its power to say – all in truth, when it attempts to give even the unnameable a name ... What I decipher in this desire, which every truth puts on the agenda, is the very figure of Evil. For the forcing of a nomination of the unnameable is tantamount to the denial of singularity as such ... We shall call this disaster. Evil is the disaster of a truth, one that comes when the desire to force the nomination of the unnameable is unleashed in fiction ... The ethics of a truth consists then wholly in a sort of restraint with regard to its powers. (Badiou 2008e: 126, 127)

This is a sharp cautionary counsel intended to safeguard the 'unnameable' from apocalyptic politics. Thus, Badiou seems to impose a principled limitation on 'the combined effect of the event, the subject and truth' (2008e: 127). More generally speaking, cautionary tales appear, more often than not, as a posteriori rationalisations of inner anxieties and courageous undertakings, when they manage not to regress to covert moralising or self-hating rituals of personal catharsis. But, it is true, they may also operate as masterly antidotes to narcissistic delusions of grandeur in which significant portions of the speculative far Left were trapped in the post-'68 sequence. It is equally true that Badiou's poetics of the unnameable unavoidably reiterates eclectic postmodern moods and sensibilities against 'authoritarian and totalitarian pathologies'. Badiou certainly did not need to wait for the consolidation of the postmodern zeitgeist in order to be able to identify the voluntaristic tendencies of leftist deviationism. That was after all one of the charismatic crafts of good generic Maoism and its dexterity to always situate itself at the centre. There remains, however, the missing pole of right-wing deviationism, an equally indispensable adversary that enables the identification of the centre in the (still) trialectical schema of post-Maoist topology in which, as we know, the subjective poles shift as ever according to the challenge of the historical conjuncture. For instance, it is highly uncertain that anyone can readily classify Žižek's anti-capitalist outlook and incontestably assign his radical state-oriented politics in particular to the fixed category of speculative leftism. In addition to this complication, why should we consider any practical assistance to immigrants for purposes of self-organisation and citizenship, claiming this as 'prescriptive supplementation' of a situation and as being consistent with a sober, non-speculative 'communist hypothesis', when NGO agencies glamorously and quite profitably facilitate the same process? Unless a principled polemical confrontation with the performative power of the impolitical does take place in this field of the metastructural operations of empire, it will not be easy to elucidate the difference between political internationalism, on the one hand, and the cosmopolitan chyle that sustains the clientship of empire on the other. An excessive philosophical emphasis on the disastrous consequences of speculative leftism may equally direct attention away from the possibility of what Oliver Feltham calls 'right-wing Badiousianism', regardless of whether we agree or disagree on the elementary traits of its profile (Feltham 2008: 116–23).

On the occasion of his acute reading of Derrida, Simon Critchley has in fact raised this Möbian possibility of a convertible Left into a philosophical task:

> why oppose this extraordinary chrematistic energy with a defensive reactive strategy? Perhaps what is required is some kind of exacerbation of the enormous creative energy of contemporary capitalism, where those energies are comprehended, criticized and transformed, where rather than opposing capitalism with a reterritorialization on the level of economy, the state and law, one would try to accelerate its deterritorializing effects. Such might well be the task of philosophy. As Deleuze and Guattari write, 'Philosophy takes to the absolute the relative deterritorialization of capital.' Absolute deterritorialization, then. Is this not a spectre of Marx? (1999: 172)

I am not sure that this logic of absolute deterritorialisation can be traced to the spectre of Marx without foregrounding first and foremost its immanent logics of imperialist expropriation, reappropriation and so on. Still, I may defend Deleuze and Guattari's *A Thousand Plateaus* as an anti-imperialist tract in its own right; although, as Eyal Weizman has uncannily demonstrated, the Israeli Defence Forces have effectively integrated into their counter-insurgency tactics Deleuzian 'swarm intelligence' concepts, and have employed with equal success non-linear analytical tools for destructive ends. They have even consciously assimilated the Situationist technique of *détournement* and Bernard Tschumi's postmodern urban theory into their military operations, thus coupling effectively soldiers with architects (Weizman 2006). This military simulation machine proved itself unbeatable on the ground until its fateful encounter with Hezbollah in southern Lebanon. In the neighbouring island of Cyprus we witness an imperial site of experimental zoning, of doubling-halving tactics and deconstructive dissemination of the effects of Turkish occupation, whereby colonisation is represented as an act of multicultural immigration, thus pre-empting any critique as racist! Occupation forces appear as peace-keeping troops, NGOs as peace-making agencies, and UN engineering schemes that legalise the *faits accomplis* of the Occupation appear as methods of a 'fair balancing of differences' and so on.

I therefore suggest that the major problem or risk facing the kind of politics Badiou is trying to conceptualise is not speculative leftism as such but *simulationism*, what Badiou himself calls fidelity to the simulacrum, or what Susan Buck-Morss identifies as the political promiscuity of the mass ornament (Buck-Morss 2002: 154). However, this is neither a sort of pathology peculiar to speculative leftism nor a symptom of thermidorian repentance. Rather, it recalls a logic of biopolitical montage, juxtaposing disparate signifiers of change whose performative effect is both 'representational and cinematic' (Buck-Morss 2002: 156). This is presently the vernacular romance of empire, which is equivalent to both the delegated act of the broker or agent and counsellor, and what I would call the cinematic act literally rendered as a 'funded sequence' of 'movements' and non-governmental activism. What I mean by 'cinematic act' is precisely this simulated mode of action that capitalises and feeds parasitically on representation. This 'cineplex' action is the subject of empire.

Politics, then, designates a singular task: passing through what Badiou, again, refers to as 'the efficacy of semblance as real' (2007: 49). Badiou's conceptualisation of Brechtian politics 'at a distance' from the state is intended to break with this necessity that joins the real to semblance. The wager for the politics of forcing is whether it can designate the gap between real and semblance and pass through it. Badiou maintains strong doubts about this possibility. He thinks instead that

> the crucial point (as Hegel grasped long ago with regard to revolutionary terror) is this: the real, conceived in its contingent absoluteness, is never real enough not to be suspected of semblance. The passion for the real is also of necessity, suspicion. Nothing can attest that the real is the real, nothing but the system of fictions wherein it plays the role of the real. (2007: 52)

Have we, then, been misled into a paranoid dialectic between Stalinist purges and semblant politics? Although Badiou has undertaken a defence of the singularity and greatness of politics, he is equally at great pains to deflect the anti-political implications ensuing from the 'fictionalisation of the real' and its implied maxim: simulation is destiny. Is Badiou ultimately caught up into this double impasse between the Stalinist logic of paranoid purification and the imperial logic of politoid simulation? To be sure, he does give free rein to the logic of purification in the field of painting and mathematics. But what could possibly be the political counterpart of Kazimir Malevich's *White on White*? Elements of this staggering equivocation are also found in *Ethics*. There Badiou does not simply disapprove of the Red Guards' voluntarism during the Cultural Revolution and their willingness to completely suppress 'self-interest'. He goes as far as identifying the Red Guards with nineteenth-century Romanticism and its 'Literary Absolute', and even further with the positivist claim that scientific statements could 'replace opinions and beliefs about all things' (Badiou 2001: 84). This view is reinforced by a stronger philosophical assertion: 'The Good is Good only to the extent that it does not aspire to render the world good ... So it must be that the power of a truth is also a kind of powerlessness' (2001: 85).

This could not have been Badiou's final word on the singularity of politics. In fact, Badiou's assessment of Maoist fashions and far-leftist mannerisms during the '68 sequence isolates some formal traits which have become generalised standard trappings of the biopolitical promiscuity of the present. What Badiou's insightful comments on the surprisingly widespread phenomenon of *Gauche Proletarienne* indicate is not the perils of extra-parliamentary, far leftist politics per se, but a tracing of its unnamed, biopolitical moods to the present state of politoid apoliticism, a state that is defined by the universal interchangeability of political semblances:

> they made 'revolution in the head', 'melted into the masses', always with a very keen eye to the media. The organization was highly centralized in secret; in public it dissolved itself every five minutes in order to 'liberate' the energy of the masses ... What attracted these intellectuals and artists was an aura of activism and radicalism, and they didn't look closely at the actual politics the *Gauche Proletarienne* was conducting, which often involved trickery and throwing dust into people's eyes. Almost everything put out by GP propaganda was half untrue – where there was a kitten, they described a Bengal tiger ... Godard's film *Tout Va Bien* gives a good picture of this kind of sympathy – simultaneously bourgeois, activist, distant and fashionable. (2008h: 4)

What Badiou has described above is not simply the pivotal operation of the simulacrum within French factions and fashions of Maoism. He has described the kinky revisionism of the simulacrum that threatens with supplementation not only Badiou's proposal of 'prescribing the State' but the event itself. Just one year before May '68, the master mystic of this revisionist disposition of the simulacrum said: 'The supplement is always the supplement of a supplement. One wishes to go back from the supplement to the source: one must recognise that there is a supplement at the source' (Derrida 1976: 304). Is there a spectre of Derrida haunting Badiou? Is this deconstruction's dispassionate revenge against politics? After all, 'the supplement is neither a presence nor an absence. No ontology can think its operation . . . One can no longer see disease in substitution, when one sees that the substitute is substituted for a substitute' (Derrida 1976: 314). Substitutionism is destiny! Is not this the ultimate truth of politics as well as the legacy of deconstruction?

If that is the case, then the Rousseauean-Maoist opposition to substitutionism, the heroic *liaison de masse* that was the key to political invention in the '68 sequence, is lost for ever and 'may be', 'perhaps', 'possibly' for good purpose! Then, there is no plausible reason why people's subservient conscience or 'political incompetence must be attacked by affirmative commitments that are untied to electoral concerns and measured against principles alone' (Badiou 2006b: 96). Then, inventing new sites of the general will to equality and 'procedures of political work internal to the popular masses' becomes a meaningless task, as meaningless as 'a firm indifference to posts of state, and a constantly sustained cordial scorn for electoral pretends' (Badiou 2006b: 96). If it is impossible to identify the cinematic movement of supplementarity and semblance due to the 'always', 'already' and necessary powerlessness of truth, it is at once obvious that there is no longer any urgency for new manifestos or sites of equality and justice, but only 'scenes of writing'. Politics in the light of the Derridean scene appears as a technical question caught up in logics of deferral and apparatuses of representation:

> Everything begins with representation. Always, already: repositories of meaning which was never present, whose signified presence is always reconstituted by deferral . . . The call of the supplement is primary, here, and it hollows out that which will be reconstituted by deferral as the present. The supplement, which seems to be added as a plenitude to a plenitude, is equally that which compensates for a lack. (Derrida 1978: 211–12)

For Derrida, 'representation has no end ... To think the closure of representation is to think the tragic: not as the representation of fate but as the fate of representation. Its gratuitous and baseless necessity. And it is to think why it is fatal that, in its closure, representation continues' (1978: 250).

Thus Derridean pharmacy redoubles the errant excess of the state, supplements the alterplex operations of the empire and so on. Badiou knows that he needs a moment, an act that will cast away the pharmaceutical cup of Derridean consolation by way of a political cut. Badiou is equally aware that if he wants to sustain the Rousseauean idea of the general will as the singular point of a communist hypothesis with universal resonance, he also has to find ways to pass through the sophistic sorcery of imperial simulacra. This alterplex empire 'seems to have achieved a *miserable fusion of what is and what can be*; this is no mean feat' (Badiou 2005c: 101, emphasis added). Empire, then, has managed to become itself the vanishing mediator and sophistic resource of this global confusion and disorientation which explains our political impotence. Consequently, 'to identify the rare sequences through which a political truth is constructed ... is in itself a stringent intellectual discipline. What is even more efficient is to attempt, in the realm of "doing politics", to be faithful to some axiom of equality by unearthing those statements that characterise our era' (Badiou 2005c: 101). Given the formidable difficulty of political construction under conditions of imperial simulation that define what is reasonable and feasible and what is not, Badiou also realises that he has paid excessive respect to 'self-interest'. Now, 'we must certainly sacrifice many preferences. This is where philosophy can help since, in its most general inspiration, it teaches us that the universality of truth is preferable to mere preferences' (Badiou 2006b: 97). Even in *Ethics*, where Badiou takes reassuring measures of deconstructive prophylaxis against Evil as the absolutisation of the power of truth, he argues that it is only 'in the last analysis' that a truth process 'does not have the power to name all the elements of the situation' (2001: 85). What is implied is that there will be junctures and critical points when a political sequence may force its truth procedure cum general will against self-interest and individual preferences, but respecting the unnameable element of the situation 'in the last analysis'. All the same, Badiou makes his most dramatic overture in this direction in the last chapter of *The Century*: 'The century will have been the century of univocity.

This is what I hope will outlast the current Restoration, which is all the more mendacious and equivocal in that it claims to be both humanistic and convivial' (2007: 162).

Consequently, it is impossible not to suppose the 'all power-ful truth' of a duration in default of the alterplex state. That is a point of inscription, an evental caesura, a stage of the subject that 'forces the situation to accommodate it . . . to the point of becoming presentation . . . finally recognized as a term and as internal' (Badiou 2005a: 342–3). In the final analysis, this generic term or condition is unappealable. It is not answerable to self-interest.

Subtracting Rousseau

Badiou's philosophical hero of the political condition is, after all, Rousseau. But, again, as with every incarnate avatar of the concept, Rousseau is a double figure of unfailing irony, for good and for bad. He embodies the subjective paradox of a political aristocrat and patron of the coming bourgeois revolution. Rousseau is a prudent hypothesist of restraint action who antici-pates that 'In a word, it is the best and most natural arrangement that can be made, that the wise must govern the masses, provided that they govern them always for their good, and not selfishly' (Rousseau 1960: Book V, 235). He is at the same time the master instructor of the general will. This Rousseau thinks the conceptual prerequisites of politics, the revolutionary being of politics whose 'unnatural' truth is the masses. The social contract of the masses is 'the *evental form* that one must suppose if one wishes to think the truth of that aleatory being that is the body politic' (Badiou 2005a: 345, original emphasis). In the revolutionary constitution of the masses we come to realise 'the *eventness* of the event in which any political procedure finds its truth' (Badiou, 2005a: 345, original emphasis). The revolutionary constitutionalism of the masses is precisely a novel political procedure that creates freedom in its genericity, forced against the natural necessity of being dominated by particularistic wills. Necessity is apolitical. Freedom, instead, is commensurable to the political event of the general will that constitutes it as collective humanity. The constituent power of the masses is then presupposed by any constitutional act. The political wager is the following: how to force freedom against the necessity of factional interests implied by the nature of particular wills, while remaining consistent and faithful to the norm of the constituent will, namely equality. What is, therefore, implied by Rousseau's concept of the general will is equality as the generic norm of the becoming of politics, emancipated from the tutelage of the state, the vested self-interest of opinion, and the opportunistic domination by strong factional wills. Roussseau's difficulty is precisely the passing from the generic principle to its realisation.

The principle of unanimity implied by the general will cannot be consistently maintained. That being the case, Badiou asks: 'How can the generic character of politics subsist when unanimity fails? This is Rousseau's impasse' (2005a: 349). Therefore, he introduces the supplementary concept of 'qualified majorities', distinguishing between important and urgent decisions. But who, Badiou rightly asks, 'decides whether an affair is important or urgent? And by what majority?' (2005a: 352). How generic or political, then, could be a will that is contingent upon the necessity of circumstances and the inevitably casuistic technique of evaluating it?

This encyclopaedic impasse of the general will is further aggravated by its inflexible laws. By virtue of their inflexibility the laws dictated by the general will cannot respond to or regulate a state of exception cum emergency. The terminal crisis of the general will is consequently resolved by dictatorship. Casuistry is the supreme manifestation of the dictatorship of necessity, yet another sophistic technique that reduces the generic equality inherent in the political will to self-interested determinations. Dictatorship suspends the laws dictated by the general will in order to salvage the latter from the inflexibility of the former! Thus, dictatorship is the sufficient form of the general will 'once it provides the sole means of maintaining the condition of its existence', that is, the founding condition of the event which institutes politics as truth (Badiou 2005a: 353).

This disingenuous reasoning has anticipated Carl Schmitt's legalistic casuistry in the twentieth century. Let us recall that for Carl Schmitt 'the arcana of political-technical secrets are in fact just as necessary for absolutism as business and economic secrets are for an economic life that depends on private property and competition' (Schmitt 1988: 38). The difference is that Schmitt, as a defender of the modern *arcana respublica*, posits state secrecy as a necessary protection of the public interest from the corruption of public opinion, whereas for Badiou one simply replicates the other. The state cannot be a subjective figure. For Badiou, this Schmittian *arcana respublica* is by its very nature 'indifferent or hostile to the existence of a politics that touches on truths' (Badiou 2005c: 100). Its objective function engineers consensus while in its 'subjective dimension' it duplicates capital's economic necessity: 'This is why every programmatic or statist definition of justice changes it into its opposite . . . harmonising the interplay of conflicting interests' (2005c: 100).

Authority and equality: transference as a political paradox

How then is Badiou extricating himself from the Rousseauean impasse of authority? In the first place, he is not shunning at all the highly controversial issues of leadership, organisation and mediation. In fact, he seizes these most contentious and polarising issues of the political procedure, not only with the expected polemical resolve but also with masterful displacements and philosophical subtractions that engage their force in unexpected ways. The comparative lessons Badiou draws from Jacques Rancière's work provide a vantage point for evaluating the scope of his critical intervention on these issues.

As was argued above, the crisis of the general will and Rousseau's casuistic recourse to dictatorship posit dramatically the problem of political authority in terms of a dialectic between knowledge and power whose hierarchical implications tend to neutralise the egalitarian hypothesis that is immanent in the political condition. Being a condition of semblant ultrapoliticity, this dictatorship of the master opinion appears as a rescue operation of the generic truth of politics against its failed embodiment in an ignorant subject.

Thus, we end up with the sophistic oxymoron of delinking the generic will as the egalitarian condition of potential self-constitution from the political procedure of its realisation. What is inherent in this substitutionist logic is the forcing of the general will into passivity in order to treat the symptoms of a perceived infantile disorder, namely, inflexibility, lack of foresight, prudence and so on. Rather than the general will prescribing the state, the latter prescribes the former in a perverted pharmaceutical dialectic of Derridean supplementation that ministers to the self-destructive drives of the political body. Rousseau marks off two separate levels of this delegated nursing power; one that provides for administrative Bonapartism so to speak, expediting law into a series of administrative acts; and another that suspends the sovereignty of law without permanently abolishing it. This is precisely what Carl Schmitt aptly calls commissarial dictatorship (Rousseau 1960: Book IV, VI, 290–1; see also Schmitt 2013). Unavoidably, however, both levels of the state of exception are coimplicated and duplicated. We therefore need to perceive the ersatz biopower of the state of exception as a normalising operation of governmentality which relieves the general will of its political impasse. The point is that this commissarial logic of medicated restoration of the political body to normalcy, which entails a recovery process in terms of passivity and pacification, implicates diachronically the authority of the party as well as the standing of intellectual and managerial elites; in short, all the 'therapeutic' or ministerial professions that tend to the process of pedagogical transmission and take care of the general will as being always and already in a state of permanent infancy and pure potentiality.

All the same, the hierarchical transmission of knowledge by the 'university discourse' of the state, the party, the union bureaucracy, the factory bosses and engineers, the academic professoriat and so forth was, as we know, forcefully challenged in the last century by the Cultural Revolution and May '68. They were the first, unequivocally anti-hierarchical revolutions in history which focused acutely the politics of emancipation on the contradiction between mental and manual labour as the major state-capitalist loop of the spectacle's domination. That trajectory of the '68 sequence illuminates sharply the Badiou–Rancière controversy, foregrounding not only its singular legacy but also putting into perspective the pivotal stakes of the politics of emancipation in the present. The key question, then, is the following.

The condition of transmission as a condition of *passing on*, of *passage*, of *transference* in the psychoanalytic sense is necessarily a condition of mastery. It combines the double authority of the discourses of the university and the master. Is there a model of proper transference that is compatible with the egalitarian condition of the politics of emancipation? Moreover, could we conceptualise the master risking his mastery in a procedure of counter-transference without endangering the emancipatory operation of transmission? Could counter-transference itself have emancipatory effects? Could there be a possibility of forcing the master logic of transference in an emancipatory direction? How could we possibly know that this passing on of 'emancipatory knowledge' is not a disciplinary loop of pastoral biopower?

Badiou's attempted solution to the thorny issue of transmission draws on Plato's vision of the *Republic* and the virtuous idea of a disinterested communist aristocracy, but its modern pedagogical edge is Wagnerian. It is both pragmatic and radical, but no less controversial and not necessarily egalitarian. All the same, Badiou's pedagogical hypothesis displaces Plato's collective figure of transmission, namely the guardians of the communist Republic, considered 'as a metonymy of a polyvalent humanity' (Badiou 2012a: 112). This oxymoron of an unprivileged but talented and experienced 'communist aristocracy' of masters insulated from the corruption of wealth embodies an ideal combination of the Athenian virtues of dialectical philosophy and mathematics along with the Spartan austerity of discipline and martial arts. Badiou subtracts from Plato's republican communism a polyvalent, universalisable paradigm of generic humanity 'as the real support of an authentic equality' (2012a: 113). Badiou, then, forces, contra Foucault, a dialectic between knowledge and power which grounds emancipatory politics within the disciplines of virtuous education and organisation. One could even argue that he supplements pastoral power with emancipatory protocols, affirming a communist discipline of the new against its self-assuring narcissism. In sum, the conjunction of knowledge and authentic mastery is not necessarily conducive to normalisation. Rather, it is propaedeutical to a communist *cura sui*. I find the wider implications of this daring logic of transmission compelling. It brings out the urgency of reckoning with the biopolitical narcissism of a cheap, impatient and untalented internationalism that presently sees no reason for anti-imperialist thought. However, Badiou's polemics with Rancière is of a different order and character. It is a discord within communist discourse, so to speak.

For Badiou, the overturning of the question 'Who educates whom?' by Rancière's figure of the 'ignorant schoolmaster' impoverishes precisely that 'form of knowledge which is equal to the status of one truth at least'.[4] The prescriptive form of transmission can only be 'an education by truths', marked by conviction and principle.[5] Without fidelity to this generic form, transmission cannot be addressed to all. Even Socrates' professed ignorance had a singular polemical edge against sophistic conceit and encyclopaedic particularism. At variance with Badiou's logic of transmission as a condition of emancipation, Rancière foregrounds emphatically emancipation inherent not in the possession of knowledge itself but in the equality of intelligence. The pedagogical fiction of knowledge necessitates the transmission of hidden truths by masters of explication (see Rancière 1991). The logic of unequal knowledge presupposes the arbitrary authority of an apparatus of explication run by masters who infantilise the popular classes, the poor, children and so on. Badiou responds, asserting that Rancière's 'ignorant schoolmaster' as a counter-figure of transmission 'poses a false dilemma between the assumption of the figure of the master and that of anarchy, where knowledge and non-knowledge are equivalent in the capacity of life. If everyone educates everyone else, then no one educates anyone' (2012a: 124). Obviously, Badiou approximates affirmatively the Platonic idea of a republican aristocracy of talent and experience with his own version of a militant aristocracy of vanishing instructors, coming out of mass anonymity in order to construct a set of consequences with regard to an egalitarian declaration.

However metonymic Badiou's displacement appears to be, there is a significant caveat in the Platonic rendering of this idea which confirms that there is absolutely no guarantee concerning its universalisability. In discussing the communist ethos of such political excellence, Plato designates it as a condition in which the *pleistoi*, the greatest number, only will feel this kind of solidarity (Plato 1937: Book V, 462C). The rest, without being slaves, are still not and cannot be on a par with the guardian class that protects the communist constitution of the polis. Plato's republican communism is not addressed to all but to the 'greatest number', possibly to the guardians. This is the same difficulty encountered by Rousseau in the *Social Contract*: in other words, the moment when the general will relapses into the 'pragmatic' state of the 'will of all', summing up by necessity only the will of some faction.

What I find particularly problematic in Badiou's conceptualisation of the 'communist aristocracy' is that it is discursively framed as an oxymoron or paradox rather than in terms of the political concept of contradiction. Oxymorons and paradoxes are steeped in arcane and equivocal loops, whereas contradiction is amenable to the labour of the negative and subject to transformation if not resolution.

Interestingly, Badiou's supplementary master figure of 'communist transmission' is subtracted from Wagner's opera *Mastersingers of Nuremberg*. The Wagnerian character Hans Sachs appears to lend credence to Badiou's anticipatory idea of crossing the aporetic 'non-relation' between master and apprentice, old and new, tradition and novelty. The pedagogic authority of Hans Sachs is the catalytic mediator that ultimately enables the new master song to be sung by the young knight and to be acknowledged by the mastersingers' guild. In the figure of Hans Sachs, Badiou finds a subjective confirmation of the idea of a coaching communist aristocracy operating as the vanishing mediator of the new. The talented tenor, Walther, a young, impatient, as well as ignorant and arrogant knight who wants to compete in the contest of the mastersingers, evidently lacks sufficient knowledge of the structure of corporatist authority carried by the guild. He thus typifies the example of an untutored genius, desperately in need of moral correction with regard to his perceptions and expectations, and, of necessity, in need of a training period for learning the art of working through the established order of the situation. An *enfant terrible*, a young genius, but also a young fool uncomprehending of 'Wagner's lifelong idea that art is for the whole community, and is to be attended and judged by the whole community' (Magee 2000: 246). This is the *Bildungsroman* of transmission. No apprenticeship, no mastery. Yet a successful working through the formidable obstacles of the state of the situation presupposes not only a Platonic but also, it turns out, a Schopenhauerian ethos of old age and maturity, a 'mild, sad, noble and resigned' aristocratic subject, prepared to cede magnanimously wooing space to Walther and Eva – the *objet petit a* of the opera – although Hans Sachs could usurp that too (Magee 2000: 244).

Wagner's allegory of the fusion of great art and the mass and, by analogy, revolutionary politics with the mass remains an evental communist vision too. Badiou, however, acknowledges in passing that transmission in the *Mastersingers* comes out successfully because of the 'cunning and intrigue' of Hans Sachs (2012a: 128). The problem with the arcane master in general, and not with Wagner's figure in particular, is that he is an unpolitical figure that may lend his charismatic aura to any idea. Insofar as the pedagogical *arcanum* is sustained by arbitrariness appearing as necessity, then any logic of transmission that appeals to it reproduces inequality as necessary.[6] Badiou, of course, qualifies this point: 'All told, the master of the whole process, *as recognized by the people*, is the miserable cobbler [Hans Sachs].'[7] Should we conclude, however, that the political inscription of the new pre-supposes a necessary stage of receptive passivity, regulated by the pastoral power of a hidden science as a necessary supplement to a truth procedure?

This obscure zone of indistinction regarding the just measures, proportions and transitions between obedience and freedom, actu-ality and potentiality, is all the more important as it evolves into a privileged fold for Wagner's identification of mastery with empire:

> Honour your German masters
> If you would advert disasters!
> For while they dwell in every heart
> Though should depart
> The Holy Roman Empire, still remains with us
> Holy German Art![8]

Despite the spiritualist veneer of German mastery, we cannot bypass lightheartedly the mocking caricature of the Jew in the figure of Beckmesser, 'desperate for acceptance by German society' and incapable of interpreting German music authentically 'as is shown in his climactic performance of Walther's purloined song' (Rose 1996: 112). What, then, if Wagner's allegory is not 'prospective, anticipatory, and a temporal beacon of the becoming eternal of the idea', as Badiou argues (2012a: 130), but instead projects the fantasy of imperial art as a site of harmonisation between factional corporatist forces? What if this is the hiero-glyphic point of reconciliation that would have been the new mil-lennium of the Reich? What if *The Mastersingers* (1867) provides the necessary matrix of a cultural discipline that is faithful to the drift of nineteenth-century Germany towards *imperialsozialismus*, namely, a fusion of radical conservatism with the masses?[9] Indeed, here Badiou's masterful investigation of the flashy spectacle of political mimicry could not have been more relevant: 'Fidelity to a simulacrum, unlike fidelity to an event, regulates its break with the situation, not by the universality of the void, but by the closed particularity of an abstract set [ensemble], the "Germans" or the "Aryans"' (2001: 74). What is at stake in *The Mastersingers* is the real of the simulacrum. That being the case, shortly afterwards Wagner's operatic dice throw from Nuremberg would have an unexpected impact. In 1871 the dice did land on the heads of the Paris communards – like bullets. Here is Stéphane Mallarmé, a

French admirer of Wagner, uncannily anticipating the ballistic trajectory of this obscure dice throw:

> It travels ancient through the fog, and penetrates
> Like an unerring blade your native agony;
> Where flee in my revolt so useless and depraved?
> *For I am haunted!* The sky! The sky! The sky! The sky!
> 'The Azure', 1864 (Mallarmé 1982: 15–16)

Coming much later on the scene of forgetfulness, in the age of imperial ordo-liberalism, we may not be able to recast the dice, but we can certainly venture, again, the wager of fighting our way to the sea, with Badiou among us as a chief pathfinder:

> Nothing, not those old gardens eyes reflect
> Can now restrain this heart steeped in the sea . . .
> 'Sea Breeze', 1864 (Mallarmé 1982: 17)

The Contributors: Partisans of the Swerving Affirmation

We know that the hysteric comes to the master and says: 'Truth speaks through my mouth, I am *here*, you have knowledge, tell me who I am.' Whatever the knowing subtlety of the master's reply, we can also anticipate that the hysteric will let him know that it's not yet *it*, that the here escapes the master's grasp, that it must all be taken up again and worked through at length in order to please her. (Badiou 2005d: 1, original emphasis)

There is certainly no 'she' among us in accordance with the political correctness of 'affirmative action', but we are all supposing and affirming her, in taking her place, in hystericising the master, barring him from complete mastery so to speak. However, this we-formation of contributors that assumes a she-function sustains in the arrangement below 'forms of knowledge in such a way that some truth may come to pierce a hole in them' (Badiou 2005d: 9).

Badiou's intervention in this volume provides a new twist in his debate with Jacques Rancière. By finally overcoming persistent reservations of the past, he now comes to affirm democracy as a political concept; not as a representative institution and notably not as a momentary revolutionary rupture, but as another name for the elaboration of the consequences of collective action that determine a new political subject. He thus emphasises, in the context of a new communist anthropology, that the human animal standing today before the market as a consumer, or for that matter disposing himself as an imperial *clientulus*, is not generic at all but desperately particular. Consequently, as affirmed by Badiou's concept of political communism, this exceptionally demanding, yet not impossible passage from animal particularity to anthropological genericity obtains a heroic tenor.

Frank Ruda unpacks the political implications of this philosophical struggle in the context of a communist critique of biopolitics which remains liberally oblivious to the exception of the idea as a foundation of life. He emphasises Badiou's notion of intermediate infinity as a founding term of the political condition that breaks with preceding successions, and hence becomes the point of recommencement. Drawing on Badiou's book *La République de Platon* (2012), Ruda reposits the controversial question: how do we transmit what will have been an egalitarian exception to the existing order? He points to the possibility of an answer by reactualising the Socratic pretension to ignorance. The Socratic gesture is thus valorised in terms of communist recollection which summons the political subject as he who does not know, who struggles with what is necessary – though impossible and not known. Could this possibly be a Platonic bridge between Badiou and Rancière regarding the controversy over transmission?

Ed Pluth engages with the logic of active and passive numbers and considers the question whether democracy as a state form is necessarily incompatible with Badiou's politics of the active number. In direct dialogue with Badiou's critique of democracy, Pluth turns the tables by prioritising a political critique of capitalism instead. He radicalises Badiou's thesis that philosophy is not the master of the political condition, namely, that it cannot and should not define the essence of politics, calling urgently for the need to introduce a narrative dimension into the political procedure. The abiding question is whether a narrative supplementation of politics provides also for representation at the expense of the narrative's own void and the idea it recalls. The challenge for every narrative, as always, is not to forget ideas and ethos.

Dominiek Hoens examines Badiou's qualification of the political truth procedure through a critical analysis of the Pascalian wager in *Can Politics Be Thought?* (forthcoming from Duke University

Press). Hoens explains Badiou's sympathetic engagement with Pascal in terms of the latter's conjoint thinking of reason and fidelity, whereby reason acknowledges not only its own limit but also a surplus which operates both as an obstacle and a motive for the wager of thought. Hence, political praxis or intervention presupposes a 'faithful subject' which summons comparisons between a Pascalian Christian and the figure of a political militant, whose belief is neither outside nor opposed to reason. He then proceeds to juxtapose Badiou's Pascalian conceptualisation of politics with Lacan's analysis of the notorious wager, suggesting that Badiou overlooks the masochistic constitution of the wagering subject. Badiou's emphasis on the political affirmation of the event, Hoens' Mephistophelean argument goes, makes him oblivious to the possibility that the political militant might just as well be the object of a dark and ungrateful God.

Marios Constantinou takes issue with Badiou's reclaiming of Paulian universalism as a counterpoint to the present Pétainisation of the state. He argues that the real of Saint Paul's intervention is the universal emancipation from all forms of slavery, a procedure which occasionally escapes even the mental hold of the intervening subject. He engages the spectres of Paul in an anti-imperialist perspective in order to reconstruct and affirm what is present but implicit in Badiou's perception of the imperial condition and its unofficial biopolitical dogma of 'democratic materialism'. To this effect, he proceeds by way of a subtractive genealogy to a) re-actualise Paul as a political name that prescribes a break with the collaborationist norms and postures of contemporary Pétainism; and b) reiterate Badiou's gesture of emancipatory universalism in an anti-imperialist direction, as the only strategy of consistent political change that cannot be duplicated by the 'Pétainist transcendental'.

Jan Voelker examines the relation between the vanguard logic of the pure act and the formula that counterbalances its intensity in the form of the manifesto. The vanguard manifesto subjects the power of simulation to the real of politics, inventing a future that it still cannot name. Voelker valorises the programmatic character of the genre of the manifesto as the formal protocol shared by both twentieth-century avant-garde art and revolutionary politics, highlighting its significance in the articulation of Badiou's thinking. He then considers the deleterious impact on politics of a weak relation with militant art. This is precisely a condition that needs to be reversed by a new political paradigm inspired by the inventive capacity of militant art to create new forms of the real.

Christopher Norris draws on Badiou's idea of transitory ontology to investigate the mode of existence of 'political song' and its singular power to inspire protest movements across time, passing on its elusive force of resistance to later generations of militants. He posits the 'anti-genre' of political song as a test case for Badiou's concept of 'inaesthetics', defending it as the capacity of artistic practices to challenge established norms of aesthetic validity, while lacking sufficient means of conceptual articulation. Thus, Norris's philosophical intervention elucidates against any relativist temptation the link between art and politics as intersecting conditions of philosophy with truth-generating power. Aesthetics, then, encounters politics in the figure of the political song and its diachronic force of truth.

In yet another interesting coupling of philosophy's compossible conditions, Norman Madarasz suggests that Badiou's 'communist hypothesis' must break with secularism and accept instead the logic of reinvention that is immanent to love as one of the strong conditions of politics. No truth procedure can be consistent with politics, Madarasz argues, without such a metaphysical supplement. The 'logic of love' which implies the possibility of anticipatory life in the Pauline sense of living *as if* a new world is coming into being should supplement the practical reasoning of revolutionary politics, regardless of whether the social condition allows for its generalisation or not. Madarasz, thus, points to a consequential ellipsis of the communist hypothesis. The underlying question is whether the communist hypothesis is affirmable by a liberation theology of love. There seems to be an ontological hiatus between emancipation and liberation, and Madarasz suggests that its crossing is a major political task.

Sean Homer intervenes in the ongoing philosophical construction taking place between Badiou and Žižek, articulated as it is by divergent perspectives primarily on Lacan. This intermittent intellectual trajectory, consisting of several other disjointed tales besides Lacan, explains to a large extent their differing responses to the outbreak of anti-austerity movements and urban riots in southern Europe, as well as with regard to the Arab Spring. Despite Badiou's sarcastic 'bipartisan' assurance that 'the future lies in our hands' (2009a: 563), Homer argues that the philosophical and psychoanalytic contradictions that traverse the

Badiou–Žižek comradeship harbour discrepant anticipations which affirm incongruous passages into politics.

A. J. Bartlett and Justin Clemens end this intellectual adventure into the political Badiou with a psychoanalytic affirmation of the force of restraint action that is immanent to the political procedure. They argue that Badiou's philosophy remains literally unthinkable without a thorough investigation of its long and obstinate confrontation of the challenges posed by psychoanalysis. Badiou, they argue, can only become 'Badiou' – that is, a thinker of Being and Event and beyond – by using psychoanalysis as a method of intervention in the disjointed conditions of philosophy – science, art, love, politics – which sorts out their possible confusion and maintains their mutual distance. This means that not every subject is a subject of politics – and the subject of politics must be carefully discriminated through its singular relation to the infinite. Observing boundaries is a good antidote to the temptation of overpoliticising the conditions of philosophy, although, in the final analysis, 'philosophy makes disparate truths compossible and, on this basis, it states the being of the time in which it operates as the time of the truths that arise within it' (Badiou 2005d: 14).

The scope of this introduction was to delineate in constructive form the conceptual high-points of Badiou's attempt to renew the anti-sophistic gesture of philosophy in terms of the politics of emancipation, while also pointing out the obscure loops attached to this heroic commitment. It marked off Badiou as the singular thinker of our age, the thinker of political sequences par excellence, and has also integrated in a non-partisan way the crucial debates that surround his work. Moreover, it valorised new resources and anti-imperial paradigms of emancipatory affirmation relevant to Badiou's conceptualisation of the political condition and to the present predicament.

A last but not least note of due remembrance: El Lissitzky's swerving letter on this book's cover is both a tribute to children and a call for politics. In discussing *Antigone*, Lacan asks: 'Have you noticed that she is only ever referred to throughout the play with the Greek word η παῖς, which means "the child"?' (1992: 250). What is at stake in the incrimination of the child's death drive is not necessarily her blindness, inflexibility, lack of prudence, immaturity and other pious phobias. The political real of Lacan's anxiety is not Antigone's suicidal act in itself, but the 'child's *autonomy*' as a 'bearer of' a potential 'signifying cut' that confers on her 'the indomitable power' of being what she is in the face of everything that may oppose her (Lacan 1992: 282, original emphasis). What is executed by state action is precisely this suspension of the political possibility of autonomy, of *parrhesia*, of frank and unrestrained speech. The punishment of the child consists in 'her being *shut up* or suspended in the zone between life and death. Although she is not yet dead, she is eliminated from the world of the living' (Lacan 1992: 280, original emphasis). What is being pre-empted by the state's sentencing act is the risk of parrhesiastic truth-telling, turned into a political procedure. Moreover, it remains a particularly strong reminder of the association of politics not only with the wager but also with daring courage. To continue the same intriguing question that betrays the political angst of psychoanalysis: 'Have we not noticed' that in Aeschylus' *Prometheus Bound* we encounter the same fidelity to the child-event? Io asks the sentenced Prometheus in line 771: 'Who then is to loose thee against the will of Zeus?' 'It is to be one of thine own lineage – εγγόνων εἶναι χρεών', Prometheus replies (Aeschylus 1973: 772). Astonished, Io asks, 'How sayest thou? A child of mine release thee from thy misery?' – ἦ 'μός παῖς σ' ἀπαλλάξει κακῶν; (Aeschylus 1973: 773). This Promethean, uncanny child-figure is the real of Badiou's parrhesiastic pedagogy: the child-figure that 'will have to educate itself, that will have to grow up by itself', 'reversing the course of time'. In that sequence, we too can become 'a new historical child, as it can be a new historical animal' (Badiou 2006b: 130). Antigone's lament that she won't be able to beget children will thus have been redeemed, by a surplus truth in excess of parentage.

Notes

1. Certainly, Badiou and Lyotard's reading of Leibniz goes contrary to Deleuze's more dazzling example whereby the self-sufficient monad slides through baroque deterritorialisations of organic and inorganic matter into nomadic folds and singularities. See Deleuze's paradigmatic statement *The Fold* (2006).
2. Bosteels 2011a: 173. For the wider ramifications of the Badiou–Žižek debate, see also Sean Homer's chapter in this volume.
3. For a thorough treatment of Žižek by Bosteels see chapter 4, 'In Search of the Act', in Bosteels 2011b.

4. Badiou 2012a: 125, 124. Badiou's essay, 'The Lessons of Jacques Rancière: Knowledge and Power after the Storm', translated by Tzuchien Tho, was published in Gabriel Rockhill and Philip Watts (eds), *Jacques Rancière: History, Politics, Aesthetics* (Durham, NC, and London: Duke University Press, 2009).

5. For a sustained treatment of this argument see Bartlett 2011.

6. On this issue see Rancière's studies in *The Philosopher and his Poor* (2004) as well as Marios Constantinou's chapter in this volume.

7. Badiou 2012a: 128, original emphasis. Badiou treats the same issue in his book on Wagner without revising his position. See Badiou 2010c: 86, 106–10.

8. Wagner, *The Mastersingers*, Act III. For an excellent account of this passage in the wider context of Germany's imperial mandate and Wagner's solicitation of patronage regarding the Bayreuth Festival, see Rose 1996: 110–14. Badiou disregards entirely Wagner's intentional equivocation which forces the mutual supplementation between empire and art, arguing, instead, that high German art replaces empire. For Badiou, the chorus simply lets the empire go (2010c: 108). In my perspective, empire is the Wagnerian real of Germany. The fidelity of High Art to the imperial simulacrum is the presupposition of the 'new Germany'. Hence, the presence of the signifier 'Holy' as a common qualifier of 'Roman Empire' and 'German Art'.

9. On the issue of *imperialsozialismus*, see the excellent essay by Domenico Losurdo, 'The Adventures of the Revolutionary Subject from the 19th to the 20th Century', *brumaria*, 22 (2010).

Part I: The Crisis of Negation and the Political Condition

From Logic to Anthropology: Affirmative Dialectics

Alain Badiou

The fundamental problem in the philosophical field today is to find something like a new logic. We cannot start out from considerations on politics, life, creation or action. We must first describe a new logic, or, more precisely, a new dialectics. This was that way that Plato took. And it was after all the one Marx proposed too. Marx's work is not to begin with a new historical vision, a new theory of class struggle and so on, but instead a new general logic that he developed in the wake of Hegelian dialectics. Marx was perhaps the first, after Plato, to forge an explicit relation between revolutionary politics and a new dialectical framework. Our problem today is the same. To be sure, after two centuries of successes and failures in revolutionary politics and, in particular, after the failure of the state-form of socialism, we must have something to rectify. But what we also have to find is a new logic, a new philosophical proposition adequate for all forms of creative novelty. Thus, the difficult question of dialectical and of non-dialectical relations is a pressing one. Our problem, if you will, is the problem of negativity.

When the logical framework of political action is of the classical dialectical type, what is fundamental is negation. The development of the political struggle is fundamentally something like a 'revolt against', an 'opposition to', or a 'negation of'. And the newness – the creation of the new state, or of the new law – is always a result of the process of negation. This is the Hegelian framework: you have a relation between affirmation and negation, construction and negation, in which the real principle of movement, and the real principle of creation, is negation. And so the very definition of the revolutionary class is to be *against* the present state or *against* the present law in the precise sense that revolutionary consciousness, as Lenin would say, is basically the consciousness that one stands in a relation of negation to the existing order.

But this vision as such cannot be sustained today. We are living through a sort of crisis of trust in the power of negativity. And we have known two forms of this crisis.

Adorno thinks that the classical Hegelian dialectics was way too affirmative, far too subordinated to the potency of the Totality and of the One. He proposes a sort of hyper-negativity, the name of which is 'negative dialectics'. Today we know that by proceeding in this way, all we ultimately end up with is an ethics of compassion, a vision where the hero of our consciousness is the suffering human body, the pure victim. And we know as well that this moralism is perfectly adequate to capitalist domination pursued under the mask of democracy.

Negri and Althusser, on the other hand, argue that Hegelian dialectics was overly negative, way too subjective and all too indifferent to the absolute potency of Nature, Life, or the movement of History. They find in Spinoza a model of philosophy that is ultimately devoid of negation. Today we know that by proceeding in this way we are left with an acceptance of the dominant order, in accordance with the conviction that this order is full of newness and creativity and that in the end modern capitalism is the immediate strength working, beyond empire, towards a sort of communism.

What all my work has sought to do is to propose a new dialectical framework, neither via a return to the young Marx or to Hegel, nor via the negative dialectics of Adorno, which is like an aesthetics of human rights, nor via the affirmative construction proposed by Negri, which destroys all forms of dialecticism and amounts to a sort of Nietzschean Gay Science of History.

I think the problem today is to find a way to reverse classical dialectical logic inside of itself, so that affirmation, or the positive proposition, comes before negation instead of after it. Differently put, in some sense my attempt is to find a dialectical framework where something of the future comes before the negative present. I'm not advocating a suppression of the relation between affirmation and negation – revolt and class struggle certainly remain essential – nor a pacifistic orientation or the like. The question is not whether we need to struggle or to oppose; more precisely, it concerns the relation between negation and affirmation. So when I say that there is something non-dialectical, whether with regard to Paul or to the field of concrete political analysis, I am putting forward the same idea formally speaking. We have to try to understand the exact conditions under which we are able to have something like a possibility of concrete negation. And this can only be achieved, it seems to me, in the field of primitive affirmation, through something that is primitively affirmative and not negative. To use my own terminology: it is a question of event and subject.

Ultimately, what I am saying is very simple. First, that to open up a new situation, a new possibility, it is essential that there be a new creativity of time and a new creativity of the situation. There has to be something that is an actual opening, which is what I name 'event'. What is an event? An event is simply that which interrupts the law, the rules and the structure of the situation, and thus creates a new possibility. So an event is not in the first place the creation of a new situation; rather, it is the creation of a new possibility, which is not the same thing. In fact, the event takes place in a situation that remains the same, but this same situation is inside the new possibility. For Paul, for example, the event is the resurrection of Christ, and this event does not directly change anything in the Roman Empire. So the general situation, which is the Roman Empire, remains the same. But inside the situation an event transpires, thus opening a new possibility. Things are the same in the political field. In May 1968 in Paris, for instance, no real change occurred in the general situation of the state: De Gaulle remained in power and the government continued to operate, with its police and so on. But there was the opening of a new possibility, and this is what I mean by event. After that comes the possibility of realising / materialising the consequences of this new possibility, the elaboration of which amounts to the creation of a new subjective body.

A new subjective body is the realisation of the possibility opened by the event in concrete form, and is thus the development of some consequences of the new possibility. Among these consequences different forms of negation are, of course, to be found: struggle, revolt, new possibilities of being against something, the destruction of some part of the law and so on. But these forms of negation are consequences of the birth of the new subjectivity, not the other way around: the new subjectivity is not a consequence of the negation. So, this logic is actually non-dialectical – in Hegel's and Marx's sense – since it does not start with the creativity of negation as such, though the site of negativity is certainly included in the consequences of something which is affirmative.

With this, I can return to a book I wrote many years ago about the Apostle Paul. This book was written in order to put forward a clear example of this new logic, that is, of a new logic for *all* truth procedures, those in the political field included. Paul offers a very clear example of how to think through the relation between an event and a new subjectivity – this was my main point. Paul provides a new, very acute perspective on how this logic operates in the field of law, and specifically in the new subject's relation to the old law. Indeed, Paul explains very clearly that whenever an event occurs that is truly the creation of a new possibility in the situation, a new body must first be created and a new subjectivity affirmed prior to all negation or negative consequences. The first thing to do is to create, to affirm the new subjectivity. What, then, stands at the very beginning of the new subjectivity and the new subjective body? It is the group of people that affirms that there really is a new possibility – they affirm the affirmation. In the case of Christianity, they affirm the resurrection. After such an affirmation, a lot of practical and symbolic consequences will follow for the situation in question. It is interesting to see in the example of Paul, however, that the very beginning of something new is always something like a pure affirmation of the new possibility as such. There is a resurrection and you have to affirm it! And when you affirm the resurrection and organise that sort of affirmation – because affirmation occurs with others and is directed towards others – you create something absolutely new, not in the form of a negation of what exists but in the form of the newness inside of what exists. And so we no longer have negation, on the one hand, and affirmation, on the other. Instead, there is affirmation and division, or the creation that grounds the independence of new subject from within the situation of the old. This is the general orientation of the new logic.

Within this orientation, it becomes possible to propose a novel examination of all the old words in such-and-such a field of knowledge or action. As an exercise, I propose that we discuss the word 'democracy'. The word democracy is indeed the common term of all ideological dispositions of the imperialist states today, in fact of pretty much all the reactionary states. So we must declare a first rupture by saying that we do not accept their ideological line, since it ultimately amounts to the idea that their 'democracy' cannot be resisted except if one is a terrorist, an ally in despotism and so on.

This means, however, that we are in a situation where we have to clarify for ourselves not only the content of the concept but also whether we want to use the word. Is there a possible good use of the word 'democracy' today? That is my subjective question. It is not exactly a theoretical one. Why? Because I can always name 'democracy' something else. There can be both good and bad uses of the word democracy today. And there is probably something genuinely confusing about the use of the word itself insofar as one generally understands it immediately in terms of its present meaning, which is basically that given it by all the reactionary forces in the world today.

I have ultimately decided to keep the word. It is generally a good thing to keep a word, for the reason that there is something problematic about leftists saying, for example, 'I am not interested in "democracy" at all, because it has become practically meaningless.' On the other hand, it is true that when you talk about democracy you continue to operate on the terrain of the common ideology. The situation is difficult, because we have to criticise the actual 'democracies' in one sense and in a different sense we have to criticise the political propaganda made of the term 'democracy' today. If we do not do this we will become paralysed. In the first case we would be saying 'Yes, we are in a democracy, but democracy can do something else'; however, this would ultimately put us in a defensive position, which is the opposite of my conception, since my position involves starting with an affirmation, not at all with a defensive posture. So, if we stick to the word, we must divide the signification of the word classically and differentiate between good democracy and bad democracy, between the reactionary conception of democracy and the progressive conception of democracy. But what is the basis of that division? In classical Marxism, there is a clear basis upon which to divide everything, namely according to class distinction. We can distinguish popular democracy from bourgeois democracy, or perhaps, to be more contemporary, from yuppie democracy. And the possibility of that sort of division is also the possibility of thinking democracy as something other than a form of state. It is a distinction not only between popular democracy and yuppie democracy, but between true democracy and democracy as a form of state, as a form of oppressive state, as a class state.

But this strict duality is not convincing in the framework of a new dialectical thinking. It is too easy to determine popular democracy negatively as being all that the state democracy is not. To escape the game of negation and the negation of negation, I shall now present three understandings of democracy – not a division into two, but into three. That is always my trick. When I run into a difficulty with a division in two, I create a division in three. And this is why, in general fashion, as Giorgio Agamben was the first to remark, I ultimately have, for every problem, four terms. Hegel has three terms, because after the negation and the negation of negation, there is the totality of the process, the becoming of the absolute knowledge as a third term. But for me, after two different affirmations – the conservative one and the affirmation of the new possibility – there are two different negations. This is because the conservative negation of novelty by the reaction is not the same as the negative part, directed against the conservative position, of the new affirmation.

On the question of democracy, I give the three primitive terms. First, there is democracy as a form of state, which is actually democracy in its commonplace meaning, that is, representative democracy or parliamentarian ideology. Secondly, there is democracy understood as movement or a 'democracy of places', which is not democracy in the directly political sense, but perhaps more in the historical sense. So when democracy takes place, it is democracy in the form of an event. This is the sense of democracy in the work of Jacques Rancière, for example. For Rancière, as for me, democracy is the activation of the principle of equality. When the principle of equality is really active, you have some version of our understanding of democracy: that is, democracy as the irruption of collective equality in a concrete form, which can be protest or insurrection, or popular assembly, or any other form in which equality is effectively active. So, this understanding itself has many forms, but we can perfectly understand exactly what this form of democracy is, and it is in fact a recurrent form of revolutionary democracy. But as you know it is actually rather the form of a sudden emergence in history, and ultimately of the event, than the form of the consequences of an event, or of the creation of a new political body. As such even if the moment of revolutionary rupture is a true meaning of democracy, it is not exactly the political concept of that meaning. I think it is a much more historical concept of democracy, that is to say, a concept that stands in relation to the event. And so we have to find a third sense of democracy, one which is properly the democracy of the determination of the new political subject as such. This is my ultimate conception. Democracy for me is another name for the elaboration of the consequences of collective action and for determining the new political subject.

So in the end we have four terms: classical representative democracy, which is a form of state power; mass democracy, which is of an historical nature; democracy as a political subject; and, finally, the process of the progressive vanishing of the state, which is the historical and negative inscription of politics in history, under the name of communism.

So, for the clear classical opposition between the dominant false democracy and true popular democracy, we thus substitute a sort of complex, with three places – state, revolutionary event and politics – and three processes – affirmation of people's access to politics outside the state, negation of this access by the state, and victory for the political organisation of people. And as a totalisation of the entire complex, the advent of communism by concrete results, or all results which are proofs of the weakness of the state and finally of the possibility of its vanishing.

Another example is precisely the relationship between politics and power. Classically, the goal of political action is to seize power, to destroy the state machinery of the enemies. The name for this process is the master name of all political classicism: revolution. Today, at the beginning of constitution, at the beginning of a new subjective body, it is not possible to be inside the state or more generally to aim for power. The word 'revolution' can no longer be our master name. So we have to stand entirely outside state power. But the state is always in the field of political questions and in the space of action. If our political subjectivity is not inside the state, if on the contrary it is on the outside, nonetheless the state is in the field of our action. To take a concrete example from my own experience, if we must do something about workers who are without papers, say African immigrants, and we want to organise and change things in this field, then we will quickly find that the state is in our space. We will have to confront new laws and state decisions. And we will have to create something that will come face-to-face with the state – not inside the state, but face-to-face with it. So, we will have to have a 'discussion' with the state, or otherwise organise various forms of disruption. In any case, we will have to prescribe something concerning the state from outside. We will have to prescribe something that establishes a relation with the state. And the major difficulty will be to maintain the possibility of being outside while prescribing something that concerns the inside. In the development of politics, then, there is a sort of topological difficulty, namely, the relation between the outside and the inside. Because the state is always inviting you inside and asking that you not be outside.

I have had many very concrete experiences of this. A good instance is when I go with workers to discuss matters with some minister or other, because the state refuses their 'regularisation'. And the state representative will always ask, 'Who are you?' And we always answer, 'We are a political organisation with people'. And the reply is always, 'OK, but who are you?!' The problem is simple: to be somebody is to be inside the state, otherwise you cannot be heard at all. So there are two possible outcomes. Either there is ultimately a discussion and some political outcome. Or else there is no room for discussion because we are nobody. Once more, this is the precise question of affirmation: how can we be somebody without being on the inside? We must affirm our existence, our principles, our action, always *from outside*.

I know that some critics of my thought, who also aim to represent possibilities for a complete transformation of our situation, object that I am too far 'outside' this process, that I'm ultimately a 'prophet' and not really an active player in the immanent and concrete world. I completely disagree with this sort of objection because in its theoretical analysis of global society it forgets the real logic of prescription and the necessity of having a new conception of affirmative dialectics. Without the French Revolution, without the great revolt of workers in France, without the real and concrete movement of the Parisian proletariat, Marx certainly would never have fathomed this concept of the proletariat. The movement is not from the concept of proletariat to the proletarian movement. The real becoming is from the revolt of workers to the new proposition. So, in the end, the true discussion is not at all about the concrete analysis of global society, but about our relation to the state. The real question is whether to be outside or inside the state. The fundamental idea is that to be in the new affirmative dialectical framework, you must be outside the state, because inside the state you remain precisely in the negative figure of opposition. And thus, once more, negativity, the appearance of negativity, comes first.

I want to insist on the fact that the new logical framework is not only a vision of politics, or even a vision of some particular practices. It prescribes, much more generally, a sort of anthropology.

First, I think we are animals. I speak of human animals and living bodies, and, in contrast to all classical humanism, I include a lot of things in our definition of animals. Ultimately, this definition encompasses all our concrete existence as such, not including anything else or any supplement. And I indeed think that capitalist anthropology is the conviction that, fundamentally, humanity comprises nothing else but self-interested animals. That is a very important point. I think we have to engage in some propaganda on this point. Modern capitalism is always speaking about human rights, democracy, freedom and so on, but we can in fact see very concretely that under all these names there is nothing else but human animals with interests, who have to be happy with products, and its subject is something like animals-standing-before-the-market. And this is in actual fact its definition of the human. We have a hierarchy, at the bottom of which are the poor, who stand facing the market but without means, and at the top of which are the rich, who also stand facing the market but who have far greater means. And the protection of all this is really nothing else but capitalist anthropology. Now, the possibility of being something other than animals in this sense is actually the becoming subject of a human animal. And it is through the incorporation of a new body, which is something other than standing before the market, that you can become something like a subject. 'Infinite' is another name for this process, because what we have with this kind of incorporation is an affirmation of a new possibility with infinite consequences. The new possibility has infinite consequences – this is always the case.

So, we can say that human rights, rights that are the subject's rights, are in fact the rights of the infinite. It was Jean-François Lyotard who first coined this expression in his most important book, *The Différend*. And it is one that I take up.

But what, ultimately, is the anthropological question? I propose that this question runs as follows: what exactly is the singularity of mankind, of human beings? We know that, today, there exists a species of human animals, defined by their inclusion in the global market. And, by contrast, we can call 'humanity' the capacity to become the subject of an event, of something that happens. The capacity to accept the possibility of incorporation within a new subjective body; the capacity of drawing its practical consequences in the situation of incorporation which itself is the becoming of the new subject. And in the becoming of the subject, beyond the support of all that which is one or some human animals, there is something infinite, a new creation of something infinite, and for me the name of this infinite something is: truth.

We can say, then, that the incorporation of the subject is the incorporation of some human animals in something like a process of truth. And that is the global field of what we can name humanity or human beings, in the context of affirmative dialectics.

I agree ultimately with the young Marx on one point: only in the successive creation of new forms of subjects is there something like a generic humanity, because generic humanity is infinite humanity – it is the same thing – and the human animal standing before the market is not at all generic; it is absolutely particular.

All this comes to a new hypothesis about the subject, and it is also a new hypothesis about human life, about what it means for humans to live. In my book *Logics of the Worlds*, I oppose human rights in their ordinary meaning to the rights of the infinite, by making a contrast between today's 'democratic materialism' and the project of 'dialectical materialism', which is a possible name for affirmative dialectics. What makes these forms of materialism antithetical are their respective understandings of human life: either there is nothing but languages and bodies, or else there is a third term, something like the production of 'truths' that cut through the hegemony of our animal existence. The title of the conclusion of *Logics of the Worlds* is 'What is it to live?' It is clearly the end question of anthropology.

In fact, there are two completely different conceptions of human life. The first reduces human life to common animal life: the satisfaction of all natural desires, happiness, security and so on. The second one is what we are speaking of: human life has to be identified with the incorporation to a truth-body. So, a human being is properly 'living' only when he or she is the agent of a passage from particularity to universality, from a local process to genericity, from a singular world to an eternal truth.

All these passages operate under a new idea, which is, for a concrete individual, the mediation between his or her practical singularity and the common or generic relationship to universality. For example, in politics, the name for this idea, which is the mediation between the concrete situation of political action, and a form of eternal truth, is communism.

Maybe this conception is a bit heroic. Indeed we know that many philosophers affirm that the time for heroism has passed. But perhaps Althusser was right to affirm that philosophy has no history. The fact that an idea is old-fashioned is not, for the philosopher, an objection to this idea. In any case, even if the conception is a bit heroic, I affirm before you: it's mine. And I, certainly, am too old to change on this point.

Edited by Steven Corcoran

2

Conditioning Communism: Badiou, Plato and Philosophy as Meta-Critical Anamnesis

Frank Ruda

Socrates . . . inaugurated the new being-in-the-world that I here call a subjectivity.

Jacques Lacan

[T]he better part of our memory exists outside of ourselves . . .

Marcel Proust

Philosophy makes things endlessly difficult. One reason for this is that philosophy in its very practice opposes forms of oblivion that make certain ways of life possible to begin with. It might be argued that one of the last thinkers to make this the centre and kernel of his overall philosophical writings was Martin Heidegger. He infamously proposed to conceive of the complete history (of being and consequently also of mankind) as a history of the forgetting of one of the most important distinctions: that between being and beings (Heidegger 1996). For him this type of forgetting was precisely the defining kernel of the totality of metaphysics. Metaphysics is the most influential mechanism of oblivion as it takes the distinction between being and beings and interprets it by reinscribing it into one of the two sides of this very distinction. That is to say, there is no distinction between being and beings, yet there is a hierarchy on the side of beings which implies that there can be a highest being (traditionally this being goes under the name of God, but, as Heidegger argues, it structurally defines the place of the 'subject' in terms of the underlying ground to everything, that is, as *subjectum* [Heidegger 1991]). This move – taking the distinction and reinscribing it into one of its elements – is what makes metaphysics structurally ontotheological (it takes being as being the highest being) and implements a fundamental oblivion that in the history of philosophy first occurred with Plato. He put the truth of being

56

(*aletheia*) under the 'yoke of the idea' (Heidegger 1998: 170) and thereby reduced 'being' to the very presence that is implied in the concept of being 'a being'. Not only have the consequences of this very ontotheological manoeuvre led to the most cata-strophic effects (mostly inaugurated by different means of subjec-tive empowerment under the heading of 'technique' [Heidegger 1982]), but with it also came a forgetting of the very act of forget-ting. In this sense the totality of – at least – Western history is a history of forgotten oblivion. Philosophy, for Heidegger, therefore has the task of countering this forgetful forgetting that is meta-physics by returning to the beginning, to its origin and advent. It is able to remind us that there was once thought that was not yet forgetful (not even of its own forgetfulness). Only in this way can philosophy oppose or overcome (*verwinden* in German) the for-getful state we are in.

Yet the proper medium in which such a non-forgetful thought can be situated is not in itself philosophical. Why this is the case may become clear when the framing of oblivion is taken into account. For what needs to be recalled cannot simply be 'a being' (a somehow present memory, something experienced yet forgot-ten, and so on). What needs to be recalled is a distinction that never takes the form of an object (a being). Thus philosophy can point us to the fact that remembering this is the most crucial thing to do. Yet the proper medium of this recollection is not philosophy but that which Plato – who is the truly bad guy in this scenario – seems to have really despised: poetry. In poetry – poetic thought before and to a certain extent after Plato – there is something that can be used to fight the forgotten oblivion that functions as the structuring principle of our contemporary world. The difficult task of philosophy, then, is to point us to this reminder, to demonstrate that there is something that we need to recall in order to help us understand what has been lost by forgetting that we have forgot-ten. In this precise sense, philosophy for Heidegger is – although against Plato – an anamnesic practice. However, there are few things more difficult than not to be forgetful – and the poets know this best.

Alain Badiou is one of the few influential philosophers today who claims to be a Platonist. In his first *Manifesto for Philosophy* (originally published in 1989), he branded this peculiar kind of Platonism 'a *Platonism of the multiple*' (1999a: 103, original emphasis). This proclamation not only sounds very counter-current today, but also radically anti-Heideggerian. Indeed, it is a counter-affirmation of Plato against the whole of the twentieth century, which was – with very few exceptions (see, e.g., Koyré 1968) – unanimously anti-Platonist (at least from Nietzsche to Deleuze [Badiou 1999a], including the Marxist tradition, the Vienna Circle and the positivists following it, and so on); and it is anti-Heideggerian, as for Badiou Plato is not the philosopher in whose thought one can first (and foremost) situate the beginning of a catastrophic and powerful history of oblivion.[1] Rather, it is with Plato, precisely, that philosophy as a historically specific and peculiar form of practice first saw the light of day. Against Heidegger (and the majority of contemporary philosophers), then, Badiou affirms that there is something – not in pre-Socratic poetic thought but in Plato – that is still contemporary to and relevant for all philosophical thought;[2] but, with Heidegger, Badiou somehow insists that this very 'something in Plato' is worth remembering. So Badiou's gesture of reaffirming a Platonist position can also be read as a gesture of anamnesis. Yet the question emerges as to what it is that philosophy needs to remind us (and itself) of. Is there also a diagnosis of oblivion at work in Badiou?

What Badiou calls 'democratic materialism' (2009a: 1–40) – the contemporary form of ideology suited to what he calls 'parliamentary-capitalism' – can be said to endorse a peculiar kind of forgetting. This can most easily be rendered in the following way: if – following a statement of Louis Althusser – what has determined both philosophy and the whole political field throughout practically their entire history is the old struggle between materialism and idealism, after the disappearance of idealism and the complete takeover of materialism – everyone being a spontaneous materialist – this struggle has now entered a new phase. Although taking an idealist position seems impossible right now, it cannot be said that materialism has simply won the battle. Although the predominant version of materialism – which is precisely democratic materialism – denies that there might even be a struggle any more, the ideology-critical approach of Badiou consists in demonstrating that this denial, this repression, cannot be upheld.[3] There is always a return of the repressed (in this case of the struggle). Therefore, it can be said that the struggle between materialism and idealism today reappears and returns within materialism, splitting it into two: a materialist materialism and an idealist materialism.[4] Yet this return of the struggle within materialism also contains a moment of reversal. It is precisely not, as one might expect, that the materialist materialism has taken the place of the formerly solid materialism and the idealist materialism that of the formerly idealist position. It is rather that the ideological structure – the denial on which it is based – of democratic materialism functions in such a way that by attacking the kernel of the former idealism it also attacks the dialectical moment it was based upon. To put it simply: democratic materialism was only able to overcome idealism by getting rid of the materialist kernel of idealism itself. Due to the return of the repressed struggle within materialism, materialism is now – ideologically – split into a materialism which denies there is anything materialistically relevant to idealism and one which seeks to stick to the materialist kernel of idealism itself.

But one might ask here: in what does the materialist kernel of previous idealism consist? Two interlinked answers can be given: first, the materialist kernel of idealism (let's say of thinkers commonly treated as idealist such as Plato or Hegel) is dialectic;[5] second, the materialist kernel of idealism is linked to what Badiou calls an 'idea' (2011a: 105–16). Democratic materialism has become the predominant ideology of today's world by ignoring the dialectic (for example, by ignoring the dialectic which makes it impossible for materialism simply to become the only fitting ideology for the contemporary world)[6] and in doing so it denies the very existence of what the previous idealists called an idea. Or, to put it simply: what appeared with the disappearance of idealism is a materialism that seeks to be everything there is and that, by problematically totalising itself (there are only bodies and languages), turns itself into a weird form of idealism (idealising the 'matter' of bodies and languages by treating these as the only matter there is). So what one ends up with in this very formal account of Badiou's diagnosis of the contemporary present is, in terms of ideology, also that there is oblivion, or, more adequately perhaps, that there is amnesia. Democratic materialism forcefully forgets, denies and represses the very existence of the dialectic, and consequently becomes amnesic of the idea. Democratic materialism can thus, referring again to Heidegger, be called a metaphysics, or in Badiou's terms an ideology.

Democratic materialist metaphysics or ideology – which wants to be neither one nor the other – not only forgets the distinction between materialism and idealism (and therefore the dialectical kernel of idealism which is also linked to the concept of the idea), but also performs the very move that Heidegger criticises as that of metaphysics par excellence. If, for Heidegger, metaphysics relies on the understanding of 'being' in terms of a highest being, this implies that metaphysics takes 'being' as something constructible[7] (in terms of the highest being). Insisting on constructibility – and the oblivious denial of an antecedent split or distinction that opposes this constructibility – is for Heidegger the crucial move of metaphysics. Democratic materialism also insists on constructibility, insofar as everything is constructible in terms of bodies and languages, or of individuals and communities.[8] But, much like Western metaphysics for Heidegger, democratic materialism relies on a very special manoeuvre that gives its specific constructibility a peculiar shape (and makes intelligible why it is perfectly well suited to the contemporary form of capitalism).

The metaphysical manoeuvre of democratic materialism as the ideology of contemporary capitalism can most easily be accounted for by relating it – as Heidegger would never do – to a simple scientific, that is, mathematical, insight.[9] Consider the order of whole natural numbers (1, 2, 3, 4, and so on): each of these numbers is in itself finite (each of them names the finite point or position where it stands) and so each of the numbers and the whole series of numbers preceding it is also finite, yet each of them has a potential infinity of successors. One can easily find a greater number to any number thinkable by simply applying one of the most simple mathematical formulas, namely $(n + 1)$ to it.[10] Thus there is a dialectic of finitude and (potential) infinity with regard to the series of natural numbers. A number is thus an element of an infinite set (of potential progression ad infinitum) precisely by its standing between the finite (of the preceding series of numbers) and the infinite (of its potential successors) (see also Lavine 1998). This is the precise definition of what one can call numerical finitude, as each number forms a point between the finite series before and the potentially infinite series after it. It should be clear that even numerical finitude is nothing but a peculiar relation between the finite and the infinite. Simply considering the numerically finite as being finite thus already relies on a specific kind of oblivion (since what is forgotten is the potential – but constitutive – infinity of successors). What is forgotten is the possibility of (potential) infinity. Indeed, simply by considering that the realm of the (infinite set of) natural numbers derives from the very constitution of this very set – the essential finitude of the number (its element) – already works to hypostatise one side of the defining criteria of what a number as element of the set of natural numbers is. Put simply: to claim that number is finite implies a 'decision for finitude' (Badiou 2012–13) that forcefully forgets that the possibility of infinity is as constitutive of the number as the finite series of predecessors.

This forgetful decision in favour of the finitude of number can be translated into direct political terms: the numericity of commodities, of money, of electoral votes, opinion polls, the very idea of majority votes, and so on – all that constitutes our 'era of number's despotism', 'the empire of number' whose main imperative is 'count!'[11] – relies on the oblivion of the latent, that is, potential infinity that is constitutive of the very number that the contemporary 'politics of administration' (Badiou 2012a: 311) (a possible name for the link between democratic materialist ideology and parliamentary capitalism) employs as one of its most crucial tools (if not *the* most crucial). Number relies on an orientation that constructs everything there is as being countable. This very countability relies on constructibility, which in turn relies on a decision to finitise the very concept of number. And as we have all been counted – as voters, as mobile phone owners, as mere existing bodies, and so on[12] – the type of subjectivity that is implied within this alleged political system is a 'voided Subject' (Badiou 2012b: 459), a subject that is precisely voided by being finitised (purified and reduced to nothing but an individual body with communal language capacities) by the 'seduction of commodities and money' (Badiou 2012b: 460). Oblivion here is thus not only a decisive and decided forgetting of democratic materialism, and thus an ideology, but it simultaneously engenders a production of oblivion (of one's own potential infinity) in each and every individual. But this very forgotten production of oblivion (a more traditional name for which is 'naturalisation') thus perfectly endorses and reproduces, produces and enforces the contemporary capitalist order. And it endorses materialism since – against Heidegger – one cannot actually interpret this in any ontotheological way (by claiming that there is something like a highest of all beings).

Yet the forgetting of the possibility of infinity (of the number) is perhaps not even the most radical dimension of this ideological forgetting and the proper dimension of the implicit decision for constructibility can only be grasped by taking this into account. There is a twofold forgetting here. To outline this let me once again turn to mathematics: in mathematics it can be demonstrated that there is an infinity that is higher, or, to be more precise, more powerful, than the (potential) infinity of the natural numbers (that is, infinite progression). Therefore, there are the whole natural numbers (a series of predecessors and successors) and then there is 'something' that cannot be considered a successor of the series of natural numbers (otherwise it would simply be another natural number); let us call it ω.[13] One way of rendering ω's position is by calling it an actual infinity (the mathematicians' name for it).[14] ω as infinite point can be said to surpass the potential infinity of successors precisely by not being a successor; instead, it is the place or space where the succession can take place.[15] But, by being excluded from the potentially infinite succession, it is simultaneously the horizon of this very succession (that which is the totalising limit-point of the potentially infinite series).[16] ω is thus an infinite point, which is also an infinite place (by retroactively totalising the potentially infinite series and simultaneously not being a successor) and takes the function of a limit-point (infinite horizon). In this threefold determination ω can be said to interrupt the repetition of the succession (the repetition of the repeated engendering of new successors) which defined the realm of whole natural numbers. Yet a successor to ω (which is itself not a successor) can now be generated by again applying the simplest mathematical formula ($ω + 1$), and this can of course be repeated indefinitely. This amounts to reopening a further succession,[17] to the reinscription of a new repetition. But as ω – and this is important – is at the jointure of two successions, it is itself not a successor of the first series of succession. This is why Badiou calls it an 'intervallic infinity' (2012–13), since it can itself be considered to be the support of a new series of (potentially infinite) succession. Here it might be said that the best example of such an intermediate infinity in political terms is a revolution[18] (because – at least in its traditional understanding – it embodies the function of the infinite point, of the place and of the horizon); it breaks with the previous succession and order of succession and creates a new one. ω is an infinite number that breaks with repetition but that also makes it possible to recommence. What does all this tell us? It tells us that finitude, which is the most crucial momentum of contemporary ideology (a result of its constructibilism), consists in an oblivion of the very existence of the different functions of infinity (point, place, horizon, interruption and recommencement). The philosophical and political (but also artistic and amorous) consequences of this forced and forceful forgetting are far-reaching.

A first consequence is that this oblivion implies the denial of the significance of the infinite point *tout court*. It denies that there can be something that is not a successor and thereby also the very idea of an interruption of succession, that is, it denies eventality as such. This leads to an endless extension of the quantitative dimension of finitude by forgetting that there can be something like a qualitative leap, an exception. This is one way of rendering the fact that democratic materialism forgets the dialectic, since any dialectic worthy of the name is a dialectic of exception. The extension of the quantitative implies that there is no exception to that which is, this is to say that there is no dialectics and no option for political action, for in the last instance everything has a price (in other words, there is no politics that could not be reduced to the mere number game of the economy).[19] This very operation (of constructibility) might be considered to be one of the most crucial capitalist operations *tout court* (that is, the assimilation of a point of exception to the normality of repetition), since it implies the translation and transfixation of something qualitatively different into something quantitatively equivalent, and thus comprehensible and accessible (this involves turning an exception into a new commodity that simply has a price like all the others). This implies, of course, that everything that does not have a price (that is, is not quantitatively accessible) does not count, that is, is insignificant, or imperceptible from the perspective of the quantitative regime. This is what makes intelligible the fact that in capitalist democratic materialism true love does not count for much (and is constantly subjected to attempts at being quantitatively grasped);[20] that art is only what can be sold on the art market; and that science is only truly worth thinking about when it yields new, marketable results. Everything that seems incapable of being grasped in quantitative terms is insignificant, and thus negligible, and can be (indeed needs to be) forgotten. Quantity governs everything; quality is forgotten.

A second consequence lies in the fact that ω, in its precise determination as place of potentially infinite repetition (constitutive for number), gets forgotten. This consequence is realised by hypostatising relation, that is, the relations that obtain between the finite (numbers), and by giving them primacy over the place where their relation is situated. That is to say, number is treated as a mere relation able to be comprehended in terms of equality and inequality.

This ultimately comes down to the matter of holism versus ontology. What is thus established is that the only way in which a thing can be worth more than another is by the position it takes in the series (7 is more than 4 but less than 13). With this operation it is not that the exception as something qualitatively different is obstructed, but rather that it is forcefully forgotten that there can be (and is) something absolute. This is why, within the political field, this leads to cosmopolitism or cultural relativism (no political organisation or party within the parliamentary system can claim that its agenda is fundamentally different from any of the others; it can only claim that its proposition is – numerically – better than the others). For better or for worse, this is what counts; absolute difference is forgotten.

A third consequence is that the very definition of ω as infinite horizon, as limit-point to the potentially infinite series of numbers, is denied and forgotten. This can be translated into the claim that, although it might seem that there is something beyond the mere repetition of finitude, in fact there is not. This operation can also be translated into the following claim: that the repetition that is recommenced after ω, after the interruption of the first series of repetition, is worse than the first (it is criminal, destructive, dangerous, horrific and so on). All these consequences are consequences of a forgetting of the infinite. This forgetting takes the precise form of forgetting the status of ω as non-successor (with its different characteristics). So Badiou has in some sense diagnosed, like Heidegger before him, the forgetting of a difference, of a qualitative difference (or more precisely, the qualitative difference between quantity and quality), of the difference between finitude and infinity (more precisely, between the constitutive infinity of finitude), and therefore of the difference between the denial and the existence of something absolute. If, for Heidegger, philosophy was able to counter metaphysical forgetting (and its social, political and cultural consequences) by revealingly recalling the truth of being (and insisting on the ontological distinction between being and beings)[21] through his pointing to the language of the poets, Badiou's opposition to ideological oblivion functions differently. So why and how is philosophy anamnesic for Badiou?

One might start to answer this question by taking two things into account: Badiou not only defends a philosophical position that could not be more counter-current to the contemporary (ideological) doxa, namely Platonism, but is also one of the few thinkers who has openly begun again to endorse a political position, one that also could hardly sound more out of date with respect to today's mainstream political positions, namely communism. My claim is that in order to properly understand Badiou's take on how to counter the above-delineated oblivion of democratic material- ism, these two commitments have to be read together. Badiou is not only defending a renewal of Platonism, he is – and very much so – defending a renewal of what he calls the 'communist hypoth- esis' (Badiou 2010a). These counter-affirmations[22] (of Platonism and communism), as I see it, have to be read together. This is not an arbitrary or merely contingent take on Badiou's position, brought to it from the outside. The necessary, and maybe at the same time impossible, link in his double commitment already becomes perceivable when, somewhat empirically, two things are taken into account. 1) Badiou reconstructs the history of the com- munist hypothesis in its different sequences (two of which are thus far completed) in terms of different historical types of organisation of what Badiou calls the 'communist idea'. The communist idea – which must be systematically distinguished from the 'communist hypothesis'[23] – is that which is always marked by a historically specific exception to the given realm of the (politically) possible; a conversion from something previously regarded as impossible into a new 'impossible possibility' (Badiou 1985: 101). The idea whose political name is communism then marks an exception, an interruption of the repetition of the previous succession of pos- sible actions, types of organisation, political agendas and so on. The idea, a Platonic name par excellence, is that which names the motor of the very organisation of these exceptions.[24] One of the most crucial metapolitical[25] concepts of Badiou's thought, then, is already a Platonist-communist bastard. But I will leave this point of the investigation aside, since my claim is that it can be under- stood even more adequately when one takes into account 2) that Badiou has been working for a long time on a 'hyper-translation' (Badiou 2010–11), as he once called it, of Plato's politeia, to which he gave the provisional title 'On Communism' (Badiou 2007–08). To my mind it can be instructive to take this book (now published under the title Plato's Republic) as offering clues to understand- ing the anamnesic practice of philosophy within Badiou's system as well as why Plato and communism have to be read together. In other words, Badiou's Plato is deployed to counter political oblivion.

In his preface to the hyper-translation, Badiou claims that one of the questions that had been occupying him while working on the project was 'What does it mean to "treat" the text?' (2012b: 10). Against the background of what has been said thus far, this could be rephrased as follows: 'What does it mean to render a Platonist text under the heading of communism and simultaneously under the condition of the hegemony of democratic materialism?' What does it mean to translate one of Plato's most famous texts – one dealing mainly with the question of politics and justice – at a time when there is only democracy (as the best of all the worst options) and its materialism (as the only one of the worst ideological options)? How are we to understand this gesture of re-translating Plato under a new title in a specific historical context?

Some brief digressions will be instructive here: in the 1960s Pier Paolo Pasolini embarked on a rather unusual project that he was never able to carry out (at least not in the form of a film). He was working on a screenplay about the life of Saint Paul. The film was intended to 'transfer the life story of Saint Paul to our own time'.[26] Pasolini's project can help shed some light on the questions I raised above. Why? Because Badiou comments on the same project in his book on Saint Paul.[27] What Pasolini, according to Badiou, sought to do was to 'turn Paul into a contemporary without any modification of his statements' (2003b: 37). That is to say, what Pasolini tried to do is show that Paul (as for Hegel the absolute) is with us.[28] The aim of transplanting Paul into the contemporary world was linked to three diagnostic effects: 1) 'today the figure of the saint is necessary, even if the contents of the initiating encounter may vary'; 2) 'by transplanting Paul, along with all his statements . . . one sees them encountering a real society . . . [one] infinitely more supple and resistant than that of the Roman Empire'; and 3) 'Paul's statements are endowed with a timeless legitimacy'.[29] If one takes these three claims together as part of an endeavour that seeks to demonstrate that 'Paul emerges strangely victorious' (Badiou 2003b: 39) when faced with the contemporary world, it might become clear why re-actualising a seemingly outdated position, notably that of a religious militant, can indicate the forgotten, concealed impossible-possibility of a subjective position and of subjective action. But for Pasolini to fulfil this task it was necessary to effectuate a 'series of transfers' to 'resurrect' (Pasolini 2007: 16) Paul's position in and for the mid-1960s. So how can this reference help us to understand Badiou's hyper-translation of Plato? Is Paul to Pasolini what Plato is to Badiou?

To start to answer this question, it might be claimed that what is at stake in both endeavours is the task of transmitting something and how to transmit it.[30] Therefore, what both Pasolini and Badiou aim to do is to provide adequate tools for a 'message', for something to get through. Yet while Pasolini's project involved placing Paul without any modification to his statements in a more contemporary context in order to demonstrate and remind us of his eternal legitimacy, Badiou's project goes a step further. Of course – and the above-mentioned mathematical references teach us this – Plato was the first to delineate the very conditioning of philosophy by non-philosophical forms of practice (art, politics, love and science, i.e., mathematics) and this very claim is what for philosophy – from a Badiousian perspective – has an eternal legitimacy.[31] Yet to make Plato's text legible and to counter the oblivion induced by democratic materialism, a different kind of renewal is needed. The very name 'Plato' stands for a dimension that has been forgotten within the reign of democratic materialism. However, in order to recall what this name stands for, even the means for remembering have to be reshaped, since Plato stands charged not only with being an utter idealist defending an unsustainable philosophical position, but also with being totalitarian (in his conception of the philosopher-king).[32] So what is surprisingly attacked in the name 'Plato' is also in some sense (although, of course, from a different perspective) that which is attacked under the name 'communism': a totalitarian model that is not suited for the real life-world, that has been proven wrong by history, and that is criminal not only by accident but in its essence. So by seeking to revamp the very text in which Plato deals with the question of justice and political organisation (and the critique of the different types of organisation from oligarchy to tyranny), Badiou links the question of how to render Plato's 'message' transmittable to that of how to transmit the very conception of an idea. It might be said that his hyper-translation is an attempt to realise not the transmission of a concrete idea that could be put into practice proper, but the very form of an idea, since what is forgotten today is not this or that concrete idea, but rather the very (possibility of the) existence of the idea (that is, of something infinite in its different dimensions). To actualise something that seems to have been invalidated and forgotten, what is needed is not only to transplant artistically the very position one seeks to defend into the new context, but rather a renewal of the means of revamping the forgotten position. Simply put: one cannot simply translate Plato's theses unmodified into a contemporary context, as this would precisely not demonstrate their validity. Since the ideology of democratic materialism works precisely so as to make certain things unintelligible, unreadable (by rendering them as utterly absurd, nonsensical and so on),[33] a simple gesture of transplantation would only further enforce the alleged nullity and meaninglessness of a Platonic position. But if communism might be said to have been an idea and if *the* philosopher of the Idea is of course Plato, the following question emerges: how can one revamp the idea of an idea? This is the question that might be seen as standing behind Badiou's hyper-translation of the Platonic text.

To rephrase the argument thus far: both Heidegger and Badiou seem to understand philosophy as an anamnesic practice, and both argue that what needs to be recalled is not 'something' but rather a forgotten distinction. For Heidegger the forgetting of the ontic-ontological difference leads to a hierarchised structure of the ontic sphere (and in the last instance thereby to an empowerment of the subject); whereas for Badiou the forgetting of the distinction between finitude and infinity leads to a privation of the very notion of the subject and its practice. Heidegger counters the effects of oblivion by referring to a forgotten truth by pointing to the poets, who stand somehow as the bearers of the knowledge of the truth of being's very existence. For Badiou, things are a bit more complicated: the forgetting of the distinction somehow instructs his return to Plato and his use of the allegedly idealist category of the 'idea'. Yet the very concept of a practice that returns to the idea – in its Platonic forming – does not simply return to the forgotten infinity. What philosophy – among other things by means of mathematics – recalls is that there is also and necessarily a dialectics of finitude and infinity at work that constitutes the very form of the idea. What has been forgotten is in some sense the very dialectics that is constitutive of the idea.[34] So what does it mean to remind the human animal of that which has been forgotten under democratic materialism? Badiou himself once answered as follows: that for which philosophy has to struggle is an alternative to the form of life (and practice of living) that democratic materialism defends (one with oblivion at its basis; a life without any exception whatsoever and thus without any idea). Life can exist under an idea. And of course the political name for such an idea, for Badiou, is communism. Yet how with the change of circumstances can philosophy remind the human animal of this?

What philosophy needs to recall, or resurrect, from Plato is precisely the concept of the idea (which Heidegger deemed to be at the origin of metaphysical oblivion). But things start to get difficult here. What does it mean to recall the conception of the idea in Plato? Badiou does not want to mimic a (traditional) Platonist position. Indeed, he wants to insist on the fact that the only real way in which philosophy can be anamnesic is by re-actualising not only what has been forgotten but also the very means by which this anamnesis can be achieved. Philosophy does not recall the idea by recalling its dialectical constitution; it can only do this by dialectically working through the very concept of anamnesis itself. This implies 1) that philosophy is anamnesic for the sake of introducing a distinction,[35] a distinction between two ways of living, for example, a distinction that forces one to take sides;[36] 2) that therefore the anamnesic practice that is philosophy is militant: it is a militant anamnesis; 3) that philosophy is critical in the very literal sense of the Greek verb *krinein*, of distinguishing and deciding;[37] and yet 4) that philosophy can do this only by recalling that the very means of reminding the human animal of this forgotten distinction need to be reworked, too, taking into account the historically specific situation and the hegemonic ideology within it. Thus philosophy cannot simply be anamnesic for the sake of being critical. It has to be meta-critical (critically re-actualising the very means of anamnesis) in order to fulfil its anamnesic task.

So what does all this mean when one looks at Badiou's revamping of Plato's text? Maybe the best way to answer this is to rephrase the question: is Badiou's hyper-translation of Plato a book by Badiou or a book by Plato? The most obvious answer might be: both. And indeed, it is a book in which Badiou re-actualises Plato against the background of his own philosophical enterprise. Yet this is to say that we have some sort of recursive loop when dealing with the text. The book itself is neither simply Badiousian (as Badiou is a Platonist) nor simply Platonic (as it is Plato revamped, retranslated). Therefore it presents one way in which philosophy can be anamnesic by reshaping the very concepts (and their presentation) by which it brings back to life what has been forgotten.[38] Its essential operation is to remind the human animal of the fact that, despite ever-changing historical conditions, something impossible can happen, although it will always and ever again seem (or will have seemed) impossible. We are thus here dealing with a meta-critical and anamnesic book. Hyper-translation thus names a crucial operation of meta-critical anamnesis. Indeed, meta-critical anamnesis is another name for philosophy (in Badiou's sense).

One of the most crucial claims that can be derived from the book – one intimately linked with the question of how to recall the very idea of an idea – is presented close to the very end in the discussion of what justice is and furthermore of what 'happiness' is (Badiou 2012b: 489–528). It could in some sense be argued that this passage provides Badiou's-Plato's answer to how to comprehend the being of an idea. The background to this presentation might be best summed up with Badiou's own words as follows:

> In the Republic, the generic form of being is the Idea. When it is a question of designating the principle of intelligibility of the being of the Idea ... we must have recourse to the transcendence of the Good. Now, what does Plato tell us immediately afterwards? That the Good is not an Idea, and thus that with regard to the ontological disposition, what is the root of being and the thinkable stands in exception to being, in the form proper to non-being that is the non-Idea. (2012a: 314)

This means that one cannot simply recall what an idea is by presenting the concept of an idea. Rather the very being of the idea – which is the Good, itself not an Idea – necessitates recalling the very status of an exception. But how can an exception be transmitted? This is what the already delineated chapter of Badiou-Plato deals with. So, then, what is happiness? Happiness is misconceived when rendered as something that could describe the objective state of a subject (since then it would be quantifiable and we would be in the thick of democratic materialism). Instead, it has to be conceived of as that which can only be grasped when there is an exception to the seemingly unchangeable laws of the world and of one's existence. This means that one can only comprehend what happiness is by partaking in the unfolding of the consequences of an exception. This also means that happiness names the very affective state comprising the link between a subject and an idea. An idea enters the world via an exception – as the very nature of the idea is exceptional – and the idea only becomes what it is if it in some sense materialises in the very world in which it introduces an exception. Happiness – the subjective and affective name for the Good in Badiou's Plato – can thus only be grasped from the subjective interiority of the very process that constitutes the material effects of an exception to the world. Thus if philosophy aims to bring into existence the very improbable and allegedly impossible possibility of an idea, what it needs to do to fulfil this task is also to affirm in ever new ways the impossible possibility of an exception.

Linking together Plato and communism once again – the double commitment constitutive of Badiou's endeavour – it might be said that philosophy as meta-critical anamnesis has to remind the human animal of what cannot be known. What is recalled has the character of a peculiar non-being (the being of the idea, that is, the Good that is non-being, that is an exception even to being). And it cannot be known because it can never be anticipated, deduced, derived, inferred. It is necessary, yet impossible. Meta-critical anamnesis consists in recalling the necessarily impossible. This is what philosophy can achieve by defending Plato. And as in its principles[39] communism is and always will have been an exception to the given state of things (qua real movement abolishing the present state of things), then to defend Plato is to struggle for the very impossible necessity of communism. All this is somehow akin to what Lacan said with reference to what happens in true love when he claimed: 'to give one's love, is very precisely and essentially to give as such nothing of what one has' (Lacan 1998: 384). Philosophy as love of wisdom does something similar: it recalls as such nothing of what one knows, it recalls precisely the Nothing of what one knows as this is what is the subject. *It insists that one has to remember what one never knew*. This is why true philosophy at least for Badiou remains (and will remain) Platonic. Philosophy as meta-critical anamnesis defends Plato by forcing us to remember what we never knew and this is the very precondition for communism. So to affirm Plato is the first necessary, yet impossible, communist gesture.

Notes

1. I am, of course, very well aware that Badiou is not a Heideggerian (although to the best of my knowledge there is thus far no detailed investigation of their relationship that would go further than

Badiou's own criticism of Heideggerian thought) and I will return to some elements of difference between the two in the points below. For a direct comment on the forgetting of being from Badiou's side, see Badiou 2005a: 443–8.

2. In what follows it shall become clear that I limit my remarks to a specific moment that is implied in Badiou's reference to Plato. For a more detailed study on their relation, see Bartlett 2011.

3. This is perhaps nowhere more clearly to be seen than in the claim by former French president Nicolas Sarkozy that it is absolutely necessary to 'forget 68'. The simple point to be made here is if there is nothing more to it, why claim that it has to be forgotten? For this, see Badiou 2008b.

4. I also elaborate this argument in greater detail in Ruda (forthcoming). A similar point has been made by Žižek (2012: 41ff.).

5. And any true dialectic is a dialectic of exception. That is why democratic materialism seeks to totalise itself and foreclose the possibility of an exception altogether. See Badiou 2009a.

6. To render this in even simpler terms: the claim that there is nothing but democratic materialism is a quite non-dialectical claim.

7. I use this term here in the sense that Badiou has introduced. See Badiou 2005a: 265–326.

8. And the axiom of democratic materialism is, of course, that there are only bodies and languages, or nothing but individuals and communities. See Badiou 2009a: 1–40.

9. Here I am basically reconstructing a point that Badiou has made in his recent lectures. See Badiou 2012–13.

10. Yet what is important here is that this creation of new successors functions on the basis of one and the same operation, repeated within the potentially infinite series of numbers generated. Thus there is something like repeated finitude, finitude in and through repetition.

11. For this quotation and a pointed characterisation of all the realms today governed by this finitised definition of number, see Badiou 2008a: 1–4. Therefore it helps to counter this very operation first and foremost by comprehending what a number is and on what it constitutively relies.

12. As Badiou puts it: 'But we don't know what a number is, so we don't know what we are' (2008a: 3).

13. This argument is also linked to what Badiou calls the second existential axiom within the set theoretical setting that he employs (2005a). It should also be remarked that if ω is not a successor, this also

implies that it breaks the repetition mechanism that was fundamental in the case of natural numbers.

14. I again refer here to Lavine 1998. One way of rendering this is to say that potential infinity is an infinite succession of numbers taking place. But as soon as one claims that there is a number that is not a successor, one comes across a different phenomenon, as ω totalises potential infinity.

15. It might be said that all natural numbers belong in the potentially infinite series to ω, and thus that ω names the very space where their succession can take place (by belonging to ω, that is, by being smaller than it). See Badiou 2008a: 93–8.

16. This can also be put as 'the place of succession does not itself succeed' (Badiou 2008a: 95).

17. This second succession can be said to run up maximally to ω + ω.

18. This example is given by Badiou in his lecture on which I base my reconstruction (Badiou 2012–13). For a detailed account of the structure of the conception of revolution, see also Ruda 2013.

19. This is, to my mind, a risk that anyone denying the constitutive separation of economy and politics has to take into account. This is, of course, not to say that there could be something like a pure politics (of emancipation) that pays no attention at all to economic issues. But it is to say that as soon as one forgets or denies this distinction one risks deducing the very existence of politics from economics (which comes down to not being able to think politics at all – at least as long as one remains within the democratic materialist framework. Things, of course, stand differently with regard to Lenin, although even here one should take care not to fall into the same trap.) The danger here is a problematic form of objectivism that fetishises (quantitative) finitude.

20. This operation proceeds mainly by focusing on the quantity of things one objectively has in common, of things that one 'owns' together or is able to achieve in the future by exchanging useful favours (which has become the principle of many so-called dating agencies). For this, see Badiou 2012c.

21. Heidegger's rendering of anamnesis is paradoxically far more traditionally Platonic than Badiou's. For a detailed account of Plato's anamnesis doctrine, see Huber 1964.

22. That there always is what I call 'a determinate affirmation' in philosophy, I have demonstrated in Ruda (forthcoming).

23. This distinction has rarely been taken into account, but I think it is a crucial one. An idea names the active procedure of unfolding the

consequences of an exception, while the hypothesis names the very affirmation of the possibility of the existence of an idea. To confuse the two is to a certain extent to confuse philosophy and politics.

24. Badiou himself argues that there are symbolic, imaginary and real aspects to what he calls an idea. In a free reformulation one might say it is the inscription of something real (mass movement, for example) into a historically specific context (symbolic) which at the same time enables the vision to participate in the emancipation of the whole of humanity (imaginary). See Badiou 2010a: 229–60.

25. Metapolitics, as is well known to the reader, names the relation of philosophy to its political condition. See Badiou 2005b.

26. I here translate from the German version of the text (Pasolini 2007: 16).

27. And also because Badiou himself is working on a movie on Plato's life titled 'The Life of Plato'.

28. Pasolini alludes to the liturgical saying about Christ's lasting presence when he claims that 'Paul is *here, today amongst us*' (Pasolini 2007: 16).

29. Badiou 2003b: 37. In Pasolini this reads as follows: 'What is clear is that Saint Paul destroys, with the simple force of his religious message and in a revolutionary way a society that was based on the violence of class struggle, imperialism and particularly slavery' (2007: 17).

30. That this is one crucial element of philosophy can be seen in many of Badiou's texts. First and foremost one might read this as an element of what he calls a 'philosophical institution' (2008e: 26–32).

31. For this, see again Badiou 1999a.

32. For one famous formulation of this claim, see the (hopefully soon to be forgotten) book by Popper, *The Open Society and its Enemies, Vol. 1: The Spell of Plato* (Popper 1966: 68–168).

33. Compare, for example, how democratic materialists deal with political figures such as Mao or Stalin. These latter are rendered as the embodiment of evil and thus as representing a complete absence of sense or meaning. To transplant Stalin's statements – and of course I am not defending Stalin here – into a contemporary context would not be to endorse Stalin; instead, it would work to invalidate the very gesture of transplanting these same statements.

34. This might be rephrased by saying that Badiou insists, against Heidegger, that truth is not the truth of being but rather something that emerges in a specific historical situation. In itself this goes to indicate that there cannot simply be one truth (of being) but that

there needs to be multiple truths. The latter claim can be derived from the following consideration: if everything that is is, for Badiou, a multiple of multiples, the same goes for truth. This immediately leads to the dialectical insight that not only are truths composed of multiples of multiples, but that one can only have an adequate understanding of truth if truth is by definition also multiple: truths. It thus cannot ever be the same truth (not even one that is constantly present only as being absent truth, as Heidegger conceptualised it).

35. As Badiou claims: 'It is reasonable to assume that a philosophy always unfolds its arguments between two imperatives – one negative, the other positive – which define, on the one hand, the vice that destroys true thought, and on the other, the effort, or even the ascesis, which makes true thought possible' (2006c: 39).

36. For this, see also Badiou's definition of a 'philosophical situation' (Badiou and Žižek 2009e: 1–48).

37. This is also one of the defining characteristics of what Badiou calls a philosophical act (Badiou, n.d.).

38. It is thus of quite some importance that one of the chapters is entitled 'What is an Idea?' (Badiou 2012b: 339–80).

39. For this, see again Ruda forthcoming.

3

The Narrative Politics of Active Number

Ed Pluth

I

In an interview with Bruno Bosteels and Peter Hallward from 2002, Alain Badiou suggests that, politically, 'in order to think the contemporary world in any fundamental way, it's necessary to take as your point of departure not the critique of capitalism but the critique of democracy' (Bosteels 2011a: 339). Many of his recent works have affirmed this line of thinking. Badiou has also expressed scepticism in the past about the political utility of critiques of capitalism, when those critiques are only economic: 'any viable campaign against capitalism can only be political. There can be no economic battle against the economy' (Badiou 1999c: 118). The distinction Badiou seems to rely on here, between the economic and the political, is what will be my focus in this chapter.

It is perhaps helpful to point out as early as possible that one of Badiou's biggest concerns with democracy is that the term currently has a mostly ideological function. He refers to democracy as a siren song, for example, and wrote, in an essay I will analyse in some detail, that 'what is needed is the wax Ulysses used to keep from yielding either to the songs, or to the sirens, or to the blackmail of "democracy"' (2006b: 97). Thus, the critique he proposes aims to keep us from falling into some kind of trap when it comes to the idea of democracy in political life. In his earlier essay titled 'A Speculative Disquisition on the Concept of Democracy' he makes a similar point, observing that 'the word "democracy" concerns what I shall call *authoritarian opinion*', in that it is taken to be the uncontestable desire of every human being, and questioning it is entirely taboo (2005d: 78, original emphasis). He then notes that any time there is such widespread agreement about a term, philosophers should get suspicious.

The problem Badiou sees with democracy has to do largely with its subjective effects, I claim, and the political consequences of those effects; a point that I will be exploring in detail. With respect to his position on the shift in priorities, from a critique of capitalism to a critique of democracy, my questions are as follows: to what extent is the disjunction he poses meant to be an exclusive one? Badiou is arguing that pursuing a critique of capitalism, in a certain style at least (and I will clarify what I mean by this) may actually *dissuade* one from critiquing its frequent partner, democracy; and overlooking a critique of democracy makes the emergence of the form of political life Badiou has in mind more difficult. But what kind of relationship is there, then, between economics and politics if this can be the case?

Pursuing answers to these questions helps to draw out several crucial aspects of Badiou's general position on politics. In particular, this inquiry will show how Badiou's orientation is very much focused on the importance of what I am calling the subjective dimension. Badiou's position is that a critique of capitalism, if it is an economic, historical and sociological endeavour, must rely on references to *objective* economic, historic and sociological categories. As such, a critique of capitalism engages in basically the same kind of work that he thinks the state of any situation engages in: it places quantitative categories over qualitative ones. As we shall see, this displacement of focus and interest from qualities to quantities in politics is part of what Badiou thinks accounts for the disappearance of politics today. For Badiou, politics should be distinguished by the possession of certain qualities that are associated with the notion of the Hegelian infinite (although I will not be able to do everything I should to explore or justify this point here). A critique of capitalism, so the reasoning must go, lacks these qualitative features since it requires necessarily a quantitative, objective orientation.

As we shall see, this inquiry will reveal some problems in Badiou's philosophy when it comes to thinking the connection between the qualitative and the subjective, on the one hand, versus the quantitative and objective, on the other. Ultimately, my conclusion will be that Badiou's concerns about the roles of historical, economic and sociological objects and quantities in politics may be overstated. He does not really point to much more than a loose association between how a state operates and how a critique of capitalism operates. (Again, the association has to do with the approach each has to their objects, which relies on quantification.) But I will argue that a critique of capitalism still does far more for politics than provide what Badiou describes, almost dismissively, as mere background material for it: especially when it comes to Marxism as providing a science of history. He does concur that 'the part of Marxism that consists of the scientific analysis of capital remains an absolutely valid background' for politics. But it is clear that this aspect of Marxism need not play much more than a trivial role as far as he is concerned, and this is because of his worries about the subjective effects that an emphasis on quantities has in politics (1999c: 117). These worries are not enough, however, to lend credence to an argument that a critique of capitalism should be set aside or even de-prioritised; in fact, Badiou's orientation overlooks the important subjective, and let's say counter-ideological, effects such critiques can have.

2

I wish to start with a discussion of Badiou's essay on the presidential elections in France in 2002, included in *Polemics*, titled 'On Parliamentary "Democracy": the French Presidential Elections of 2002'. This essay touches on basically all of the points I want to focus on. The 2002 elections were noteworthy for the fact that the far-right candidate Jean-Marie Le Pen received second place in the first round of voting, which allowed him to be on the final ballot in a contest against the incumbent, Jacques Chirac. This put the socialist candidate, Lionel Jospin, out of the running altogether; and he was, of course, expected to be the one on the final ballot against Chirac, giving voters a typical Left/Right option. Instead, every French citizen had to make a final decision between a right-wing candidate and a far-right candidate! Badiou discusses in this essay, with obvious glee, the resulting anguish of the Left: out of fear of Le Pen, the parliamentary Left found itself in a situation in which it had to urge people to vote, and to vote for Chirac specifically! And the situation was put in rather hyperbolic terms by many of them: France needed to be saved from Le Pen, who was portrayed as a threat to democracy and the republic themselves.

Badiou points out that of course Le Pen posed no threat to the existence of the French republic and its democratic form at all, even if he had won the final election. So, he wonders, what was all the fuss about? Why was there so much outrage, when there did not have to be? For Badiou these are legitimate questions because as far as he is concerned the Right and the Left, insofar as they participate in parliamentary politics (and perhaps those labels don't really make sense outside of that space) are not really *heterogeneous* to each other. What is meant by this is not the familiar old complaint one often hears in the US – that 'there's no difference between the two parties'! I do not take Badiou's point to be that there are not genuine and meaningful differences that result from one party winning an election over another. He does claim, however, that there is a 'principle of homogeneity' that reigns over the democratic state-form and its elections (2006b: 80). In other words, there is something – albeit not at the level of content, doctrine or policy, but instead, as one might expect, something formal and structural – that renders political parties participating in elections *homogeneous*.

In an initial articulation of the principle of homogeneity, Badiou puts it as follows: 'anyone can be a candidate, but only those who are in line with certain norms may have a place pre-coded for potential power. In truth, this means those who one knows for certain will not do anything *essentially different* from those preceding them' (2006b: 79, emphasis added). At this point, Badiou is discussing why so many felt that Le Pen was not a legitimate candidate. It was because Le Pen was perceived to be too extreme, and that his victory would violate this not-explicitly-articulated principle of homogeneity. He would be too different. Hence, his potential victory was perceived as a threat to the French democratic republic. No one would have contested Le Pen's right to be on the ballot – it's a democracy, after all! But the expectation was that his candidacy would go nowhere . . . except, it went somewhere.

However, Badiou thinks the homogeneity principle actually goes deeper than this notion that the places of power in a democracy are 'pre-coded', that only some leaders and parties may ever 'have a place pre-coded for potential power'. Badiou's reference to a politics that would be or do something 'essentially different' is a crucial part of his point about the homogeneity principle. There is, of course, for Badiou a *kind* of politics that is simply not present in an electoral form. Thus, he writes, 'as regards decisive transformations in a country's politics, nothing will ever come to pass if left to a vote, because the homogeneity principle stands above' the conduct of elections (2006b: 80). In other words, the homogeneity principle grinds down alternative political movements. Those desiring a certain type of change from democratic elections, where this type of change concerns a certain type of social and political life itself, are fooling themselves. So the homogeneity principle is not just a rule about who can be on the ballot; stronger than that, it is a structural rule that even orders what politicians and parties are able to do, and even what politics is deemed as being. This is why Badiou has little trouble mocking the Left's overreaction to Le Pen's first-round victory. For, although Le Pen was on the far Right, there was little reason to think that he would ever even be able to do anything 'essentially different' from what France was already doing – continuing crack-downs on immigration, to take just one of the points Badiou considers. This practice was assured to continue to some extent, regardless of the electoral outcome.

So an important, and basic, claim in Badiou's critique of democracy is that *democracy perpetuates a model of politics which actively rules out another model of politics*. But in what manner does it do this? Already in this claim one can discern a distinction between the objective and subjective sides, or effects, of a structural rule such as that of the principle of homogeneity. Objectively, what this means is that any party or candidate that obtains power via elections is going to leave some basic aspects and policies of the democratic state-form intact despite the different policies that it wants to pursue. In other words, the point is that there is a possible form of political life that is ruled out by elections. Subjectively, it means the following: mere participation in the electoral form has consequences on what its participants are *willing* to do. This is a reference not only to what is objectively possible, but also to the subjective desires or inclinations of politicians and voters as well. Power may corrupt, yet it is not just being victorious in elections, but merely participating in elections that is its own, prior corruptor. And what is more important is that this point applies not only to politicians and parties, but *to the voters in a democracy themselves* as well.

Democracy becomes then an anti-politics, a sort of negative politics, like a negative theology: in a paraphrase of Meister Eckhart, who prayed to God that he be rid of God, according to Badiou voting would be a political activity in which one hopes precisely to be rid of politics. Thus – and here we are getting to a nice paradoxical thesis – the vote is depoliticising, and is not the ultimate expression of a people, or a political will – except as a will to resignation: 'People vote to persevere, not to become,' he writes, and a politics that would involve what he calls 'real decision' and becoming 'is entirely foreign to the vote' (2006b: 91).

3

The distinction that Badiou is emphasising here between models of politics, or forms of political life, can be approached in another way – through the difference between what he calls in the same essay on the 2002 elections passive versus active number. Democracy, Badiou claims, embraces the rule of passive number. We can associate passive number with a quantitative approach to groups, or to the people. Passive number would be passive because it promotes and relies on counting; the tallying-up of opinions in polls, or votes in elections, for example, or the notion that the legitimacy of a protest, rally or movement depends on the number of people involved. But it is also passive in delegating activity to others – to elected representatives, or to the general will. Badiou finds this reliance on both quantity and representation – as well as the expressive model of politics that it relies on – thoroughly irrational: 'why should number have any political virtue? Why would the majority, modifiable at will thanks to the rise of infinite modes of balloting, be endowed with the attributes of a norm' (2006b: 93)? This is one way in which Badiou's critique of democracy resembles a classical philosophical critique. Truths are not things that one puts up to a vote. They have an authority all of their own, one that anyone can recognise and acknowledge; and is indeed obliged to. Thus, for Badiou, if voting is the paradigm of political activity, this means that politically one is content with the dominance of mere opinion over truth – a dominance, he points out, that we would never allow in other domains such as art, science and love (2006b: 93). Of course, this argument requires the assumption that there *are* political truths. If there are truths in politics, then there is a type of politics, or some variety of political principle, that is not dependent on the results of a vote, whose validity is independent of the opinions of a majority; and thus, there is a crucial aspect of politics that would (or should) have nothing to do with elections.

In contrast to passive number, active number is the descriptor Badiou uses in this essay for the politics he is pursuing. To get at what is meant by active number, he initially considers the half a million or so people who protested against Le Pen's victory in the first round of the 2002 election versus the nearly five million people who voted for him. Even though Badiou does not ultimately think that this protest qualified as an instance of active number, since size did matter for it – it was, after all, an attempt to get out the vote against Le Pen – he does use the protests to show how it is the case that 'active number, however large it is, is in reality always tiny with regard to the passive number' (2006b: 93). This is because passive number, involving mere quantity, always potentially includes anyone who is not doing anything at all politically – which is usually a vast majority of the people.

Badiou makes a similar point in some of his earliest works, although the terminology is a bit different. In fact, the older discussions can still be used to shed light on what is going on in this distinction between passive and active number. In *De l'idéologie* Badiou discusses how politics creates a system in which 'the logic of places' prevails 'over the logic of forces, the individual over class, the quantitative over the qualitative' (Badiou and Balmès 1976: 119). Making quantity more important than quality (think: making popular opinion more important than truth) is exactly what he says democracy does in his essay on 2002. In fact the same term as in the 2002 essay, 'heterogeneous', is also used in this context to describe a political fight against what he calls the 'logic of the homogeneous' (1976: 120). And in *Théorie de la contradiction*, from 1975, this political heterogeneity is also described in terms of a dialectical relationship between force and place, where force is, again, associated with 'quality' and place with quantity. And significantly, the qualitative is also associated with the emergence of the new (1975: 109).

Consider this as a distinction between *types* of number. Each type of number can be said to be strong in different ways: active number is strong due to its qualities, not its quantity; passive number is strong by virtue of its quantity, and not its qualities. But what are the qualities of active number? I have already been making use of the idea that one quality Badiou associates with active number is its relation to truth, in contrast to opinion. Without being able to go into this in enough detail now, I also want to say that some of the other qualities this type of number has should be associated with what was called good infinity in Hegel's philosophy – an infinity that is not merely an endless series, not merely an infinite quantity (the limitless), but instead one that possesses qualitative attributes not present in an infinite quantity, such as independence and autonomy, or being self-grounding. Thus, active number is for Badiou a descriptor that is going to pertain to groups that have such qualities, regardless of their size.

In a description of active number that highlights these features, Badiou writes that 'a meeting, a demonstration, an insurrection, all of them proclaim their right to existence outside any consideration that is not immanent to that existence' (2006b: 94). This type of self-grounding or self-reference is a quality that was also given to truth procedures generally in *Being and Event*. There, Badiou claimed that an event is a multiple *'composed of, on the one hand, elements of the site, and on the other hand, itself'* (2005a: 181, original emphasis). A violation of the axioms of set theory, that is, the very rules for the organisation of multiples, this is what renders the status of events and the truth procedures based on them undecidable for the situations in which they occur. Certainly, this is a way of thinking their autonomy from situations and states too. They are not able to be subordinated within or judged or determined by what Badiou called the 'encyclopaedia' of a situation, that is, the particular way in which elements of a situation are organised and counted by it, an idea which is closely associated with the idea of a state of a situation. While this quality of active number can indeed be considered a type of autonomy, it is of a distinct sort and should not be thought to be identical to freedom on the model of liberalism, which enshrines the right of individuals to act, develop and think freely in civil society under certain constraints that preserve the common good (such constraints being provided by the state, the social contract, etc.). What is distinct in this case is that the elements involved in active number mark a becoming-other within the situation itself. Yet this self-referring, self-grounding quality of a politics of active number may well make it out to be formal and empty; for, beyond its self-grounding, what is its content?

4

Active number involves the possession of certain qualities, then, rather than the possession of a quantity. Earlier, we saw Badiou suggest that certain types of activities are themselves, as such, in possession of the qualities that active number has. But can it be that phenomena such as protests or riots, as such, are things that make the number of a particular group active? Think, by contrast, of a rally in favour of Le Pen, or any other political candidate during an election. However large or small it may be, it no doubt would not qualify as a manifestation of active number for multiple reasons. It would lack the kind of signifying autonomy Badiou has in mind, for one thing (from the state, from electoral politics and so on). Some rallies, protests and riots contain a clear reference to the state and can be said to occur fully within its space, and are such that quantity is more important than quality in them: they are, after all, quite often attempts to increase the number of votes a candidate might receive, to increase turnout for the election itself, or to show popular legitimacy by means of the sheer number of people at the rally supporting candidate X (more people are at our rally than at theirs . . . we're bigger, we've got the people on our side . . .). In fact, it is doubtful that there is any particular *form* of activity that would automatically allow one to distinguish between active number or passive number – except, Badiou suggests, the absence of one: for voting in parliamentary democracy amounts to concurring with putting passive number above active number. The homogeneity principle guiding elections ensures that any qualities one particular group might have over others, when voting, are levelled down, or ignored, in favour of the reign of sheer quantitative number.

It is the rationale for this strong claim that I would like to explore further at this point. The two types of number seem to occupy quite distinct realms. They are, after all, heterogeneous to each other. So why would this not instead mean that it is possible to vote with one's eyes open, so to speak, and to inhabit both worlds at once? To participate in elections without letting this activity corrupt one's politics? And is this not what many on the Left in France in 2002 were doing (and what many in the US do in nearly every election)? Many people vote, keenly aware that it is a trap. They vote to avoid the worst, and they expect little if anything at all from the result. In fact, many vote and still fully expect to have to continue some form of political activity outside of state institutions and mechanisms, where real political life, according to Badiou, occurs in the first place. Call this preventive voting – something at which the Left in most democracies seems to excel.

One could, then, be content to allow passive number to reign as far as the state is concerned, and let active number do its work elsewhere. On this reading, Badiou's orientation potentially endorses some kind of 'render unto Caesar what is Caesar's' view. Let the vote be the vote, let the state be what it is. One can consistently fulfil one's duties as a citizen by voting, and yet, as a political activist, continue on guided by the insight that ours is another (political) kingdom. These questions bring us to the heart of Badiou's critique of democracy. For is there anything in what Badiou is claiming that really offers an argument *against* participation in democracy? While democracy, as a state form, is clearly not the definitive model of political life, is it incompatible with a politics of active number?

Something needs to be added to the critique of democracy. We've seen that Badiou holds that to vote is to concur, regardless of what one thinks one is doing, with rendering active number *subordinate* to passive number. This is the heart of his critique. To vote, then, is to abdicate what for Badiou is the political dimension altogether. Or, as he puts it in the essay on the 2002 election, 'to want to abdicate is to vote' (2006b: 92). Thus, participation in electoral democracy is claimed by him to be subjectively toxic. The subjective or psychological or ideological effects of participation in democracy are such that active number, which is the strength of genuine political organisation, is rendered illegitimate and fruitless. Because when it comes to quantity, active number cannot compete, and voting endorses the importance of quantity.

So the full argument must include this idea: voting makes the very qualities of active number that are its strengths appear trivial even to its own participants. How can militants for a truth subjectively keep doing what they are doing when they are forced to see, during elections, how entirely marginal their activity, and their number, is? They look like fools, compared to where the majority of the people are politically. And this may well be the case, even when the number of participants in rallies and protests is quite large. Hence, democracy is very much a siren-song; a subjective danger to the kind of political activism Badiou has in his sights. Best stop up one's ears when approaching it.

Peter Hallward's observation that Badiou's position sounds very much like a politics of the Hegelian unhappy consciousness makes some sense, then. In what is a rather harsh assessment, he suggests that Badiou's position encourages 'the stoical affirmation of a worthy ideal or subjective principle ... divorced from any substantial relation to the material organisation of the situation'

(Hallward 2002: n.p.). For, when it comes to political activity, we have already seen that size matters not. It suffices to be a few people, articulating the right kinds of principles. But if size matters not, success would hardly seem to matter either. And since seizure of the state is not at all the goal of politics, it is not even clear what success would be. Mere participation in a politics of active number may be success itself, and all the success that is needed. This is why Hallward connects Badiou's views to the unhappy consciousness position in Hegel.

The unhappy consciousness also embraces a dualism, a two-worlds view. Pertaining to politics, this implies a situation in which one can continue with one's virtuous political activity regardless of how effective, or ineffective, it is, with respect to the state and the domain in which quantities matter. It does not matter how many people recognise a truth, it is still a truth (a very un-Hegelian point, by the way). The lesson one might draw from this is even a stoic one: learn to control what you can (your own activism) and do not try to control what you cannot (the state, for example, and the number of people who appreciate the truth); and in fact, do not even let the latter get you down. Stop up your ears.

Badiou's basic ontology seems to endorse such a division. His model allows one to see the state as an epiphenomenon, albeit a quite powerful one. To what is it epiphenomenal? To a political situation proper: a situation that is represented and expressed, or more precisely, not, in the state. Badiou's critique of the state does not rely on claiming that its representation of a situation is inadequate. It is based on the mere fact that it represents at all, and that it establishes representation as the model of political life. This is a significant factor in his argument against placing quantity, or passive number, above quality and active number. But if the state is epiphenomenal to its situation, is this not all the more reason to let the state be the state, and to be content with seeing political activity continue in a different direction, in a different space, in total indifference to it? Such that, when it comes to the matter of participating in democracies, by voting, for example, one could very well vote now and again, or not – and, for politics as Badiou construes it, it should not matter whether one did or didn't, unless his case about the ill subjective effects of voting is convincing.

5

At this point, I want to return to my initial and main question: what, in all or any of this, endorses the view that, politically, a critique of democracy should take precedence over a critique of capitalism? I've presented part of what I think the case is for this point: the ill subjective effects of democracy, and the fact that participation in elections is not what political life is, or ought to be, about. We've seen, however, that these points do not strike a decisive blow against participation in democracy. What they suggest is rather a two-worlds view as far as politics goes, at least, and there is no strong reason given for why one could not participate in both at the same time (again, unless one finds Badiou's points about the ideological and psychological or subjective effects of democracy and voting convincing). Now I want to explore how these points are related to the other half of Badiou's claim: that a critique of capitalism can, in principle, be set aside in politics; that it may, but need not, play a role, and that, if done in the wrong way, it may even have the same ill subjective effect as participating in democracy, to the extent that a critique of capitalism also relies on representation and an analysis of quantities.

What exactly is the economy, for Alain Badiou? What is the space or situation or world within which economic practices occur? Economics is not one of the four situations that Badiou considers to be historical: there would thus be no such thing as a truth procedure that pertains to economics. Of course, as a science, economics may be susceptible to truth procedures. But my question is this: what does he consider to be the space of economic life itself – the space not of the science, but of the object of the science of economics (if we can call it a science)?

From what I can gather from Badiou's writings on this, economic life seems to be in roughly the same space as that of politics; but more troublingly, it seems at times to be identified with the *state* of a political situation. For example, in his *Peut-on penser la politique?* he directly associates civil society, in which economic life would traditionally be placed, with the state, claiming that 'politics must be thought as an excess over both the state and civil society, however good or excellent they are' (1985: 20). Badiou also proposes in *Metapolitics* that not only the state but the economy as well is characterised by a *surpuissance*, or superpower, over its situation:

a fundamental datum of ontology is that the state of the situation always exceeds the situation itself. There are always more parts than elements, i.e., the representative multiplicity is always of a higher power than the presentative multiplicity. This question is really that of power. The power of the State is always superior to that of the situation. The State, *and hence also the economy*, which is today the norm of the State, are characterised by a structural effect of separation and superpower with regard to what is simply presented in the situation. (2005d: 158, emphasis added)

Of course, what I am interested in here is the identification of the economy with the state. Why is the economy associated with the *representation* of a situation? Economics as a science certainly does this. And to some extent some forms of economic activity may be situated at the level of the state. For example, what is called the political economy would fit under this heading. But what is it about economic life itself – as distinct from the science of economics and from the policies and practices of the political economy – that would be involved in representation? What would make it also a *surpuissance*? And if the economy itself, economic life and practice, is not among those things that qualifies as what is 'simply present' in a political situation, what else is?

Thus, on this view it does not really make sense to claim that economic life *itself* is in a structural excess and separation from a political situation. There is no doubt a way of studying the economy, or a way of making the economy all-important (for example, as a norm for state politics, a measure by which we judge the effectiveness of politicians and their policies), that does this. This is what allows Badiou to conclude, correctly, in his interview with Peter Hallward from 1999 that the collection of economic data, and the analysis of and knowledge about economic facts, should be trivial for politics: knowledge of such things is 'useful but by itself provides no answer' (Badiou 1999c: 117). Indeed, he claims that 'the position of politics relative to the economy must be rethought, in a dimension that isn't really transitive. We don't simply fall, by successive representations, from the economic into politics. What kind of politics is *really* heterogeneous to what capital demands? – that is today's question' (1999c: 118). It is certainly true that the relationship between politics and economics is not transitive. Not all economic matters are necessarily political matters (in Badiou's sense of a politics of active number). But it must be the case that a politics of active number engages with significant parts of economic life. Otherwise, it would be far too abstract. Economic life, certainly a large part of life in civil society, must very much be part of what a political truth procedure is about – what it encounters, what it makes decisions about transforming, leaving alone and so on. And this is entirely unlike the status of the state and its mechanisms for it, which Badiou argues, fairly, a politics of active number can and should largely ignore.

This certainly gets us closer to what Badiou has in mind when he claims that what is needed is a political, and not economic, critique of the economy. Consider this quote from Bruno Bosteels:

> what do Badiou's critics mean when they deplore the fact that he would not (or not sufficiently) be a Marxist? 'Marxism' in this context seems to stand alternatively for a philosophy, a science of history, or, above all, a critique of political economy. Badiou, according to these accounts, would not be able to give us an updated critique of global capitalism or of the new world order dominated by an unprecedented explosion of immaterial labor caught in the meshes of new and ever more flexible regimes of control. No matter how sophisticated they may well turn out to be in their own right, such readings nonetheless fail to grasp the strictly political significance of Marxism. (2011a: 280)

To be clear, my point is not that Badiou cannot provide an updated economic critique of political economy; I would not expect his philosophy to be capable of that, and it is not a mark against his philosophy at all that it cannot do so. The argument I am considering from him instead is that we should not, or need not, make use of a critique of capitalism in politics – that we should in fact be wary of such a use – and should instead explore, and prioritise, a critique of democracy. Bosteels is right about Badiou's Marxism being primarily political. To clarify this insight about the nature of Badiou's Marxism, he also quotes from *Theory of the Subject*. Badiou there rejects the idea that Marxism is primarily a science of the economy or of history: 'Science of history? *Marxism is the discourse with which the proletariat sustains itself as subject*. We must never let go of this idea' (Badiou, qtd in Bosteels 2011a: 280, original emphasis). The political nature of Badiou's Marxism is highlighted well here: Marxism is for him a discourse that is not rooted in objective facts about a political situation, or economic life, but is a discourse that instead bears the traits, the qualities, of what was studied above as active number – autonomy, self-grounding, self-reference. Marxism is *'the discourse with which the proletariat sustains itself as subject'*. This makes it sound like a Munchausen type of discourse, pulling itself up by its own bootstraps.

Clearly, for Badiou, is not because of Marxism's ability to analyse and critique capitalism that it has efficacy – in other words, it is not because it is true, in the sense of offering objective insights into the nature of a political and economic situation, that it is great, or omnipotent (in an antipodal paraphrase of Lenin's famous 'Marxism is omnipotent because it is true'). Yet of course Badiou is wont to maintain that there is a truth associated with this purely political Marxism: it is just not an analytical truth. The strength of Marxism does not derive from its ability to unearth objective truths about the political and economic situation: economic laws such as the inevitable decline in the rate of profit, or the fact of increasing, global proletarianisation, the historical and ongoing expropriation of the commons, and so on. It is its subjective, or perhaps better counter-ideological, effects (particularly its effects against the siren-song of democracy) that account for its strength, for him. Earlier, I associated this point about a purely political Marxism with the manner in which a politics of active number bears the traits of the Hegelian infinite, yet may also be a politics of empty signifiers.

6

Another part of Badiou's rationale against quantitative or objective orientations in politics should be considered before concluding. When Peter Hallward studies some of the writings of Badiou's *Organisation politique*, he points out that one of their goals is to contest the view that the economy decides everything, politically. If the economy decides everything, then quantity reigns, and a politics of qualitative difference is set aside. With respect to a critique of capitalism, for Badiou, it is easy to see that its emphasis on the objective, and quantities, is the main danger that is encountered. Since the science of economics is about an objective reality (at least this is the model it seems to require), the better a Marxist or any other orientation is at describing economic life, the more prone we are to the error of basing politics itself on facts about objects and quantities. Thus, politics becomes dominated by representation, and continues to be in proximity to the state of a situation.

But perhaps there is a simple confusion here. The study of economics is certainly not identical to economic life. When a political movement engages in or uses the former, we can concede that it is prone to the errors and dangers that Badiou points out. (Although we do not have to agree that the subjective dangers posed by an economic politics are as serious as Badiou thinks they are, as I argued above.) But this does not mean that economic life itself should be separated from a political movement in the same way that a politics of representation and the state are supposed to be. Indeed, economic life is still what could largely be interrogated by such a movement. How else to give any real, and not abstract and formal, sense to ideas of equality and justice?

To avoid a politics that would be overly economistic, but also to avoid a politics of active number that would be overly formal and empty, I suggest that the political utility of Marxism not only as an economics but as a 'science of history' be reconsidered. This would be Marxism not as a Second-International-style science, but as a narrative, as a story that is not simply about the laws, origins and inevitable demise of capitalism, but that tells the very human story of proletarianisation and expropriation, without which capitalism does not exist. This is the kind of story that a politics of active number needs, since it is a story that gives substance and context to the eternal ideals of equality and justice by referring to a historical process in which inequalities and injustices continue to be advanced.

Badiou himself suggests at the end of his 2005 paper 'Politics: a Non-Expressive Dialectics' that in order to create a political space in which 'the generic' can emerge, what is needed is a 'new great fiction' (2005d: 12). However, there is no need to invent such a great fiction out of nothing. And it is not enough to promote, as Badiou does in his recent *Rebirth of History*, the idea that Marxism is

neither a branch of economics (theory of the relations of production), nor a branch of sociology (objective description of 'social reality'), nor a philosophy (a dialectical conceptualisation of contradictions). It is, let us reiterate, the organised knowledge of the political means required to undo existing society and finally realise an egalitarian, rational figure of collective organisation for which the name is 'communism'. (2012d: 8–9)

This crucial negative work is still not sufficient for a description of what a political Marxism does. The articulation of such goals really requires that a specific content from the political situation itself, the one that is being negated, be retained and reworked. This content must in part involve economic life, since that is an intrinsic part of any political situation.

Keeping in mind that economic life is in part distinct from the *state* of a political situation is a crucial lesson. With this in mind, a critique of capitalism continues to be of great importance, and does more than provide mere background material for a politics. It is true that it is never merely facts and data about economic life, or capitalism itself, that are politically useful for a politics of active number; instead, it would be the overall story in which such data is placed. This is what I have in mind by narrative. In fact, without addressing the content of economic life as well as other matters, it is difficult to see how fidelity to a political event could ever be maintained. For if it is the case that a political situation contains more than signifiers and slogans, but practices as well; and if these practices consist of some other form of political activity than voting, electing representatives and so on; then these practices, insofar as they have to do with the social reality, the social being of individuals, must be in part economic practices. It is hard to imagine what people in a political situation on Alain Badiou's model *do* if this is not the case, other than rally and protest now and again.

It is true that capitalism permeates contemporary economic life, and dominates it to a great extent. But it is still not true (hopefully) that it does so entirely. Without getting into debates about the persistence of archaic modes of production within capitalism, and of course the emergence of new, rival, alternative modes of production within capitalism, let me refer here to the work of David Graeber in his *Debt: The First 5000 Years*, and his concept of a baseline or everyday communism: types of activity and exchange in which we see actual applications of the communist ideal 'from each according to their abilities, to each according to their needs' (Graeber 2011: 98). This persistent and existing form of exchange among individuals and groups is one aspect of social and, I would say, economic life that is certainly not part of the political economy, the state or capitalism. Highlighting it as a form of economic life and contrasting it to the kinds of activities and exchanges that capitalism requires us to engage in brings about an important historicising of capitalism itself. In this way, capitalism's increasing encroachment on non-capitalist forms of economic life can become a clearer target in a politics of active number. One basic thing a critique of capitalism needs to be able to show is that capitalism is not the only form of economic life – not historically, and even not today.

It is true that the use of, and orientation towards, any kind of content in this type of politics can be a problem, since it threatens to narrow the goal of a political movement to the accomplishment of just one task. The hermetic, formal quality of a politics of active number is therefore something that Badiou holds to be very important, and this does count as a valuable insight. In his study of the Paris Commune, for example, he points out that without referring continually to the importance of a particular date, 18 March 1871 – the date on which the Commune was declared – the organisation of the Commune would not have been sustained. And that date is an example of a self-referring, self-belonging multiple: nothing outside of the declaration of the Commune on that date justifies the declaration, or the continued existence of the Commune; thus, it is a site that supports its own appearing, one whose being is not rooted in anything else in what was then the contemporary political situation (Badiou 2006b: 276).

But the role of such a self-referring site is only part of the story and lesson of the Commune. And as Badiou notes in one of the final sections of his study, 'everything, then, depends on the consequences' (2006b: 285). But the main consequence he discusses is nothing other than the sustained appearance of what had formerly not existed – the Commune itself, whose main point Badiou takes to be the appearance of the figure of the worker as someone capable of ruling politically. A politics of active number seems largely, then, to be about sustaining a form of organisation, continuing the existence of a new form. This seems to be the key feature of a politics of active number, and it explains why Badiou is so insistent on avoiding letting certain kinds of content become too important: economic data, the traps of the state, the siren-song of democracy, etc.

But, to close by returning to my main question, it remains puzzling what the content of a 'new great fiction' in a politics of active number might be, for Badiou, or where it might come from. In other words, it is the narrative of a politics of active number that is difficult to think within Badiou's framework, especially when it is drained of a critique of capitalism. Can we expect the ideas of justice, equality and freedom to suffice on their own? Badiou's position may in part be due to his view that philosophy is not the master of politics, and should not be providing politics with content, analysis, criticism, etc. I agree with Badiou on this point. But the call to prioritise a critique of democracy over a critique of capitalism is a political, and not purely philosophical, call. And at this level, my concerns about the formalism that we are left with if a critique of capitalism is avoided remain. While the self-naming and relative autonomy of a politics of active number are supposed to be among its main qualities, the nature of the kind of operation or procedure that sustains its appearance remains obscure. This must involve a consideration of the relationship between the evental site and its situation. This, it seems to me, requires more content than can be supplied by upholding the site itself, continuing its appearance and maintaining its intensity. This requires, at least, what I here call narrative: that which is developed only by putting the evental site in relation to its situation. A site is not a monad. At least, it should not be. And while Badiou is certainly keen on not letting the situation, and certainly not the state of the situation, overrun the contents of the site, it is not clear enough what it means for the site to overrun the situation; or the precise manner in which this occurs is not clear, without a further inclusion of content in a politics of active number. And I am saying that a significant part of this content must be economic life itself – it is difficult to think of our social being without it. More strongly, any account of our social being that misses it threatens to be too abstract.

Fidelity may well be based solely on an evental site and its uniqueness, its apartness. And the organisation of a politics of active number relies in large part on something just like that. I do not mean it as a criticism when I say that there is something hermetic about a politics of active number. But the danger, or the problem, is when this is a politics that has no more to do than gaze at (or show demonstratively?) its glorious new navel. The state of a situation is in excess of the situation, as Badiou claims. But this also means that a situation itself is relatively innocent. Why should any bit of its content be suspect? A politics of active number can and should engage whatever there is in its situation to engage, apart from the state. And economic life is part of what it must engage, since economic life is so pervasive and critical a part of our social and political being. Thus, continuing with a critique of capitalism, the pervasive but not yet exclusive form of economic life in our political situation, and doing so not in a purely economic or objective mode, but in a narrative, historical, mode, seems at least as important for such a politics as Badiou's cautions against the siren-song of democracy.

4

The Pascalian Wager of Politics: Remarks on Badiou and Lacan

Dominiek Hoens

> Even so then at this present time also there is a remnant according to the election of grace. (Rom. 11: 5)

Alain Badiou is well known for making a distinction between what he does, philosophy, and what may look like philosophy but is not – sophistry and antiphilosophy. Surprisingly the authors belonging to the latter category, the antiphilosophers, are undeniably of great importance for and exert a thorough influence on Badiou's ontology and ethics. Also the idea that truth – which philosophy itself is incapable of – needs to be situated outside of it, that is, in its conditions, seems to have arisen under the influence of antiphilosophy. In brief, one cannot imagine Badiou's philosophy having taken shape without a detailed engagement with and borrowing from the work of such antiphilosophers as Lacan, Kierkegaard and Pascal. To this list one should first and foremost add Saint Paul, an antiphilosopher in at least the respect that he professes Christian folly against Greek philosophy. He occupies a unique place in Badiou's work, both quantitatively, for Badiou has dedicated a separate monograph to his Letters, and qualitatively, for many aspects of the post-eventual truth procedure – universality, fidelity and so on – are to be found in or can be illustrated by Paul's intervention.

Yet not only Paul but many of the antiphilosophers quoted, discussed or otherwise used by Badiou are explicitly Christian thinkers.[1] This redoubles the problem when Badiou argues in favour of philosophy against antiphilosophy, for not only does he need to distinguish philosophy's characteristics from antiphilosophy's – the importance of the subjective or intimate experience, the opposition to a reduction of thought to conceptual thought, the privileging of rhetoric over logic, and so on[2] – but, as his philosophy is clearly developed under the influence of antiphilosophers such as Paul, Kierkegaard and Pascal, he also needs to separate his philosophy from the Christian nature and aims of their thought. Stating that he is an atheist, however, easily does this.[3] It is a short but strong answer, for it makes clear that he does not belong to a Church and that he considers the founding event of Christianity, the resurrection of Christ, as a mere fable.

In this context, one also usually relates his atheism to the secularisation that Christian notions are subjected to in Badiou's treatment of them. A good example of this is Christopher Norris's discussion of *Being and Event*'s Meditation 21 which deals with Pascal (Badiou 2006: 212–22). Norris writes: 'It strikes me that nobody who has read very far into Badiou's work could suppose him to have any sympathy with this line of argument [Pascal's wager], at least as regards its moral, religious and (not least) its socio-political implications. After all, it goes clean against . . . his commitment to a thoroughly secularised, materialist ontology . . .' (Norris 2009: 169).

From this point of view, Badiou's ontology excludes any positive reference to the Christian God, and the notions of Christian thought it includes – grace, Church, love – are completely secularised. This still leaves us with the question how this secularisation, or as Norris puts it, this 'translation' of theological statements into ethico-political terms is performed and whether it is complete, that is, entirely de-Christianised. As regards Paul, one could show that the 'de-Christianisation' consists in a positive appreciation of the form of Paul's thought (especially on universality) and not in any content. Were one to recall Kierkegaard's 'teleological suspension of the ethical' (in *Fear and Trembling* [1843]), one could easily point out its analogy with Badiou's thought of the act as a break with a given state of the situation, excluding, however, any teleology or religiously inspired despair. And as far as Pascal and his wager (*pari*) is concerned – a notion Badiou uses frequently and to which he sometimes adds the adjective Pascalian – it is clear that Badiou has no intention of reinstalling God or arguing that one should bet on his existence. In each of the three cases we discern the similar movement of Badiou's thought: it is developed in proximity with a Christian line of reasoning and separates itself from it by offering a secular and atheistic understanding of it.[4]

In this chapter one aspect of this proximity will be examined. The focus will not be on the question of whether Badiou's theory of the event and of immanent infinity succeeds in the complete obliteration of any reference to a transcendent God. Rather, attention will be devoted to the question of the subject, and the political militant in particular. In the first part *Peut-on penser la politique?* (1985)[5] is the central text, for it contains the first introduction of a politics of the (Pascalian) wager in Badiou's work. His qualification of a true politics as 'Pascalian' is explicated through an analysis of the two 'formalisms' in *Peut-on penser la politique?* In the second part, this Pascalian politics is juxtaposed with Jacques Lacan's analysis of the notorious fragment from Blaise Pascal's *Pensées*, known as 'the wager'.[6] The third and last section concludes that Lacan is much more aware of the perversity of the Christian position than is Badiou. Ignoring this perversion may turn Badiou's secularised reading of Christian thinkers into a more problematic endeavour than expected, and raises the issue of whether the 'militant of political truth' is capable of avoiding a Christian and masochistic logic.

From Scission to Decision

Peut-on penser la politique? signifies a break with *Théorie du sujet* (1982) to the extent that Badiou leaves behind the dialectics of scission in favour of a first articulation of the well-known couple of the event and the subject that supports it. It also argues, against a long Marxist tradition, in favour of a politics that is neither expressive, nor representational, nor programmatic. Politics, according to Badiou, is based on an intervention whose success is not guaranteed and the reasons motivating it will only afterwards be proved as sound (or not). In order to illustrate this Badiou introduces two 'formalisms'.[7] In the first (1985: 91–7), one is invited to imagine a world in which there are only true and false statements and people who tell the truth and others who are bound to lie. This leads to a distinction into two classes, namely L and R, the class of those who tell the truth and the class of those who utter falsities, respectively.[8] To L belong those of the Left, to R those of the Right. This artificial and simple construction makes one statement impossible, that is, the auto-referential 'I belong to R'. One can belong to R, but this implies by definition that one can only say what is false. Stating that one belongs to R could either be said by someone who belongs to L – but this cannot happen for members of L always tell the truth – or by someone who belongs to R, in which case a version of the Cretan paradox appears: if the statement is true, then the speaker belongs to R, but if he belongs to R, the statement can only be false.[9] In brief, no one can claim to belong to R and this is what Badiou calls the *interdiction* inherent to the place (*lieu*). An interdiction or its transgression, however, does not make the situation into a political one. If politics emerges when one breaks with a given situation, mere transgression will not be able to make this happen, for as a transgression it does not undo, but either affirms the law or completely destroys the situation.

For a situation to be made pre-political, one needs the impossible. At this point Badiou adds two propositions to the situation, 'B belongs to R' (P1) and 'A belongs to L' (P2), which can be said by two persons, A and B. They can make each of the assertions,[10] as long as the truth and falsity of the assertions accord with the class that the speakers belong to (L or R). But in one instance P1 makes P2 impossible, namely when it is uttered first by A. In that case there are two possibilities regarding A's identity – he either belongs to L or to R. In the former case, P1 is true, which makes it impossible for B, member of the class of 'liars' R, to state the true P2. The latter case, that is, A belonging to R, implies the falsity of P1. This turns B into a truth-telling member of L, which makes it impossible for him to assert the false P2. The impossibility of P2 does not belong to the situation as a given interdiction, but as the consequence of someone stating P1. This turns P2 into a 'historical impossibility' which does not concern all, but solely the individual mentioned in P1, that is B. This leads Badiou to conclude that the impossible is a category of the subject and of the event, which means that one can only state P2 if one acts *as if P1 had not been said*. P2 is the impossible statement that subtracts itself from the facts (like P1) that make up the situation.

Here Badiou refers to the strike at the Talbot factory in 1983–84, during which immigrant workers demanded rights that, politically, they could not claim (see Badiou 1985: 69–75, 96; Pluth 2010: 166–7). According to the left-wing government it was time for them to leave the country, as they did not have French nationality and had become redundant on a professional level. In this demand for 'rights' Badiou does not read the wish to obtain French nationality or to get represented on a political level, but rather an event that can only emerge if one is deaf to what the police say ('you have no right to be here', 'you are only an imported commodity'). Stating P2 after P1 is to stop communicating and to choose the impossible instead of remaining within the realm of the possible.

Section two of the 'formalisms' (1985: 97–109) contains the discussion of a slightly more complex situation, based on the former one. First of all there is, next to L and R, a third class of people who can make both true and false statements (C). Within the situation a political crime was committed and the police bring in three suspects. One knows four things: 1) there is only one culprit; 2) he does not belong to R; 3) the three suspects belong to L, R and C, respectively, but it is not clear which one belongs to which class; and 4) the suspects do not say anything, except for 'I am innocent' (suspect x), 'x is innocent' (suspect y) and 'that is not true, x is guilty' (suspect z). Taking into account all the facts and parameters one can easily deduce these three possible hypotheses:

H1: x belongs to L, y to C and is guilty, and z to R
H2: x belongs to C and is guilty, y to R, and z to L
H3: x belongs to C, y to L and is guilty, and z to R

At this point nothing can be concluded but that z is not guilty. That leaves us with the question as to who did it and to which class he belongs. In a passage remarkably similar to Lacan's piece on 'logical time', Badiou refers to time pressure and urgency. The minimal time available allows for two questions. The first one is addressed to z and asks whether he is guilty. If he denies this, one can deduce that he belongs to L and that x is the culprit (cf. H2). If his reply is affirmative, then there are two possibilities that lead to the same conclusion: y is guilty (H1 and H3). But as it is a political crime one wants to know to which class y belongs, that is, either C or L. In order to determine this, one needs a supplementary question, namely to ask x whether z is guilty. The answer can be either yes or no.[11] In the former case x makes a false statement and one can conclude that H3 is the correct hypothesis. If x, however, denies that z is guilty, no conclusion can be drawn from this answer.

The difference between both questions is explained in the following way:

The first question produced an effect of necessary modification in knowledge. In this sense, it had the status of a guaranteed prolongation of analytical intelligence. It is not the same when I run the risk of a null effect. The suspense in what happens in the guise of the answers is complete, and balances the time of anticipation, before the retroactive seal is stamped on it, between nullity and mastery. It is this type of intervention, which is qualified only by its effect, and which stands in danger of nullity, that I call intervention by wager. Politics is Pascalian in pretending that it is any case worth more to wager, when one has come to the extreme limit of whatever the security of analysis authorises, and which is prolonged, as I have said, by the discriminating intervention. (1985: 103–4)

The difference between both questions may be clear – the first one is simply clever, the second one is a wager that may turn out to be unsuccessful – but what is less clear is the status of the subject of this intervention. From the analysis of the two formalisms one can conclude that, for Badiou, the militant can act on the basis of the facts that make up the situation, while at the same time testifying to a 'deafness' to them by choosing the impossible. The intervention, however, becomes Pascalian when one is forced to wager on a possible outcome, without any guarantee. Only afterwards, when the effects of the act emerge, will it become clear whether the intervention was sound or rather meaningless. This lack of ground is in perfect accordance with the atheist ontology Badiou is to develop later in *Being and Event*. The absence of a God leaves a gap for which the (political) subject takes responsibility through acting without any reference to superior knowledge or transcendent justice. The 'truth' of the act is entirely immanent to the situation within which it is done: it is either null, or changes the situation within which the intervention could be made.

This, however, leaves us with the question of what kind of subject is capable of such an act and whether this subject automatically emerges as soon as a situation presents its own impossibility. In order to elaborate this question, we will take a look at Lacan's discussion of Pascal's wager, only to find another Pascalian idea of subjectivity that is both diametrically opposite to and remains unthought-of in Badiou's philosophy.

You Never Know Your Luck

Although Jacques Lacan frequently refers to Blaise Pascal, the relation between the two thinkers is rarely commented on and has still to be studied in detail.[12] An in-depth discussion of Lacan's use of various writings by Pascal at many, and often crucial, moments of his teaching (the seminar he taught from 1953 to 1980) would be a task for a book. That this work is still to be done may be due to the fact that of the two seminars – *The Object of Psychoanalysis* (1965–66) and *From an Other to the Other* (1968–69) – where Lacan deals most extensively with Pascal, only one has been published in French (Lacan 2006c), and no official English translation is available of either.[13]

It is no surprise that Lacan's return to Freud makes a detour via Pascal. One of the best-known Freudian propositions is 'The finding of an object is in fact a refinding of it' (Freud 1953: 222). One way to understand this is with reference to the fundamental nostalgia characteristic of mental life: some mythical object was lost, taken away, or disappeared somehow, and since that moment the psychical apparatus has been desperately looking for it. Because the real object is lacking and thus cannot be retrieved, one must satisfy oneself with surrogates, that is, with objects that are only interesting to the degree that they remind us of the original. It is certainly possible to argue for this reading from a Freudian perspective. A slightly different reading, however, makes use of the paradox inherent to equating the finding of an object with its refinding. The simultaneity of finding and refinding indicates two possible directions. We have already discussed the first one: finding is based on a prior loss. The second one, for its part, entails a more complex operation: finding the object actively installs the loss on whose basis one can consider the object as found again. In that sense, each and every refinding of the object actively creates the separation between what is lost and what is found. What this means for pleasure, in loss and gain terms, is that pleasure, to be pleasure, must entail a loss, and that loss alone makes it possible to find pleasure in a certain object. This concomitance of pleasure and loss is already present in the German word Freud uses, *Lust*, which means both pleasure and desire or craving.

The notion that pleasure is to be kept open, that it must be like a quest in which the seeking is more important than what it leads to, is succinctly articulated by Pascal in fragment 773: 'We never go after things in themselves, but the pursuit of things' (Pascal 1966: 262).[14] We must read this passage with an eye to the world his interlocutors inhabited, the world of amusement through game-playing. Games were particularly popular among

seventeenth-century noblemen. They served as a necessary distrac-
tion from boredom and, in Pascal's diagnosis, from the miserable
condition human beings are in. What is essential to the game is not
the outcome, the gain or loss, but the playing of it, the expectations it thrives on, the tension between the certainty of the rules
of the game and of the stakes put on the table, on the one hand,
and the uncertainty of chance (*hasard*), on the other.

In this respect, it is worth noting that Pascal first became interested in games of chance when he was asked about the right way
to end such a game prematurely. His friend the Chevalier de
Méré asked him how the stake could be divided fairly between
two players should they decide to interrupt their game before it
reached the end. By way of example, imagine two players, each
of whom has invested fifty euros in a coin toss game that, they
stipulate, will end when one of the players has won six tosses.
However, they subsequently decide to end the game at an earlier
stage, when one player (A) has won five tosses and the other
(B) four. How, then, is the stake to be divided between the two
players? Pascal's quest for a rule of division (*règle des parties*) is
detailed in the (partially lost) correspondence with French jurist
and mathematician Pierre de Fermat (Pascal 1654). From what we
have of the exchange, however, it is clear that both men, although
their approaches differ, arrive at an equally sound solution to the
problem. Fermat suggests calculating the possible outcomes, and
then dividing the stake in accordance with the quantity of possible
wins that A and B can respectively count on. In our example, it is
clear that the quantity of possible wins for A is greater than for
B, and that the stake should be divided between the two using the
same ratio. The disadvantage of this solution is that it very quickly
leads to rather complex tree graphs without which it would be
impossible to show all possible outcomes of the game.[15] Pascal
proposes a different method, one that, as mentioned just above,
leads to the same division of the stake between both players.

Pascal starts from the observation that there are two possible
outcomes to each successive round: either A or B will win the toss.
Returning to our example, we can easily deduce that either player
A wins the toss *and* the game, or that B wins the toss and equalises
the chances of winning the game. In the latter case, with player B
having tied the tosses at five each, each player will again be fully
in possession of his stake, so that A has at least 'won' fifty euros,
even if he were to lose his round. The chances that the former case

will obtain, however, are split – he will either win or lose – hence the remaining fifty euros should be divided in half. The conclusion is that if both players decide to end the game prematurely, A is entitled to 75 (50 + 25) euros, and B to 25. If we now make a minor change to our example and imagine A to have won five rounds and B only three, the reasoning is then as follows: A is sure to have the right to 75 euros – based on the future possibility of B winning four rounds, as we just explained – and A can also lay claim to half of the remaining 25 euros, bringing his total to 87.5 euros, *if* both players agree to end the game when A has won five and B three rounds. The confines of this article do not allow for engaging more deeply with Pascal's 'rule of division', or with the elegant application of Pascal's triangle to it.

Our interest in this brief discussion of the problem of dividing the stakes among two players who decide to end a game of chance prematurely resides in the direct references to it in the *pensée* devoted to the wager. This fragment, titled 'Infinity – nothing', can be divided into two parts.[16] The first part is called the existential wager and argues that one has reason to bet on the existence of God. We do not know if God exists, and the aim of the argument is not to prove God's existence. Rather, it says that the fact that no one knows with certainty what to do does not take away the choice everyone is confronted with: to suppose that God exists, or that he does not. According to Pascal, one is always already *in* the wager and one has to make a choice. Simply not believing in God is tantamount to making an active choice against God's existence. Here, it is obvious that Pascal defends Christian belief as a matter of reason because it can be based on a division between what one can be certain of and what depends on chance. This implicit reference to the problem of the right division of stakes – which is also based on a precise division of what is certain and what is still open to chance – leads to the second part of the fragment, the mathematical wager.

This opens with Pascal's imaginary interlocutor objecting: 'That is wonderful. Yes, I must wager, but perhaps I am wagering too much' (Pascal 1966: 151). Wagering on the existence of God entails giving up earthly pleasures, and what if sacrificing one's life's pleasures is too high a stake compared to what one may expect as the outcome of the game? Pascal replies by pointing out that if the possible outcome is an infinity of happy lives after death, one is right to bet on the existence of God. What one can lose (if it turns out that God does not exist), that is, earthly pleasure, is *nothing* compared to the *infinite* reward awaiting us if he exists. Here Pascal makes active use of his rule of the division of stakes: it is right to bet, that is, to start or continue the game, for if one were not to enter (or to interrupt) the game, one is certain to lose more. We should also add here that, while no one knows the outcome – my forsaking of earthly pleasure could go unrewarded, either because God does not exist, or because he decides not to save me from hell – everyone knows that the game will end: death is one of the few certainties human beings can rely on. The uncertainty is treated like a chance: either God exists or he does not. But, given the minimal chance that he does exist, and the infinite reward that may entail, the only reasonable option is to bet on his existence, as my stake is, compared to the infinity of the possible, a nothing (*rien*). And Pascal concludes: 'That leaves no choice.' In French, it says: '*Cela ôte tout parti*', which means, literally, that the choice to choose for or against God was never actually a choice at all. If one follows reason, according to Pascal, it becomes clear that in this case the rule for the right division of stakes does not apply. In an ordinary game, the rule leaves the players with the choice either to continue or to interrupt the game, and, moreover, it shows them how the stakes will be divided. In the context of the wager, however, where infinity is part of the calculation, the only thing one can do, if one wants to act reasonably, is to continue the game and wager on the existence of God.

In the last section of the fragment, the interlocutor admits that the argument to wager on God's existence is convincing, but he also adds: 'I am so made that I cannot believe' (Pascal 1966: 152). Reason forces him to opt for God's existence, but that does not mean he actually believes it. Pascal's notorious answer advises him to act as if he believes, which will gradually make the aspiring believer 'more docile'; '*Cela vous abêtira*', it says, which means, literally, it will turn you into a beast. Lacan approvingly quotes this passage, stating that beasts lack the very thing that, according to Pascal, prevents human beings from believing, namely an image of the self, which is the cause of self-love and narcissism (Lacan 2006c: 137). This is a rather surprising statement at first sight. After all, when discussing the formative function of the image for the ego, doesn't Lacan use many examples taken from animal ethology?[17] The distinction here resides in the fact that an animal is open to imaginary effects, such as copying a fellow animal's colour or emotional contagion, but it does not form an ego with which it orients itself in life. In that respect, Lacan and Pascal think along the same lines: narcissism is a deadlock and, despite the intense passions it may produce (rivalry, aggression, vanity and so on), it keeps human beings in a state of ignorance concerning their own existence. For Pascal, the real question is belief, which, as we have seen, can be approached and argued for with reason. For Lacan, the (narcissistic) ego veils the true dimension of subjectivity, namely the lack-of-being (*manque à être*) or desire (*désir*) that the subject is qua subject of the symbolic order. Despite the centuries that separate them, both Pascal and Lacan agree that self-love, or narcissism, is an obstacle to confronting another dimension, respectively, reason and the symbolic order, that more fundamentally determines our existence. Still, both also point to what only appears at the margins of the logic of calculating reason (Pascal) and the signifier (Lacan's term for the basic element with which the symbolic order works). This, for Pascal, is belief, the 'reasons of which reason knows nothing' (Pascal 1966: 154, fr. 423). And, for Lacan, desire, that which articulates itself in the symbolic order, but also indicates its non-closure as it emerges where a signifier is lacking.[18]

Here the question of the object comes into play. For Pascal, the noblemen forget their miserable condition by playing games of chance; more precisely, they are not aware of it for they do not assume the Christian perspective on their own existence. Were they to do so, they would be able both to despair and to find the solution to this by converting to Christianity. This would allow them to move from being subjects of idle pastimes in which one gambles with what one *has*, to being subjects of belief, whereby one bets with one's own life, that is, on what one *is*. Of course, the nobleman will argue that he considers life also as something he has, and as perhaps too high a stake to gamble with. As we have seen, however, Pascal argues that this life is nothing (or a nothing life). The obvious question here is: how can one stake nothing?

In order to answer this question Lacan quotes approvingly (2006d: 117, 126) a passage from Pascal's *The Arithmetic Triangle*:

> In order to understand the rules of the divisions [*règle des partis*], the first thing that it is necessary to consider is that the money that the players have staked in the game no longer belongs to them, for they

have given up the property; but they have received in exchange the right to expect that which chance is able to give to them of it, according to the conditions to which they have agreed first. (Pascal 2009: 15)

This means that, whatever one stakes, one has to consider it as lost, as reduced to a nothing. Thus by entering the game, something (property) is turned into nothing (the stake), and what one gets in return is 'the right to expect that which chance is able to give'. In the case of the wager this means that earthly pleasure is actually nothing when compared to the expectation of an infinity of happiness awaiting the gambling believer. Lacan shows the surprising analogy this has with the expectation people address to a psychoanalyst: their hope is for another life, a happy life as the possible outcome of the expensive and time-consuming labour of psychoanalysis (Lacan 2006d: 146). Within the non-Christian frame of the analytical cure, one does not aspire for an infinity of happy lives but for a second life, a happy one. That is why perhaps Lacan, more than Pascal, is able to question the stake: is it something or nothing? What should one give up in order to take a chance on leading a happy life?

The promise of Lacanian psychoanalysis, however, is not a happy life, but the entering into a culture of desire. This means that one has to give up what one has already lost, a pleasure (*jouissance*) still inherent to the symptom one complains about. The analysis will make the analysand realise that this 'stake' is anyway lost and that he can only expect to desire in a fruitful and/or bearable manner. The name for this stake is *objet a*, which is qualified by Lacan as a *plus-de-jouir*, a wordplay on *plus* that contains both of the dimensions we already encountered in our discussion of Freud: a lost (*plus*) enjoyment (*jouir*) turned into a surplus (*plus*) of enjoyment. To be the subject of desire means to give up (being) the object of it and to consider its satisfaction as an extended future.

Not Without an Object

At first sight one can identify two common traits between Lacan's reading of Pascal and Badiou's use of it: first, both try to develop a theory of the subject that decentres or adds itself to the common life of the human animal. Pascal, Lacan (and Freud) and Badiou think that human beings ('individuals') misunderstand themselves if they consider life as something they have and try and live in security and comfort, the sole enemy of which is boredom. It is not that human beings should open themselves to a dimension beyond this miserable yet (for some) comfortable situation; they are from the very beginning solicited, traumatised or in some other way affected by something that cannot be integrated into the daily passion of being an individual. Secondly, the three of them refer to an act that makes subjectivity appear. This act is not unmotivated or a simple leap of faith, but is the result of a rational examination of the situation that encounters its limit and therefore requires an act whose rationality can at best be proven afterwards. At this point we also need to underline the differences. Lacan reads Pascal not only as a reflection on the human condition but also finds in him the structure of the aim of a psychoanalytical cure: a subjectivation of an object-position. In order for this to work, someone needs to occupy the position of the object to enable the analysand to deal with a loss beyond a narcissistic 'to be or not to be'.

As is well known, Badiou avoids positing the category of the object as a correlate of the subject (see Badiou 1991). For him, subjectivity mainly equals fidelity, taken from an ethical perspective, and the body that supports the development of a truth in a generic procedure, from the ontological point of view developed in *Logics of Worlds* (Badiou 2009a). Yet leaving out the category of the object, and *objet a* in particular, may be the cause of overlooking a possibility that Lacan considers as characteristic of modern subjectivity: perversion, that is, identifying with the object instead of becoming a subject.

This possibility can be clarified when one takes into account Lacan's repeated discussion of Christianity. By way of example, in the seminar on anxiety (1962–63) (Lacan 2004: 192, 256), masochism is considered as the Christian's 'second nature'. This second nature resides in a readiness to embrace self-effacing sacrifices in the name of the commandment to love, which is, according to Lacan, a masochist strategy to provoke God's anxiety. The masochism is clearly present in the acts performed out of love (for the neighbour), but the perversity is a matter of where one locates oneself with regard to castration. The perverse position is an object-position that transfers the constitutive lack of the symbolic order on to another being, that is, God. That is why both the sadist and the masochist equally desire the Other's anxiety, for it is a proof of the Other's split and castrated subjectivity, which makes it possible for the pervert to keep up the (unconscious) illusion that he is not subject to castration. To the masochist, the Christian God may appear as indifferent, absent or silent, but sacrificing oneself may provoke him to show concern and care, in brief, to get scared about what people do out of love for him.

The author who most explicitly connects Christianity with perversion, and even refers to a 'perverse core of Christianity', is of course Slavoj Žižek (Žižek 2003). The limits of this chapter do not allow for a detailed discussion of the several books and articles he has published on the 'Christian legacy'. Yet in support of the argument made here, one is reminded of Žižek's statement that the problem of Saint Paul (and other Christian thinkers, one could add) is 'to avoid the trap of *perversion*' (Žižek 1999: 148). However, perversion for Žižek does not mean that one occupies the position of the object with regard to an Other marked by castration. Perversion, according to Žižek (following Badiou on this point), is the Law that *needs* to be transgressed in order to sustain itself as Law. Transgression – as we have already discovered in the discussion of the first 'formalism' in *Peut-on penser la politique?* – does not result in an annulment of the Law, but affirms it. This vicious dynamic of guilt, the effect of a Law demanding both obser- vation and transgression, can rightly be qualified as 'perverse', yet the *subject* of it need not be. Quite the opposite, for the perversity of the Law turns us all into internally divided neurotic subjects. Therefore, the Christian attempt at undoing the 'perverse' dialectic of Law and its transgression may, instead of avoiding perversity, actually install it at the level of the subject.

This, at least, is part of Lacan's critical distance from Christianity. Unlike Badiou, Lacan does not discover Christian love as an anti- dialectical supplement to 'perverse' desire, but rather as an exploi- tation of the subject who is called to love what is indifferent to this love. If Lacan has an interest in Pascal, it is because he, like François de Sales, Fénelon and others, belongs to a long tradition of Christian 'pure love' (see Le Brun 2002; Parisot 2008). This is a love for God that can only be pure to the extent that nothing is expected in return. The God of Christianity (or one version thereof) is a God who cannot be bargained with and whose inten- tions are unclear. Some will be saved, others will not, and the decision depends entirely on God's unpredictable grace. This may lead some believers to think that he is an evil God, but the doctrine of pure love argues the opposite: the fact that we cannot expect anything in return from God proves his goodness, for this gives us, human beings, the possibility of loving 'purely', that is, giving love without expecting a counter-gift. This freedom to choose self-sacrifice 'for nothing' would not have been possible had we been dealing with a grateful, 'reasonable' God.

If Lacan, theorist of desire, discusses Pascal and other Christian thinkers, this is also meant as a critical engagement with the Christian notion of love. Lacan qualifies this love as perverse and his oeuvre can be read as a warning against the exploitation of it.[19] Badiou may very well succeed in thinking Christianity without God, but – leaving aside the problem of the object position one occupies in relation to the Christian God – this may render his idea of the militant subject engaged in a Pascalian wager a naive and incomplete surpassing of what he calls, mockingly and against Lacan, the bedrock of the Law (1985: 113).

Notes

1. Notable exceptions are Friedrich Nietzsche and Jacques Lacan.
2. For a detailed and illuminating discussion, see Bosteels 2008.
3. Which he does, for example, in the Prologue to his book on Saint Paul (Badiou 2003b).
4. In this double movement Lacanians will recognise the logic of phantasy: the subject (Badiou's philosophy) finds itself in an object (Christianity) from which it needs to separate itself in order to keep open the possibility of a symbolic identification. See also Bosteels 2008: 178ff.
5. Quotes are taken from the forthcoming translation by Bruno Bosteels (Duke University Press); page numbers refer to the French edition (Badiou 1985).
6. That is fragment 418 of the Louis Lafuma edition of *Les Pensées*.
7. These, as Badiou mentions, resemble in some respect Lacan's famous three prisoners sophism (Lacan 2006a).
8. I render the two formalisms in a slightly more formalised way and use, for clarity's sake, more and other symbolic notations than Badiou does. The argument remains the same.
9. Here Badiou refers to the French political context of the 1980s, during which the book was published. At that time no one ever said of oneself that one was 'from the right'. This qualification was, according to Badiou, always attributed to another person, not to oneself. How times have changed.

10. Except for B who cannot make P1; see the interdiction explained above.
11. The rules of the situation seem to exclude x not knowing the answer to the questions asked – a possibility not discussed by Badiou.
12. Notable exceptions are Gallagher (2001), Cléro (2008) and a special issue of *Le Célibataire* (2006). For a psychoanalytic approach to and appreciation of Pascal's work, see Penney 2006: 69–102.
13. An unofficial English translation by Cormac Gallagher is available at http://www.lacaninireland.com/ (accessed 17 July 2013).
14. The original French includes a wordplay on *chercher* (to search) and *recherche* (to re-search): 'Nous ne cherchons jamais les choses, mais la recherche des choses.'
15. If A needs x rounds to win the game and B needs y rounds, then x + y − 1 rounds are required to be sure to end up with a winner. The possible ways to reach this result, however, amount to 2r + s − 1.
16. For the ensuing explanation I rely on Thirouin 1991: 130–47.
17. See, among many other examples, the case of the female pigeon in Lacan 2006b: 77.
18. That is also why Lacan defends Pascal's choice in favour of the God of Abraham, of Isaac and of Jacob, the God of grace, instead of the God of the philosophers (Descartes). See Lacan 2006c: 135; 2006d: 102–3, 147, 150.
19. For example in neoliberalism, where one is supposed to love a system that owes you nothing in return. For an example discussed in detail by Lacan himself – Paul Claudel's theatre trilogy *The Hostage/Crusts/The Humiliated* Father – see Lacan 2001: 315–86.

5

Contra Opinionem: Politics as an Anti-Imperialist Procedure

Marios Constantinou

Introduction: The Logic of the Anti-Imperial Gesture in Badiou

According to Badiou, the fundamental task of political anti-nihilism in the present is to expose and challenge the Western state fetish that 'only designates imperial comfort' (2012a: 60). This political task a) breaks with the naked power that underlies the global imperial attack coupled by the 'one-and-only politics' of capital-parliamentarism; b) identifies the faults of this 'democratic transcendental' and works towards its logical and practical ruin; and c) exalts exceptions without ever being intimidated by the denunciation of elitism or totalitarianism (2012a: 61).

My argument is that Badiou's political anti-nihilism may obtain its full force of critical affirmation only by recasting the distance between thinking and sequences of imperial power in a new light. The contemporary task of political anti-nihilism is to elucidate this distance between, on the one hand, the state as the condensed condition of the extended order, and, on the other, the exception of political truths, by which we measure this distance and decide whether or not it can be crossed. It is the pre-coded power of the extended order that homogenises and globalises the state, law and capital logics defined by Badiou as 'capital-parliamentarism'. We may rescue the possibility of a contemporary political affirmation only by striking, and invigilating over, a distance from the state and the market as sequences of imperial episodes that are fused together in Hayek's concept of the extended order, and by assuming the consequences for this distancing 'however remote and difficult they may prove'.[1] Badiou, after all, is fully aware that a philosophical as well as a political awakening 'implies a difficult break with sleep'. As was already the case for Plato, and will be for all time, philosophy consists in the seizure of a truth that breaks with the sleep of thought (Badiou and Žižek 2009e: 15).

Thinking, I propose, is first and foremost a thinking of the event against empire and its pre-coding power. As a paradigmatic embodiment of this reorientation, consider Archimedes, the celebrated Greek mathematician of Syracuse who set fire to the imperial navy of Rome during the siege of his native city. Here it is important to follow Badiou's remarkable reconstruction of this imperial episode, since it provides the impetus for the hypothesis I shall put forward. Archimedes was involved actively in the resistance against the Roman invasion and occupation, on the occasion of which he ventured to invent anti-imperial war machines. After the fall of the city, upon returning to the 'normalcy' of the extended order, Archimedes' scientific investigations were persistently obstructed, delayed and interrupted by the encyclopaedic encroachments of imperial power: 'The Romans were very curious about Greek scientists, a little like the CEO of a multinational cosmetics corporation might be curious about a philosopher of renown' (Badiou and Žižek 2009e: 6). Not that General Marcellus, who enjoined the imperial envoy to bring over and present Archimedes before his authority, had any great interest in mathematics; he simply wanted to witness 'what an insurgent of Archimedes' caliber was like' (Badiou and Žižek 2009e: 6). Archimedes courageously ignored the injunction. He rejected his reduction to *ordinarius servus*, 'looked up slightly and said to the soldier: "Let me finish my demonstration" . . . the soldier, by now absolutely furious, drew his sword and struck him. Archimedes fell dead, his body effacing the geometrical figure in the sand' (Badiou and Žižek 2009e: 7).

What kind of fatality is involved in this *hostis caedere*? Nothing less than the generic brutality of imperial scission; a caesarian section of thought with nothing born. It features siege, manoeuvre, cutting off from behind and a courting of thought. Failing to manipulate successfully this supplementary loop in which the insurgent is converted into a protected client, that is, failing to seduce the insurgent into the Hegelian knot of master and slave recognition, there comes elimination, the foregrounding of the imperial cut, the caesura which manifests the essence of empire as a deceptive mimesis of nothingness. Now, why is this imperial hiatus a philosophical situation? Because, Badiou replies, it demonstrates that between the right of the state and creative thought 'there is no common measure, no real discussion' (Badiou and Žižek 2009e: 7). When it comes to the law of his thought, Badiou argues, Archimedes remains outside the range of action of imperial power. The temporality proper to thought defies the imperial subpoena of the invader, conqueror and occupier: 'That is why violence is eventually wrought, testifying that there is no common measure and no common chronology between the power of one side and the truths of the other' (Badiou and Žižek 2009e: 8). The same scenario might have occurred between Aeschylus and the imperial envoys of Xerxes in their world-historical encounter at the battle of Salamis had the outcome been the reverse. That was, *mutatis mutandis*, the case between the musical genius Anton Webern and the American GI, between Walter Benjamin and the soldiers of the Third Reich, and a host of other known and unknown cases. Politics, then, as generic procedure and anti-imperialist creation a) elucidates retroactively the decision involved in this encounter, and b) keeps circumscribing intensively and in detail the distance between imperial power and the fragments of truth we hold on to in the present.

Hegel and Polybius: The Sophistic Logic of the Imperial Condition

Implicated in this is, however, an intractable knot, one that concerns what Hegel, in the *Philosophy of History*, eerily calls 'the diplomatic condition – an infinite involvement with the most manifold foreign interests – a subtle intertexture and play of parties, whose threads are continually combined anew' (1956: 276). Evidently, Hegel's warning apropos of the diplomatic condition elicits an effect induced by corruption, calling attention to an 'infinite involvement with manifold foreign interests' and the 'subtle intertexture' of factionalism as integral components of imperial favouritism. Hegel, in other words, points to the corporatist dialectic of patronage as a pastoral apparatus of biopower, which works to convert a 'philosopher king' into a 'philosopher client' of the extended order. Hegel's problematic of inward slavery here is neither a formal schematism nor mere idle speculation on some archaic constellation. Instead, it should be taken as an ontological index regarding the mediation between the metaphysics of World History and the Condition of Empire, incorporating multiple levels and thresholds of bondage.

Contrary to this, there is only the courage of the egalitarian promise of truth as embodied by Archimedes' aggressive lack of interest for a courtly life of deflected thought. And this is precisely the promise of an anti-imperialist politics, that is, one's self-exemption from the relation of dialectical bondage. For Hegel, the truth of the slave's self-consciousness is 'consummate servitude', bondage brought to maturity as a progressive, humanising freedom. In the Hegelian schema, the frightened and spineless bondsman is the motor of history, the prime mover of humanity. Instead, in Badiou's narrative of political materialism, Archimedes' combative indifference to the summons of the imperial master for association and recognition indicates that any solicitation of, or accommodation to, *patrocinium* generates an exchange network of stratified corruption. In this sense the Archimedean event is not the prime mover of a progressively advancing humanity, but the bearer of a timeless and immortal truth that embodies the intensity of *universitas*, not as a Hegelian negation of the negation but as a Badiouian negation of relation: 'So that ultimately what we are told about is a break: the break of the established natural and social bond . . . So we can say that philosophy, which is thought, not of what there is, but of what is not – not of contracts, but of ruptures of contracts – is exclusively interested in relations that are not relations' (Badiou and Žižek 2009e: 14–15).

Relatedly, for every exemplary figure that, like Archimedes, becomes a scientific and political sign of the event, there appears a 'Pétainist' countersign of collaborationist nihilism embodied by a figure such as Polybius. Why is Polybius' encounter with imperial power a counter-condition, or a counter-situation, of philosophy, one that equally needs light to be shed on it as a figure of political nihilism? Hegel says:

> Looking at Greece as Polybius describes it, we see how a noble nature such as his, has nothing left for it but to despair at the state of affairs and to retreat into Philosophy; or if it (Greece) attempts to act, can only die in the struggle. In deadly contraposition to the multiform variety of passion which Greece presents – that distracted condition which whelms good and evil in one common ruin – stands a blind fate – an iron power ready to show up that degraded condition in all its weakness, and to dash it to pieces in miserable ruin; for cure, amendment, and consolation are impossible. And this crushing Destiny is the Roman power. (1956: 277)

Hegel was, like Polybius, confident that he was born at the right time, and mused solemnly over the notion of imperial succession as a general structure of universal history. Unlike Polybius, however, Hegel argued, and quite pointedly, that the '*Sophistic Principle* appears again and again, though under different forms, in various periods of History even in our own times' (1956: 269). According to Hegel, affect, opinion, caprice, deception, private interest and ultimately cultivated treason constitute the sophistic invariant of corruption that brought about the downfall of the Greek spirit. Precisely due to his critical awareness of the sophistic principle that led to the degeneracy of Greek public culture, Hegel was able to identify the imperial apparatus of corruption operant in the extended order of Rome in a way that Polybius was unable to. What Hegel was pointing at was nothing else than the cliental relation itself as 'a method of extension'. That was the *raison d'état* of what Hayek calls 'catallaxis': the conversion of the enemy into a business associate, a pacified collaborator, and so on.

Under the condition of the extended order, Polybius, unlike Archimedes, subjectivised the sophistic principle, bringing it to a state of perfection. He corrupted the Greek notion of friendship, rationalising it within the Roman system of *amicitiae* (clientships), patronage networks and *gratia*, which were bound, as it were, by the exchange of services, *fides* (fidelity to the patron) and business partnerships, solemnly called *societas* to indicate that they were tied together by *beneficia*. Polybius' illustrative counsel to Scipio Africanus, as reported by Plutarch, discloses an unmistakable trace of the founding institutional codes and structures of formation of the self in which the imperial animal was trained to engage in *regnum* and *dominatio*: 'never return from a visit to the Forum until you have made a new friend. . .'[2] Making profitable extensions by winning over new allies and clients in the marketplace, to which the imperial animal rushed to engage in business and other serviceable activities, was perforce not simply a technique of self-care or a protocol of elaborate table-manners concerning rules of conviviality. It was an imperial method of extension in its own right.

Let us not forget that this intricate question of patrician bio-power was a central preoccupation of the practical reason of empire, also exemplarily reflected in the didactic treatises of Seneca ('On Benefits') and Cicero ('On Duties'). This practical reason was literally rooted in the distribution and circulation of *beneficia* and in the patron's indispensable expectation of receiving returns on the benefits distributed to his permanent or impermanent client-age, returns cashed out in terms of public acclamation and *salutatio*. What needs to be underscored in the macro-micro context of the extended order is that this spectacular form of subjectivating biopower had profound implications for the durability of empire. Indeed, this durability was forged through varying levels of obligation and hierarchical structures of dependency among subject cities and client populations.

It was not merely circumspection or excessive tact on the part of Polybius, that historian cum client, which prompted him to consider Rome's extended order as prudent, just and uncontroversial. Arnaldo Momigliano argues that Polybius 'acts as a Greek who has a vital interest in the proper functioning of the Roman hegemony over Greece', although he adds that 'diplomatic and military history had never been so subtly and competently written before Polybius, and the brilliance of Posidonius' social analysis remained unmatched throughout antiquity' (Momigliano 1971: 29; 36). Nonetheless both Polybius and Posidonius identified with imperial fortune, never questioning the drive to world-domination: 'After the half-century or more of Roman rule which separated Posidonius from Polybius, the identification of the interests of the Greek wealthy and educated classes with the survival of Roman Empire had become self-evident' (Momigliano 1971: 35–6). It was this acclamatory *salutatio* and excessive indulgence in imperial comfort that prevented the educated (and wealthy) elites from pondering philosophically the justice not only of Roman occupation itself but of the 'extended order' in general. That was also the reason why Polybius and Posidonius 'never quite understood what was really happening in the social organism which had become the guarantee of their own survival' (Momigliano 1971: 36). They were unable to reflect on social bonds and bondage, patronisation and resistance, sophistic deception and truth, virtue and corruption as inherent contradictions of the Western *arcana dominationis*. They were unable to meet this domination with the inventive methods that pre-Roman Greeks so competently forged in order to understand Oriental empires: 'There was no attempt to see Rome, as it were, *from a distance* – as something strange, mysterious in language and religion, frightful in rituals and formidable in warfare' (Momigliano 1971: 37, emphasis added). Momigliano here delineates the contours of a phenomenology of collaborationist reason. Taken in by the Roman metaphysics of imperial succession and the ostentatious universality of its swelling *amour propre*, collaborationist historiography failed to explain the sophistic texture of the imperial condition. Instead it emphasised the Roman genius for expansion and valorised its technical acumen for ruling over it.

Even such an improbable enthusiast of the Roman spirit of patronage as Rousseau, who, incredibly, celebrated it in the *Social Contract* as an 'admirable institution . . . a masterpiece of politics and humanity [which] only Rome has had the honor of giving the world' (1988: 158–9), nonetheless dismissed *amour propre*, which, by narcissistic extension, is the terrain of imperial affect par excellence. It is, in other words, the source of self-vindicated comparison and fixated fancy, that is, the realm of sophistic *opinatio* as the universal discursive form of empire.

Elements for a Genealogy of Pétainist Reason

Nietzsche, Paul and the imperial relation

This is why Paul, himself the contemporary of a monumental figure of the destruction of all politics (the beginnings of that military despotism known as 'the Roman Empire'), interests us in the highest degree. He is the one who, assigning to the universal a specific connection of law and the subject, asks himself with the most extreme rigor what price is to be paid for this assignment, by the law as well as by the subject. This interrogation is precisely our own. Supposing we were able to refound the connection between truth and the subject, then what consequences must we have the strength to hold fast to, on the side of truth (evental and hazardous) as well as on the side of the subject (rare and heroic)? It is by confronting this question, and no other, that philosophy can assume its temporal condition without becoming a means of covering up the worst. That it can measure up to the times in which we live otherwise than by flattering their savage inertia. (Badiou 2003b: 7)

The profound political idea announced by Badiou's *Saint Paul* is that Paul is contemporary with the monumental destruction of the Greek polis and politics by the Roman Empire. Badiou is not the first frontiersman to have drawn attention to this, but he is the first to draw the consequences systematically, reaffirming its political principle as a condition of contemporary philosophy.[3] The momentous consequence of this declaration is that the universal calling of politics to justice and truth – which are identical – was thenceforth incompatible not only with the sophistic party which was its fundamental opponent in the ancient polis, but also with the empire that universalised the sophistic principle as the foundation of its constitution. The corrosive consequences and inestimable suffering generated by this fateful fusion between homegrown public market-sophistics and empire can be understood by simply noticing their ruthless, coextensive reaction to those rare moments when politics came into existence as a new creation, proclaiming an emancipatory truth with universal address and consequences. As a subjective figure, Paul comes into political being, even at times against his own will, precisely because of his confrontation with this doubling of the *Imperium romanum*. Paul works through the sophistic fiction of empire by anticipating truth. Empire is a sophistic extension that can be countered only by a universalisable truth.

Nietzsche was the first to come to this shocking realisation of Paul as an anti-imperialist. Indeed, the historical destiny of Paul as a poet, apostle of thought and militant of a truth discloses its intense multiplicity only when measured against the being and becoming of empire. According to Nietzsche, the genius of this 'holy anarchist' lies precisely in the destruction of the *Imperium romanum* as the very logic of the world, as

> the revenue of reason from long ages of experimentation and uncertainty employed for the benefit of the most distant future, and the biggest, richest, most complete harvest possible brought home ... [as the] most grandiose form of organisation under difficult conditions which has hitherto been achieved, in comparison with which everything before and everything since is patchwork, bungling, dilettantism. (1968: 180, section 58)

This supreme condition of empire became

> overnight merely a memory! Greeks! Romans! Nobility of instinct, of taste, methodical investigation, genius for organization and government, the faith in the will to a future for mankind, the great Yes to all things, visibly present to all the senses as the *Imperium Romanun*, grand style no longer merely art but become reality, truth, life ... ruined by cunning, secret, invisible, anaemic vampires! Not conquered

– only sucked dry! … Covert revengefulness, petty envy become monster. (1968: 182–3, section 59)

What Nietzsche thinks through the idol of the *Imperium romanum*, 'the harvest of the culture of the ancient world' (1968: 182–3), is a sophistic fusion of *Graecia capta* with imperial Rome. He pictures them as organically growing into a master culture of ascriptive hierarchies that reflect a superiority of spirit, which in turn bestows meaning on the suffering of the slave class, and so on. By virtue of this supreme condition of moral superiority, spiritual strength and martial force, the master culture of *Imperium romanum* miraculously trickles down to the benefit of all orders, thus justifying morally the universal foundation of inequality. By resolving imperial power into a universal culture, Nietzsche renders inequality as the necessary and inescapable condition of a master universality. After all, 'it does indeed make a difference', Nietzsche argues in a sophistic simulation of Plato, 'for what purpose one lies: whether one preserves with a lie or destroys with it' (1968: 179).

Now, what is involved in Nietzsche's polemical nostalgia for the imperial being of pure nobility, which here enjoys the sublime status of *das Ding*, or what Badiou calls 'the pre-objective basis of objectivity' (2011a: 47), is a sensualist triple strike that a) reduces Greece in captivity into an adjunct of Roman power; b) homogenises Greece with the continuum of *Imperium romanum* and its administrative genius for organisation; and c) extinguishes politics. Badiou has a different take on Nietzsche's poetic anathematism against Paul, which I consider untenable for the kind of political universalism to which he aspires. Badiou's thrilling move consists in an ingenious attempt to enlist Nietzsche's polemical operations into the service of Paul's politics. In no more than two-and-a-half pages Badiou's scintillating manoeuvre aligns Paul's declaratory tropes to Zarathustra and the 'grand politics' of life affirmation embodied by the Overman. This, however, goes against the grain of Badiou's political thought. Why? Because the subjective destination of a political truth procedure always innovates anew an egalitarian maxim which is non-equivalent to the other three subject forms: 'Science, art and love are aristocratic truth procedures … addressed to all … but their regime is not that of the collective.' On the contrary, Badiou insists, 'Politics is impossible without the statement that people, taken indistinctly, are capable of the thought that constitutes the post-evental political subject. This statement claims that a political thought is topologically collective, meaning that it cannot exist otherwise than as the thought of all' (2004a: 154).

All discerning readers of Paul and Badiou know that empire is simply an athletic, muscular name for corruption. Badiou, in my view, 'deviates' for a moment from the egalitarian thrust of his own political thought, precisely because he trivialises Nietzsche's slanderous attack rather than considering it in depth. In fact, upon closer reading, there is nothing new in Nietzsche's polemical profiling of Paul. This detail, however, ought to be of some contemporary importance for precisely the reasons that Badiou raises in dealing with similar issues in his recent polemics and interventions. This circumstance is knotted up in the same transcendental loop that spans the fundamental precepts of the standard collaborationist doxa, as it is reflected in the canon of imperial historiography and the apologetic moral sermons circulated by Paul's close contemporaries. It suffices to mention two Jewish figures of this subjective form, Flavius Josephus and Philo of Alexandria, who, among other things, are telling examples of the Pétainist transcendental of imperial history. It will be demonstrated below that the Pétainist transcendental and its collaborationist posture is not an exclusive privilege of French history alone. With this concept, indeed, Badiou has discovered, without yet naming it, the universal law of imperial being against which the truth of the political condition defines itself ceaselessly.

Sophistic anticipations of imperial biopower: the collaborationist posture of Philo of Alexandria and Flavius Josephus

Philo, an icon of esoteric opportunism and a celebrated reference point for upwardly mobile diplomatic politicos, corrupt academics and votaries of imperial loyalism down to our days, is in fact an ingenious conceptualiser of manipulative biopower and double-talk, able enough to help forestall any possibility of a Jewish revolt against Rome without having to intervene using military ferocity. Philo stigmatises parrhesiastic politics maliciously as an 'untimely frankness' (*parrhesia akairos*) displayed by 'lunatics and madmen' who dare to oppose kings and tyrants in words and deeds ... they are the guerdons of silliness, frenzy and incurable brainsickness ... they do not perceive that not only like cattle are their necks under the yoke, but that the harness extends to their whole bodies and souls (*upezevthēsan ola ta sōmata kai psychas*), their wives and children and parents, and the wide circle of friends and kinsfolk united to them by fellowship of feeling, and that the driver can with perfect ease spur, drive on or pull back and mete out any treatment small or great just as he pleases. (1988: 83–5)

Thus, again, for the 'democratic materialists' and Pétainists of all ages, only bodies and tactical discourses are available to the slaves vis-à-vis their masters: 'if we wish to gain any help from them the fitting course is to soften and tame them' (1988: 92). Philo, as one of the high sophists on the totem pole of collaborationist biopower, attributes any occurrences of wanton cruelty to the personal failures of expendable Roman governors such as Pilate, while praising the emperor Tiberius for instructing his procurators to console the Jews for their persecution, 'assuring them that penal measures did not extend to all but only to the guilty, who were few, and to disturb nothing of the established customs' (1962: 160–1). And of course Philo reserves his highest praise for Tiberius' great-grandfather Augustus and his *Pax romana*, 'this great ruler, this philosopher second to none (*tosoutos hēgemon kai philosophos oudenos deuteros*)' (1962: 318). In stark contrast, we may recall Paul in 1 Cor. 2: 6 and the 'untimely frankness' with which he declares that all 'the rulers of this age are doomed to perish'; and in 1 Thess. 5: 3: 'When they say, "There is peace and security", then sudden destruction will come upon them, as labor pains come upon a pregnant woman, and there will be no escape!'

Nietzsche simply reproduces, with aggressive impotence, the reflexes of Jewish loyalism against the Israelite tradition of popular resistance, from the Exodus and the Covenant to the Maccabean and Jewish revolts. Hence, given Nietzsche's imperial Romeophilia, Paul could be easily dismissed as a 'holy anarchist'. In the same vein, Flavius Josephus, a first-century Jew and priestly notable of Pharisaic origin and persuasion (whose predecessor was Philo and model Polybius), attributes the causes of the Jewish Revolt to incompetent Roman governors, to lack of strong leadership and to the messianic zeal of criminal rebel factions and insane bandits who exploited the rift from the fringes of the mainstream Jewish community (Josephus 1997: II, Books 1–2).

In Badiou's terms, by refusing to raise issues of justice, loyalist sophism is unavoidably caught in a schematic counter-movement from politics to piety, from militant fidelity to a truth procedure to court-favouritism, from political animal to protected client, from philosophy to self-serving apologetics that vindicate the mediating role of protégés. This posture criminalises revolt as sin and providentialises counter-revolt as a self-incurred punishment. What transpires, then, is a comprehensive, loyalist, status-stoicism that is adjusted to the *heimarmeni* of empire, which itself simply dispenses punishment for wrongdoing. In fact, Philo, in his surviving fragment included in *De providentia*, defends imperial tyranny with blustering noise, stating that 'punishment and penalties inflicted are profitable to the good'; 'for punishment has the same relation to law as a tyrant has to a people ... so God gives strength and power to men naturally fitted to rule in order to purify our race. For wickedness cannot be purged away without some ruthless soul to do it' (1954: 37–41). Hence any Jewish militancy aspiring to an alternative to empire could not but be *illico impietatis*, bringing down on itself the theodicy of punishment as meted out by those 'naturally fitted to rule in order to purify our race'. Flavius Josephus survived the great Jewish Revolt (AD 66–70), the siege of Jerusalem and the destruction of the Temple by Titus, fleeing to the Roman court where he told the history of the *Jewish War* (AD 75–79)[4] as an appalling capital offence. There he tearfully exonerated the Roman provocation and casuistically defended his client status. It is a monumental example of Roman biopower turned historiography, and a typical discourse of self-justified loyalist elites whose 'political activity consisted in dealing with the Romans, largely in flattery, obsequiousness and insinuation'.[5]

Nietzsche recapitulates the collaborationist mood of first-century Jewish client elites, shaken as they were by the death agony of recovering their rapport with Roman power, which was temporarily destabilised by the Jewish insurrection. Badiou captures this moment of imperial affect with an insight of extraordinary profundity: 'a combination of panic and shame (dissimulating no doubt the most violent instinct there is: that of self-preservation)' (2006b: 85). Badiou, of course, wants to rescue Paul from Nietzsche's polemical rationalisation, but significantly he retains its basic presupposition, that is, Paul as a destroyer of the *Imperium romanum*. Yet he does so without punctuating or reconstructing point by point the formal universality of Paul's promise as the anti-imperialist condition of politics. The latter remains largely submerged, implied and self-justified.

In order to draw the full consequences of Paul's generic procedure as a paradigm shift for thinking politics in the present (pervaded, as it is, by the 'rampant Pétainization of the State' [Badiou 2003b: 9] as well as, I would add, widespread debt bondage), we need a consistent reconceptualisation of his break with the imperial relation, one that juxtaposes the promise of his epistles to 'the Gospel of Caesar' and the contradictory potential of Palestinian Judaism. Badiou's Pauline question regarding the assignment of the subject to the universal and the price to be paid by both the subject and the law points unavoidably to the political real of breaking with the disciplines of empire as an amplification of the anti-imperialist event within Jewish particularity itself. An investigation along this line may illuminate what it is that Paul was primarily opposed to and what work Badiou expects him to perform insofar as he functions as a contemporary metaphor of the anti-Pétainist hypothesis. My argument is that unless we remain consistent in elucidating and punctuating the perennial implications of Paul's break with, or withdrawal from, the imperial relation, the outcome will be a sophistic self-trapping within the spurious and disgraceful opposition between a universal, ostensibly post-national but privileged Christianity, and a Jewish nationalist particularity. On this score, Badiou has indeed important lessons to teach us, although they are not always consistently held or reflected in his thinking about universality.

Consider Gal. 3: 28, which is the cornerstone of Badiou's reclaiming of Pauline universality as a counterpoint to the present Pétainisation of the state: 'There is no longer Jew or Greek, there is no longer slave or free, there is no longer male or female; for all of you are one in Christ Jesus.' Had Paul ended his statement at this point, it would sound to our ears like a liberal Jacobin preaching New Age trivialities. Paul qualifies his point in the following verse: 'And if you belong to Christ, then you are Abraham's offspring, heirs according to the promise.' Paul was fully aware that the only possible way of addressing the Gentiles of the Roman-occupied Mediterranean world was by turning Abraham's promise into a reason of faith outside idle custom. Thus, Paul weighed up the patrimonial ideals of prophetic Judaism against the imperial world. Abraham's promise was a promise for a new universality. Ultimately, the viability of synagogue Judaism and its anti-imperial messianism could be tested only against the possibility realised by Paul. Paul's achievement was an urgent critical synthesis of Judaism and Hellenism as a shared universal alternative to the decadence of the *Imperium romanum*. Neither of the two particularities were individually able to challenge the logic of imperial order on its own turf.

Badiou draws an invaluable lesson from Paul's response to the internal crisis of Judaism and Hellenism under imperial occupation. The core of this lesson points to a theory of dialectical universality which 'endows Christianity with a twofold principle of *opening* and *historicity*'. Paul's action is both evental and immanent 'with respect to a determinate situation, wherein it mobilises the elements of its site' (Badiou 2003b: 25). Paul thus rescues Judaism from a dead-end messianic sectarianism (which Flavius Josephus' Pharisaic legalism used as an excuse for collaboration) and at the same time restrains and suspends Gentile hostility to Judaism by preventing Christianity 'from being merely a new illuminism, one just as precarious because devoid of all basis in historical Judaism' (Badiou 2003b: 25). His is precisely a paradigmatic dialectical engagement of eventality and immanence that articulates subtractively the political principles of anti-imperialist universality.

Paul's Mass Line: The Assembled Universality

For Paul, this promise could be sustained only through an anti-imperial movement of alternative assemblies which, not incidentally, bore the name of the founding institution of Greek politics, *ekklēsiai*.[6] The ecclesiastic assemblies founded by Paul throughout the Gentile world became the crossing points of an evental encounter between Jewish and Greek anti-imperialist expectations. Paul's reclaiming of the Roman cross on which Christ was crucified captured the imagination of the Gentiles, precisely because it concentrated in a singular point the unruly multiplicity of anti-imperialist energies that was storming the Mediterranean world. The cross was the site of a political assassination, and the resurrection the beginning of a protracted intervention to reclaim, on universal grounds, the truths that were incriminated with the crucifixion in the first place. Ever since, a critical question has continued to preoccupy the revolutionary tradition, and it goes by the name of 'the colonial question' or 'the national question'. This question concerns precisely the method, the imagination and the truth by which universality is politically marked out in terms of what Bosteels calls *actual infinity* (2012: xxviii). Far from 'de-nationalising the cross' (Elliott 1994: 176), Paul reclaimed its actual infinity by inter-nationalising the anamnesis of resurrection. His summons to occupied Corinth is for a life inspired by the anamnesis of the truth of crucifixion in Judea. The Judaic event revealed by virtue of its actual infinity the consequences by which the ecclesiastic assemblies should live. Hence the urgency of the calls in 1 Cor. 7: 23: 'do not become slaves of human masters'; and 7: 29–31: 'the appointed time has grown short; from now on, let even those who mourn as though they were not mourning, and those who rejoice as though they were not rejoicing, and those who buy as though they had no possessions, and those who deal with the world as though they had no dealings with it. For the present form of this world is passing away.' This is a 'now-time'. It sounds rather different from something that is 'for the benefit of a state after death!' as Nietzsche argues (1968: 154). Had it been about insurance benefits, profits or social assistance for mutual advantage, Paul's procedure would have been simply a theological syndicalism of sorts, trading in what Lacan has aptly specified as 'the service of goods'. Instead, what is at stake is what Badiou identifies as a truth, 'the real process of a fidelity to an event: that which this fidelity *produces* in the situation' (2001: 42, emphasis in the original). Paul becomes a political figure because the material course of fidelity to the post-evental truth of resurrection he initiates entails an immanent break with the imperial situation, as well as a parrhesiastic strike that punches a hole in the encyclopaedia of collaborationist opinion. It is by maintaining the consistency of the break on both registers that Paul becomes the Badiouian figure of politics par excellence – politics, of course, as a procedure that is by definition, and not by implication, anti-imperialist. It is only in this sense that Paul comes to embody the major conflict between what Badiou schematically calls the *principle of interest* (empire) and the *subjective principle* (fidelity to a truth beyond the law of the situation that reflects the self-interest of *opinione vulgi*) (2001: 48).

More specifically, Paul's eschatological call traces back to an anti-imperial theology of the cross, the event of resurrection, which gets turned into a practical reason of redemption. It reveals that the present form of this world, in its imperial logic, is passing away. In the opening of his address to the assembly of Corinth – which, like every other Greek ecclesiastic assembly of the pre-imperial demos, was polarised by what Mao called 'secondary contradictions' and sophistic antagonisms – Paul ventures to settle differences between factions, not by means of rational persuasion like Thomas Aquinas, but by using the power of spirit, fidelity and wisdom, which is 'not of this age or of the rulers of this age, who are doomed to perish'; a secret wisdom 'which none of the rulers of this age understood' (1 Cor. 2: 4–8). Thus, even the resolution of secondary contradictions is subjected to the strong test of an anticipatory truth procedure. Sophism may only be countered by the political forcing of a generic truth procedure, not by tactics.

In Badiou's terms this genericity constitutes an 'illegality', that is, a tracing of a self-referential course of the event from (Judaic) prophecy to (Roman) crucifixion to (universal) resurrection, which is not present or comprehensible from within the imperial situation. Typically, such an illegality does not have any immediate impact on the situation. Badiou, a contemporary Paul within Paul, says:

> it is undecidable from the standpoint of the situation itself. Only an interpretative intervention can declare that an event *is* presented in a situation; as the arrival in being of non-being, the arrival amidst the visible of the invisible ... Therefore, either the event is in the situation and it ruptures the site's being 'on-the-edge-of-the-void' by interposing itself between itself and the void; or it is not in the situation, and its power of nomination is solely addressed if it is addressed to 'something', to the void itself. (2005a: 181, 182)

By the same token, Paul, a backwardly projected compeer of Badiou, argues:

> now, if Christ is proclaimed as raised from the dead, how can some of you say there is no resurrection of the dead? If there is no resurrection of the dead, then Christ has not been raised; and if Christ has not been raised, then our proclamation has been in vain and your faith has been in vain. But in fact Christ has been raised from the dead ... and at his coming ... then comes the end ... after he has destroyed every ruler and every authority and power. (1 Cor. 15: 12–24)

Paul's intervention is a Lacanian *passage à l'acte*; the parrhesi-astic act of being named after the resurrection, of being nominated and promised on the edge of the voided grave as an assembled universality, as the fundamental operator of truth in the expecta-tion of a second coming that will replace the imperial economy of corruption and the sophistic hierarchy of opinion with the divine economy of redemption by grace. Paul's politics enraptured the universal imaginary precisely because of his implicating this dis-tance matrix, a kind of ongoing political strike of actual infinity, which enabled sustained opposition to empire 'until the end of times', while invigilating over the spiritual site that voided the imperial situation itself without possibility of recovery. That was Christianity's sacred void! An empty burial pit traced to a blank name, 'the Christened one', the resurrected refuse of empire, the universal slave matter which for this very reason could be claimed by all and be realised in the name of each separately.

Here Badiou closely follows Paul's 'mass line': 'That the central activity of politics is the *gathering*, is a local metonymy of its intrinsically collective and therefore principally universal being . . . politics summons or exhibits the infinity of the situation [and] rejects "being toward death"' (Badiou 2004a: 154). What Badiou clearly implies in following the trace of Paul is that a political act exists only by constituting an assembly, a gathering cum political ecclesia that is universal in its being, by summoning immediately the infinity of the situation into the play of a truth procedure, which, ultimately, negates 'being-towards-death', that is, initiates a metonymic procedure of fidelity to 'resurrection' or what Badiou calls political immortality. In a tenor reminiscent of the young Marx in his *Philosophical Manuscripts*, Badiou, supplementing Paul's theology of resurrection, posits the principle of species immortality as a faithful trajectory of truth; as an exception to 'the rapacious flux of life, as the right of the Infinite' countering 'the temptation of wanting-to-be-an-animal to which circumstances may expose him'. Badiou places this temptation squarely within the imperial fold: 'For this "living being" is in reality contemptible, and he will indeed be held in contempt. Who can fail to see that, in our humanitarian expeditions, interventions, embarkations of charitable *legionnaires*, the subject presumed to be universal is split? On the side of the victims, the haggard animal exposed on television screens. On the side of the benefactors, conscience and the imperative to intervene. And why does this splitting always assign the same roles to the same sides?' (2001: 12–13, emphasis in the original). For Badiou, then, the subject presumed to be universal is constantly split by the imperial situation. In the wake of this failed, *légionnaire* universality, politics can exist only as an anti-imperial procedure, both at home and abroad.

The Errant Empire of *Légionnaire* Universality and its Subjective Figure: The Client Master

Badiou's rethinking of Paul provides insights into the nature of the state-form that afford a range of new conceptual possibilities for the critical research of politics beyond its monetary sign. In this age of democratic materialism, Badiou's concept of politics designates a fidelity procedure that cuts across the imperial assemblage of the state and the para-political economy it sustains, one that reaffirms its anthropological singularity in the wake of an evental upsurge. It is defined across and against its contemporary reduction to parliamentary patronage, civil society brokerage, lobby advocacy, go-between peace dealing, NGO hucksterism or a friend-at-court academic service diplomacy. This is the contemporary imperial matrix of the expanded reproduction of corruption against which politics may in rare moments come into being as a 'calling of the immortal part of men, of the inhuman excess that lies in man' (Badiou 2009a: 511). It takes, indeed, heroic courage and inhuman Homeric virtues to stand apart and defy this errant humanity of the solicitor-empire. In the face of this 'human-all-too-human' self-interest in corruption, Badiou proposes a much-misunderstood, 'terroristic' and inhuman anthropology of politics.

Let us recall that, for Badiou, a political truth is subtracted from the organisation of subjects prescribed by the imperial state-form and 'from what corresponds to the state in people's consciousness: the apparatus of opinion' (2003b: 15). It follows that the egalitarian political subjectivity that Badiou proposes will sooner or later provoke its suppression by the counter-mobilisation of the errant superpower of the state and its sophistic apparatus of opinion. What may appear as an overly abstract, formulaic and instrumentalist theory of the state turns out to be a complex research orientation based on a set of quite textured and formative principles that concern precisely the ability to measure the superpower of neoliberal biopolitics in the age of 'governance' and 'democratic materialism'. Corruption, the signature pathology of this age, has evolved into a global force of biopower whose state-function is 'the measureless enslavement of the parts of the situation, an enslavement whose secret is precisely the errancy of superpower, its measurelessness' (Badiou 2004a: 156). What may be extrapolated from this is a philosophical concept of what a critique of empire could be, if it is figured out in terms of superpower biopolitics that still retains formal state-functions, along with globalised capabilities for expanded simulation and reproduction through outsourcing, transnational brokering, huckstering, racketeering and so on.

The central feature of the errant empire that Badiou enables an exposure of is a kind of excrescent but derogated biopower with strong enslaving properties, which paradoxically empower an obscure subject. Thinking politics after Badiou sets as a primary task the identification of the new subjective figures that accommodate imperial errancy. The obscure subject to which I refer here is not Badiou's figure of the dogmatic that rigidifies truth by replacing an imaginative fidelity to the event with a sterile conformity to the past, but instead the subjective position that accommodates and is accommodated by the excessive errancy of the imperial *Dasein*. It is the vocation that puts to work the errant excess of obscure biopower. It refers to the random subject effected by this excess, the aberrant type that gains confidence by virtue of its identification with the excessive errancy of biopower afforded by empire. It is an odd figure: a kind of client master, a subservient maestro of the errant excess that both specialises in its circulation and dissolves in its ecstatic consensus. If, however, we find this subjective aberrance as form quite extravagant, we may still discern in it a sort of postmodern annotation to the old *comprador* excoriated by Mao (Mao Zedong 1926). Contemporary examples of this accommodating figure may include the Euro-parliamentary acolytes of the European Central Bank and its Eurogroup executives, the NATO-funded pacifist and the deep-green militarist squads, the Norway-subsidised conflict-resolution seminars, the Soros-sponsored Orange revolutions, the EU-financed anarchist groups and magazines, the Western patronising of the Arab Spring and so on. This random sample could exemplify what Badiou calls 'non-egalitarian, mute consciousness', clientalised by an errant metastructure that exercises the pastoral power of the count 'over all the subjects of the situation' (2004a: 154). Badiou argues that 'every situation has a state' which is also given as a state of the situation, with powers of representing collective situations in which singularities cannot be represented but only presented by a force exposed to the danger of the void. In Meditation 8 of *Being and Event*, Badiou compares this logic with the Heideggerian care of being 'or the necessity of warding off the void . . . the presentational occurrence of inconsistency as such, or the ruin of the One' (2005a: 93). Empire is precisely the superpower's anxiety of the void: 'the structure of the count reduplicated in order to verify itself, to vouch that its effects, for the entire duration of its exercise, are complete' (2005a: 94). Empire is this excrescence of the errant metastructure, which is not a term of the situation and as such cannot be counted. This could possibly be Badiou's own version of biopower. In fact, Badiou does include the indeterminacy of the financial biopower of global capitalism in his expanded and complex definition of the errancy of state excess:

> The economy is today a norm of the state . . . The matrix of inequality consists precisely in the impossibility of measuring the superpower of the state. Today, for example, it is in the name of the necessity of the liberal economy – a necessity without measure or concept – that all egalitarian politics are deemed to be impossible and denounced as absurd. But what characterizes this blind power of unfettered Capital is precisely the fact that it cannot be either measured or fixed at any point. All we know is that it prevails absolutely over the subjective fate of collectives, whatever they may be . . . This is what explains the arrogant and peremptory character of non-egalitarian statements, even when they are obviously inconsistent and abject. For the statements of contemporary reaction are shored up entirely by the errancy of state excess, i.e., by the untrammeled violence of capitalist anarchy. (2004a: 158)

Badiou's hostility to Hardt and Negri's work, incomprehensible for some, lies precisely on this normative ground. For Badiou it is the global errancy of the excessive superpower norm that impedes egalitarian logic, not excess itself: 'It is not the simple power of the state of the situation that prohibits egalitarian politics. It is the obscurity and measurelessness in which this power is enveloped. If the political event allows for a clarification, a fixation, an exhibition of the power, then the egalitarian maxim is at least locally practicable' (2004a: 158–9). What Hardt and Negri assume to be an empire of the multitude, or a commonwealth operated by governance agencies and NGO *compradors*, is a more or less nomadic and bohemian delirium of the superpower norm; an errant and measureless obscurity in which imperial biopower is enveloped. In some sense, Badiou 'anti-imperialises' Foucault and Heidegger while Hardt and Negri 'imperialise' them. Hardt and Negri explicitly fail to think through this drifting obscurity of the imperial *Dasein*, the globe-rolling, measureless errancy of the excessive superpower norm, and the necessity of measuring up to it by prescribing egalitarian, anti-imperial maxims that circumscribe its power locally. Rather, Hardt and Negri join in the rambling obscurity and indeterminacy of the errant superpower. They glamorise its wandering, unassignable errancy and consider it as liberation, exodus and so on, incarnated by migration flows but cleansed from detailed accounts of colonisation wars and the geo-monetary, geophysical division of labour that forces massive population displacements, neocolonial relocations, recolonisation and reoccupation processes. On the contrary, Badiou argues, 'people are held hostage by its unassignable power. Politics is the interruption of this errancy . . . This is the sense in which politics is "freedom"' (2004a: 156). Badiou's 'errant excess hypothesis' regarding the superpower state norm alerts us to the problematic of an empire that operates as a floating biopower of speculating markets and erratic loops of self-replication without ever folding up on themselves terminally.

Badiou and Paul in Cairo

We Chinese possess certain social and political institutions that are unique in their clarity and again others that are unique in their obscurity . . . Now, one of our most obscure institutions of all is unquestionably that of the Empire itself . . . In court circles, there does exist some clarity on the subject, though even that is more apparent than real; also the teachers of political law and history in the high schools claim to be exactly informed about these matters and to be able to pass this knowledge on to their students; and the further down the ladder of the schools one goes, the more one finds, understandably enough, people's doubts of their own knowledge vanishing and a sea of semi-education rising mountain-high round a few precepts that have been rammed home for centuries – precepts which have indeed lost nothing of their eternal truth, but which also remain eternally unrecognized amid all the fog and vapour. But on this question of the Empire one should, in my opinion, turn first of all to the common people, since that is after all where the Empire has its final support. (Kafka 2002: 65)

What in the above passage remains 'eternally unrecognised amid all the fog and vapour' is precisely the obscure sophistry of the *arcana tyrannica*. Kafka's prescient parable from *The Great Wall of China* raises anew 'the question of empire' as the critical question that politics answers. By reclaiming this Kafkaesque perspective I want to reaffirm Badiou's advanced critique of the state and simultaneously mark out some immanent aporias, eclectic evasions and assumptions that concern the problem of domination, and hence the limits of politics per se. Predictably these are a deterrent force that blocks the universalisable potential of politics. When constituent assumptions of this kind are bypassed without being problematised, they tend to become speculative necessities. I am not arguing that it is impossible to problematise the limits of politics on the basis of Badiou's anti-opinion politics. On the contrary. However, Badiou's suggestion that politics as a universalist labour is indifferent to the casuistry of opinion or to the strategy of dissimulation on the ground that they distract 'a proposition away from its universal destination' (2003b: 102) is not a sufficient safeguard against their subtle reproduction in the unfolding of the proposition during a political sequence properly speaking. What is strange is that in his *Saint Paul* Badiou acknowledges this problem by simply ignoring and hence downplaying its significance as a 'subtle strategy' of rhetorical displacement (2003b: 103). To my delight, he returns mercilessly to this issue ten years later in his Sarkozy book (2007), acknowledging it as a massive form of subjective corruption.

In *Saint Paul*, however, there are two points that are either insufficiently addressed or are considered by Badiou as of minor importance. First is the Jewish War against the Roman occupation. Paul's discourse on resurrection remains meaningless and toothless without its anti-imperial theology. It was this intense anti-imperial propaedeutics that made strong Jewish and Greek particularities susceptible to the universalisable truth of resurrection. It is Paul's power of faith and imagination to appropriate these historical presuppositions that made the discourse of resurrection possible. Badiou does acknowledge 'the event's principle of historicity' (2003b: 103) but I think he only pays lip service to it.

Secondly, Badiou understates the strategic uses of deception and sophistic devices of rhetorical subtlety that Paul employs and which are amplified by an entire tradition of biblical Machiavellianism. Badiou, again, points to this lacuna only to claim it as a virtue: 'although stubborn, even violent, where matters of principle are concerned, Paul is also a politician, one who knows the value of reasonable compromises and particularly of verbal compromises, which only slightly impede his freedom of action in the places and territories he chooses (preferably those where his opponent has the least footing)' (2003b: 19). But what constitutes on each occasion a 'reasonable' or 'verbal compromise'? How do we decide 'ecclesiastically' the occasions to which we respond? By which criteria of *arcana verbis* do we consider an intervention as cynical or political? On Badiou's reading, it is evident that Paul becomes *politico*, clashing with his politics of truth in order to realise it. But it is even more evident that there is no solid principle to adjudicate between the holy and the unholy *arcanum imperium*.[7] It all depends on the *arcana* of prudence, the 'secret leadership' of the occasion.

My dissenting point is as follows: indirectly, Badiou appears for a moment at least to accept a limit to politics, as a condition for universalising its truth. Whether this exception to politics is a hidden but sound art of truth, or a pastoral accommodation of vice and virtue to the necessity of building ecclesiastic politics addressed to all, or tactical prudence by a holy prince, is not the issue. What matters is that, by fact and discourse, it introduces obscurity into the principle of politics as a truth procedure, recasting it in terms of manipulable appearances. Is there a permissible *arcanum imperium* which is integral to the localisation of truth? Is there a private *arcana* by which the charismatic initiator of a sequence could be exempted from the principle of politics? More generally, once we accept that politics can be sustained by unstated principles and secret teachings that uphold its truth, we more or less condone the domination of inequality as the groundwork of capitalist parliamentarism. But, on the other hand, this is precisely what Badiou attacks, namely the crackbrained *mysterium iniquitatis* inherent in both the operation of representation and the capitalist logic of the 'invisible hand' of the market.

Badiou, of course, sustains still another possibility for the articulation of principle and tactic. Maxims, prescriptions or slogans, for instance, organise the consequences of upholding the principle of equality point by point. He provides specific examples from the Cairo riot in Tahrir Square in which, he claims, there is a blend of a generic Idea (of the people) and tactics (2012d: 89). The question remains nonetheless. The tension between 'people' and 'tactics' is irreducible. The self-constitution of the people appears to involve first and foremost a Pascalian wager that heroically exposes both the excrescence of the repressive state apparatus as well as the errant biopower of empire that overdetermines the former's operations. Both operations remain excrescent and errant up until the wager is ultimately decided by the people's pledge to stake their lives in the political procedure. This is where the idea of the people exists, not in secondary tactics. The political idea of the people as a wagering, non-utilitarian subject cannot be reduced to tactics. Badiou introduces the puzzling concept of 'tactics' in order to describe the political procedure of people's destatifica-tion. Arguably, he ranks these moments into separate stages, emphasising 'the time of organisation, the time of construction of an empirical duration of the idea in its post-riot stage' (2012d: 90). It is unclear how Badiou measures or thinks this critical 'post-riot stage'. Most likely, by the very necessity of the geopolitical line-up it will be forced towards new state-construction. Even if this 'post-riot stage' is destined, like the Polish movement of *Solidarnosc*, to remain self-consciously circumscribed by a prescriptive distance from the state, it will unavoidably summon repression, hence relapsing to the 'riot stage'. We are again caught up in a dialectic of revolution and counter-revolution. If the 'time of organisation' does not involve new state-construction, why then should we con-sider as a 'tactical manoeuvre' the life-and-death struggle over the framing of the constitution, immediate relief measures in favour of the poor, or the opening of the crossing between the besieged Gaza Strip and Egypt? In this case and if politics is non-programmatic by definition, Badiou needs to qualify the difference between prin-cipled method and tactical manoeuvre, in a way that corresponds roughly to Gramsci's distinction between war of positions and war of movements, with the caveat that the Gramscian dialectic is regulated by the 'princely' apparatus of the Party.

    The internal contradiction of this moment is that politics in its non-programmatic form is initiated precisely as a heroic, wrath-ful and, yes, joyful lifting of tactical limits. The people affirm a new idea by 'tactlessly' lifting these limits. That is also the reason why a political sequence is rare but possible. It is rare because it is demanding and heroic, which does not necessarily mean 'unprin-cipled' or disorganised. The confrontation with the limits which comprise the groundwork of domination and corruption is heroic and there is no way around it, precisely because it is through these limits that the depressive effects of patronage and pastoral direction are reasserted. This is what the disciplinary matrix of representation is all about, hence Badiou's invaluable conceptualisation of politics at a distance from the state. Badiou's concept corresponds ideally to a stage before the emergence of a dual power situation. Any engagement with tactics during a dual power situation is unavoidably enmeshed with state-norms and prospective logics of state-construction. But Badiou is unwilling to concede that much. It is this hiatus that Žižek's Lacanian-Leninism joyfully steps into.

Badiou's conceptualisation cannot possibly address in detail all the stakes of a political procedure in its lived moment. But Badiou's political thinking does many other invaluable things that Žižek is unwilling to do. Badiou is unique among contemporary philosophers in reviving a Platonic tradition that associates singular politics with courage 'that orients us locally among global disorientation' (Badiou 2008b: 76). Empire is precisely the errant excess of *simulacra imperii* which Badiou calls global disorientation.

Paul himself did in fact come across with the sophistic opportunism of *arcana politica* and was vehemently critical of weak forms of fidelity, such as the double prudence and receptiveness displayed by the Corinthian assembly towards obscure deacons of deception:

> But I am afraid that as the serpent deceived Eve in its cunning, your thoughts will be led astray from a sincere and pure devotion to Christ. For if someone comes and proclaims another Jesus than the one we proclaimed, or if you receive a different spirit from the one you received, or a different gospel from the one you accepted, you submit to it readily enough ... And what I do, I will continue to do, in order to deny an opportunity to those who want an opportunity to be recognized as our equals in what they boast about. For such boasters are false apostles, deceitful workers, disguising themselves as apostles of Christ. And no wonder. Even Satan disguises himself as an angel of light. So, it is not strange if his ministers also disguise themselves as ministers of righteousness. *Their end will match their deeds.* (2 Cor. 11: 3–5, 12–15, emphasis added)

Plainly, Paul's offensive addresses the *arcana* of theological opportunism in terms of a 'primary contradiction' in the Maoist sense of the class enemy, collaborator, *comprador* and so on. That the final settling of accounts will be dealt with by God himself does not remove the intensity of the life-and-death struggle between these forces in the present time. What complicates Paul's anti-sophistic and eschatological polemics against false apostles and their manipulative propaganda is that Christ himself deceived Satan by getting dressed up with sinful human flesh although he was sinless, just as Moses also deceived the Pharaoh! The issue here, however, is that, in *Saint Paul*, Badiou seems to devalorise a persistent problem of simulated political effects, equivocations, illusions of power, theatrical prudence and sophistic *arcana*, all of which are symptoms of domination and generators of enfeebled fidelity, exposed by both Paul and Kafka. Again, what is at issue here is not Paul's equivocations in his epistolary interventions, but whether the political form of his theology of resurrection, as reclaimed by Badiou, is universalisable without its self-defeating limits.

Reckoning with the Pétainist Logic of Empire: Badiou with Kafka in Vichy

It is true that the basic responsibility for it lies with the government, which in this most ancient empire on earth has been unable or else too preoccupied with other things to develop imperial rule into an institution of sufficient clarity for it to be immediately and continuously effective right to the further frontiers of the land.

On the other hand, however, this attitude also conceals a weakness of imagination or faith on the part of the people, for they fail to draw out the imperial power from the depths of Peking where it lies buried, and to clasp it in its full living presence to their obedient breasts, while at the same time they wish for nothing better than to feel its touch upon them at last, and to be consumed. So this attitude can hardly be considered a virtue. It is all the more striking that this very weakness should apparently be one of the most important unifying influences among our people. (Kafka 2002: 69)

The subjective situation of our country may be described as follows: the disorientation of minds, the factor of impotence, has been under way for a long while, at least since Mitterrand, who was a cunning organizer of confusion. But with the election of Sarkozy, the rallying of the rats and universal inertia, it has finally found its symbol, the forms of rupture that now constitute the law of the situation. In these conditions, the imperative is to orient ourselves locally, point by point, in such a way as to reconstitute courage. In circumstances such as these, local courage makes a breach in a global disposition of which Sarkozy is the name, the name of the state. But what is this breach? (Badiou 2008b: 76)

Kafka depicts enfeebled fidelity as the foundational mood of the imperial condition. Enfeebled fidelity means a failure of imaginative power, a failure to be seized by a situation-transforming truth, which is precisely what keeps not only humanity but also a political assembly 'in the service of goods' despite declarations to the contrary. Kafka's telling illustration of weak fidelity and failed imagination as unifying influences of empire is well presented today in Badiou's Pétainist hypothesis and the mass subjectivity that sustains it. Pétainism exemplifies this cataclysmic obscurantism that accrues from the reciprocal reduction of state and economy to each other. Badiou considers this hypothesis to be a national transcendental peculiar to French history, yet I think that it actually constitutes *the* imperial form of the integrated spectacle and its errant excess, one implied also in his description of the superpower norm: 'a great deal of police deployment at home, and obscure negotiations, dodgy transactions and military operations abroad, constant resort to "business", secret diplomacy and crooked deals, as well as the ostentatious display of the power of money' (2008b: 87). Is not that what the Eurozone is about? Does it not plainly uphold the *raison d'état* of the new economic Reich? This misanthropic re-zoning of southern Europe into economic 'Gaza Strips' and geo-monetary slices of meat on the chessboard of Germany and Russia, however, renders Badiou's proposal for a 'Cartesian' type of Franco-German fusion (2006b) monstrously idealist, even if this is not thought to belong to the order of truth procedures (see Constantinou and Madarasz 2009: 787). In a spirit of good generic Maoism, Badiou here certainly affirms the critical anti-imperialist force of the people-nation, an acceptable but unnamed bi-nationalism of the centre to the benefit of the periphery.

All the same, despite some minor but potentially disabling equivocations in the *Saint Paul* book regarding biblical politics, Badiou does provide in *The Meaning of Sarkozy* unmistakable criteria for identifying and combating this colossal apparatus of the Pétainist *arcanum* and its Kafkaesque loop. Insofar as it constitutes a global form of disorientation and deflected thought, Badiou's criteria provide eventful vantage points that enable a universal reorientation and reconstitution of courage as an anti-imperialist ethos. This work on the Pétainist character of the state and its subjective form constitutes, in my view, the highest and most lucid point that Badiou's political thought has reached.

So what are the features of the Pétainist situation to which politics ought to respond with a strong fidelity to the truth of an anti-imperialist universality, constructed courageously point by point? In my own reconstructed version, first, the Pétainist situation is defined by capitulation, unconditional obedience and servility to occupation forces, patrons or potentates of world capitalism, elements that get duplicated in the themes of the national regeneration and moral reform required to get the country back to work. In other words, the principles of docility, non-resistance and boot-licking 'present themselves as invention, revolution and regeneration' (Badiou 2008b: 78–9). So this is the first axiom: Pétainism appears always and everywhere as a rapturous new stage in history. For instance, the collaborationist regime during the Vichy period in France or the current accomplices of the Turkish occupation forces in Cyprus or of the Israeli occupation in Palestine have framed, or tend to frame, their discourses in terms of both 'national survival' and 'national revival', which, combined, comprise the 'national interest'. Pétainism affirms the obscure inertia of capitulation by simulating logics of change and revolution.

Secondly, Pétainism is accomplished as a curative therapy that repairs through state action the moral fibre of a decaying nation, thus working to foreclose political mobilisation and ban real popular engagement. The counter-mobilisation of the police, judiciary and other disciplinary apparatuses along with incessant moralisation campaigns thus come to replace popular politics. Moral correction through 'hard work' will establish merit and a sound household economy able to master the inherent irresponsibility of the governed (the deprived, immigrants and the weak). State Pétainism is populism from above: a populism without people and without political virtue.

Thirdly, the models of moral correction are always drawn from the imperial apparatus of biopower. The empire does 'it' better than we do, with long experience in governance, moral reform, fiscal disciplines and financial stabilisation programmes. We need foreign masters and competent local facilitators. But again, this is far from being a peculiarly French characteristic. I can personally recall a Trotskyite *Pétainiste* who thought he was practising Lenin's formula of 'revolutionary defeatism' in 2004 on the occasion of the referendum over the UN-, US- and EU-backed Annan Plan for Cyprus. The latter provided for the legalisation of the Turkish occupation and colonisation of Northern Cyprus and the cession of continental shelf-rights to the British Sovereign Base Areas. I thought that the case presented was as lucidly imperialist as it could possibly be: an imperial condominium over Cyprus, a kind of superpower constitutional patronage of its mineral resources. And yet, as this 'internationalist' was claiming (with the excessive and assured confidence afforded by the Trotskyite *arcana*), 'Imperialism knows better how to draft constitutions. We should leave this technical stuff to them. Our task is to organise the class struggle!' Leftist Pétainism of the imperial periphery, a mere candy striper of quietism, appears as an obscure half-master. But it counts as nothing less than a cogwheel in the apparatus of soft biopower: it overprizes a miserable necessity, while getting fully organised to re-perform it as rational, sophisticated and popular even against the people themselves! Consider also its liberal siblings: what else are 'transitional justice', that is, NGOs, doing in the occupied Palestinian territories as well as in Cyprus? Are they not engineering the same Pétainist high aesthetic of collaboration glossed as 'reconciliation'? Indefatigable leaders, moral crusaders and pacifist scholars with lucrative contracts, salaried bourgeois activists of the Left and Right, multicultural entrepreneurs, all try to 'rescue what is possible' in the name of prudence, for the sake of peace, of the future and so on. This, then, is the third axiom: civic-burgherly Pétainism is the *comprador*-biopower of empire.

Fourthly, the Pétainist propaganda apparatus invariably traces the origin of a crisis in which it intervenes 'back to a disastrous event, always bound up with popular demands' (Badiou 2008b: 83). In the case of the 'proto-Pétainists' of the Restoration period in 1815, it was claimed that disorder followed in the wake of the Revolution, the Terror, the beheading of the king and so on. For the Pétainist regime of the Vichy period, the breach of peace was initiated by the Popular Front in the 1930s, with the disastrous red strikes and factory seizures. In fear and trembling, the Pétainist class of the Vichy period 'far preferred the Germans, the Nazis, to the Popular Front' (Badiou 2008b: 83). Likewise, in Cyprus the collaborationist elites – Right, Centre, Left – lay the blame for all the disasters that befell the island on the anti-colonial struggle for self-determination against British rule, the failure to join NATO after independence and so on, which irritated the West and has meant it has been unforgiving ever since. Moreover, and in line with the above, the Cyprus elites prefer collaboration with the Turkish occupation forces in the name of peace, 'national preservation and protection for ever' to principled opposition against the occupation, which for them can only lead to self-destruction. In the case of Palestine, I am guessing, the source of disorder is traced to the collapse of the Oslo Agreements, attributed to the rise of the fundamentalist Hamas, and probably even to the deceased Edward Said, but never to the persistence of colonialism. The penultimate axiom: state and civic Pétainism embody a nationalism without a republican nation, a country that criminalises its own revolutionary past.

The fifth criterion for the identification of contemporary Pétainism is openly racist. We deserve better because of our special civilisation, our wondrous history and so on, vis-à-vis others. Due to our cultural superiority, this unbeatable logic would have it, we shall prevail in the long run, whatever the 'unfairness' of an austerity package imposed by foreign patrons (IMF envoys, EU commissioners and Eurogroup executives); or whatever the partiality of a peace deal enforced by the occupation army or UN delegates, or other international proxies. Under the circumstances, the Pétainist logic argues, that is the most optimal option, and hence the most patriotic peace: there is no need to join the resistance and kill yourself in vain. Instead, stay home and keep safe, work hard and trust in our bargaining for the most honourable possible deal in order to save our great nation from oblivion. This, then, is the final axiom: Pétainism embodies the cultural *raison d'état* of empire. It articulates the cultural sophistry of a client-state that clones the philistine taste of the empire of the day.

In this global simulation, the Pétainist scenario of capitulation and servility is duplicated and reduplicated incessantly. If this condition of *simulacra imperii* is the imperial condition par excellence, then, indeed, 'all courage is the courage not to be Pétainist' (Badiou 2008b: 93). But, as Badiou argues, the choice of joining the patriotic resistance against the German occupation was not sufficient: 'What was needed was a *disgust* towards Pétainism . . . what it is that withstands passive contagion by this form . . . in terms of its courage in holding on to a point absolutely at variance with what Pétainism represented' (2008b: 93, emphasis added). It is only by probing deeply the nausea of imperial hubris in terms of global Pétainism that we can start thinking politics proper. The Platonic courage of doing so is not a posture or a disposition but an enduring effort to remain within the impossible, to face up to it: *t'alla panta auton aneurein, ean tis andreios ē kai mē apokamnei zetōn* ('We discover everything else only if we have courage and faint not in the search') (Plato 2006: 81D). That is not the kind of hubristic courage that is systematically manifested today by 'transnational' executive functionaries, safely ensconced Pétainist politicians or reckless mercenaries on imperial expeditions. That thoughtless and 'programmed heroism' was precisely the 'unjust, violent and preeminently foolish' courage censured by the Spartan poet Tyrtaeus in *Laws* 630B. Badiou, as a political weaver of Platonic virtues, rather affirms what another poet quoted by Plato in 630C-D, Theognis of Sicilian Megara, exalted as the highest virtue (*megistin aretēn*), namely, *pistotēs ēn tois deinois, ēn tis dikaiosēnin telēan onomasein* ('fidelity in danger, one might term complete justice'). Badiou's emphasis on courage as the ethical form of a political procedure is already an operator of justice that makes it both beautiful and true. That is an exorbitant price to be paid by a member of parliament or a corporate executive officer. Yet in a biopolitical age of neoliberal shock and faceless imperial terror, this aesthetic and affective strength of Badiou's conceptualisation of politics sustained by the courage of justice is precisely what is worthy of fidelity.

We should take heart against the global Pétainist, who is, after all, none other than Kafka's disrobed Confidence Trickster.[8] The courage of anti-imperialist politics lies precisely in this polemical nerve to withstand the pastoral extortion of collaboration, as Sartre himself denounced it; it is also in the capacity to feel disgust, as Badiou sternly affirms, the virtue to be unreceptive and to revolt against its favourable countenance, disciplinary drift and deceptive benediction, as Kafka, sarcastically, laid it bare. Short of this noble, visceral rage and creative hatred of the sort Paul displayed, our confidence in the truth of politics and its universal appeal cannot but result in yet another 'cognitive', encyclopaedic failure of imagination. Badiou's political thought abides by the consequences of this encounter.

Notes

1. Badiou and Žižek 2009e: 13. On the 'extended order' as an imperial concept of the liberal apparatus, see Hayek 1988: 32.
2. *mē proteron ex agoras apelthein ē philon tina poiēsasthai …* (Plutarch 1969: Book IV, 659E).
3. On the gradual extinction of Greek popular assemblies and democracy by imperial processes, see de Ste Croix 1981: 300–26.
4. For a more enchanted view of Josephus' collaborationism, see Rajak 2004. My own critical perspective is drawn from Momigliano 1994.
5. Goodenough 1962: 54. Out of the vast bibliography on the issue, see further updated and critical interventions by Richard P. Saller (1982), John K. Chow (1992), Richard A. Horsley (1987; 1997), K. R. Bradley (1987), Neil Elliott (1994) and John H. Elliott (1996).
6. On this issue, see an excellent compilation of essays edited by Richard A. Horsley (2000).
7. For an introduction to this logic of domination, see Donaldson 1988.
8. See Kafka's timely comic despair and expressionistic revolt figuring in 'Unmasking A Confidence Trickster' (1981: 19–21).

Part II: Compossibilities: Conditions of Philosophy in the Wake of Politics

6

Reversing and Affirming the Avant-gardes: A New Paradigm for Politics
Jan Voelker

I

For Badiou, the Century is a time frame which can be counted threefold: as the 'communist century', from the war of 1914–18 through the end of the Soviet Union, or as the 'totalitarian century', dating from 1917 to 1976, the year of Mao's death. Then it can also be counted as the liberal Century, the 'victory of Capital', lasting thirty years from the 1970s onwards (Badiou 2007: 2). It is a complicated frame, the complication of which arises from the constellation between timelines (the count of the century), on the one hand, and inner antagonisms, on the other. What, then, is *the* Century?[1]

This threefold count stems from the opening lines of the book Badiou dedicates to *The Century*, and one could thus specify the question and ask: what is the book's method and materials? Clearly, the threefold count seems to indicate that its intention is not historical: Badiou's intention is not to count the history of the Century as *One*. Nor is he attempting to reduce *The Century* to one, two or three essential topics. Instead, the book covers not only politics, but all four of the conditions under which he has determined philosophy to exist: art, politics, love and science. So instead of an objective, historical aim, Badiou focuses on four subjective dimensions and their coexistence in 'one' century. It could thus be asked whether in this intersection of four dimensions, the notion of the avant-gardes plays a specific role, since it combines two dimensions that seem predominant in this frame named *The Century*; that is, art and politics.

But, secondly, if the notion of avant-gardist art is bound to the Century and came to an end with it, it might be asked what role this historiality plays for Badiou's philosophy. Two moments

147

may be of significance here: first, *The Century* can be assigned a special role in Badiou's oeuvre insofar as it is one of the rare works that does not analyse a sequence of one of the conditions, but that makes all four conditions coincide in a specific formula. Moreover, it is not only the coupling of beginning and end that plays an important role in this formula, but the concept of contemporaneity is also of central importance to the notion of the avant-garde. Given that Badiou's philosophical approach is one that seeks to clarify the conditions of our present, the question would thus be: what is the significance for our present of the fact that the very notion of an art that based its works on performing interventions in the present has come to a close? Furthermore, if the notion of the avant-garde significantly linked art and politics, what is the significance of the suspension of this link in the present?

However, it might prove true that the absence of a concept of art that intervenes in the present and is linked to a specific understanding of politics *is* precisely what is missing in the present, and that this absence characterises the present. Thus, both questions – the role historiality plays for Badiou and his immanent starting point from the current situation – tend to collapse into one; the reinstitution of a singular lost notion is revealed to be a task for the philosopher who works on his present situation. But even if they do so collapse, the absence of a mode of subjectivation cannot simply be objectively stated, unless it is turned into the object of a history. Thus, the question remains: for contemporary philosophy, which seeks a notion of the contemporary, it seems necessary to come to terms with the end of a subjective (artistic-political) sequence in which the notion of contemporaneity played a central role. But the paradox consists in being sure not to objectify the end of a mode of subjectivation, as the analysis of its absence can only be undertaken on the basis of a subjective stance towards the contemporary situation. Therefore, both sides – the material and its significance for contemporary philosophy – indeed collapse into one, but they do so in a difficult subjective relation, instead of being reduced to an objectified history that philosophy would be able to judge.

This difficult double relation – that between the present and the (present) past and that of the coexistence of different truth procedures – is presented in the notion of the avant-garde. This notion demonstrates what in Badiousian parlance might be called a frame of compossibility,[2] almost in miniature: a play within the play, a dialectics within an overall setting that, as will be seen, for Badiou is non-dialectical. Thus, in the notion of the avant-gardes might be grasped a philosophical concept in which not only a specific historiality of subjectivation can be seized, but with it a specific philosophical intervention wherein the specific form of a truth procedure shows itself to be linked to another procedure. Just as the past is not purely and simply the past, so too is politics never purely and simply politics.

2

Against a historical reading of the century, Badiou proposes to undertake a philosophical meditation on what 'was thought in it' (2007: 3). He rejects the category of judgement – to give a generalising account of what happened – and proposes instead to focus on the various forms of subjectivation that took place in the Century. To think the Century in this way from the inside means to grasp it from its 'immanent prescriptions' (2007: 6), to take as a starting point the declarations the Century made in relation to itself. Again, this focus on subjectivation is about the way in which the century was subjectivated, and not about an objective rendering of forms of subjectivation. *The Century* explains 'how the century has been a subjective category for its own actors'.[3] Thus, the Century is a name that floats between the different processes of subjectivation; one created by the Century itself.

Badiou draws a sort of diagonal that combines these different processes. He is thereby able to establish his central hypothesis: that the Century obeyed a 'passion for the real' (2007: 32). This passion for the real is first of all generated via the obsession of a new beginning, which at the same time would have to be the end of the old. The Century brings the nineteenth century to an end and above all wants to be new: 'The nineteenth century announced, dreamed and promised; the twentieth century declared it would make man, here and now' (2007: 32). All its projects ultimately aim to realise the desire to create a new human being: 'Basically, from a certain point onwards, the century was haunted by the idea of changing man, of creating a new man . . . Creating a new humanity always comes down to demanding that the old one be destroyed' (2007: 8).

It is in this desire to create a new man that the structure of the Century unfolds. On the one hand, there are two irreconcilable sides – the beginning and the end, nihilism and affirmation – which, on the other hand, are held together in one term. The Century is marked by a 'disjunctive synthesis' (Badiou borrows this notion from Deleuze), a non-dialectical relation that leads permanently to violent attempts to dissolve the 'missing conjunction, like a dialectical link forced into being at the very point of the anti-dialectical' (2007: 32). The structure of antagonism thus constitutes the Century, creating as its principal figure the *Two*, a *Two* without any other chance of resolving conflict than by violence. It is for this reason that war is one of the central paradigms of the Century.

The avant-garde as a movement of the arts also fits into this frame. In several ways, Badiou's reconstruction of the avant-garde can be read as repeating the 'disjunctive synthesis' of the Century in small form, for it combines art and politics as well as the presence of art and its suspension.

First of all, Badiou does not use the term 'avant-garde' to characterise all the art of the Century, but instead to name the form of subjectivation in the field of art in general. For him, it is not a notion that could be reduced to some specific movements in the field of art. Avant-gardism in this sense qualifies art as work against the classical, aesthetic imperative of the beautiful form. But because its anti-classical gesture contradicts the general idea of a 'natural norm', it breaks altogether with a complete set of norms that reaches far beyond artistic questions. 'All of a sudden, the avant-gardes are no longer simply artistic "schools", they become social phenomena, points of reference for opinion' (2007: 133). A characteristic of the avant-garde is to break with the norm of art itself, and for this reason the essential question is the definition of art as such. Defined as an excessive exceeding of the boundaries of art, the avant-gardes cannot be understood as a phenomenon inside the field of arts alone.

The avant-gardes, Badiou continues, are always organised. They are organised in a strict, almost 'military' manner, and this 'often vigorously sectarian dimension already forges a link – at the very least an allegorical one – between artistic avant-gardes and politics (in which communist parties also presented themselves as the vanguards of the popular masses)' (2007: 133). It is the will to produce a collective existence that in the first instance joins the avant-gardes with politics: a collective existence that shall be established in the present, as a break with the existing order of things.

In their orientation towards the presence of art as a vivid presence in the present, Badiou sees the avant-gardes, at least initially, as a Romantic figure opposed to the classical understanding of art. In this context, Hegel proves for Badiou to be a more classical figure than a romanticist: the famous end of the arts signifies above all that art can no longer adequately represent the idea, but also refers to the essentialist conception of art as something that has to achieve a certain perfection (the norm of which was given in the past). Art is thus understood in an objective manner and the difference between the times dissolves: 'In the end, there can be no distinction for classicism between the past and the future of art', Badiou concludes, because the present of art has to gain its past perfection. The avant-gardes, on the other hand, are the ones who 'maintain that art is the highest destination of a subject', and therefore attest to the 'ontological question of twentieth-century art', which is precisely 'that of the present' (2007: 135).

At this point, and before turning to this fabrication of the present, we may recall the three 'schemas' that Badiou developed in his *Handbook of Inaesthetics* (2005c: 2–5). These are schemas in which the relation between truth and art has been thought – so far, one could say, because it is precisely the twentieth century that proved to be incapable of inventing a new schema. The first, the *didactic schema*, is one that Badiou connects to Plato, and it contends that there is no truth in art. Art may help to educate subjects but is dangerous for the community in its will to imitate truths. The second schema, which stands directly opposed, Badiou calls the *romantic schema*. In this one, on the contrary, art alone is capable of truth, and therefore the educative function is now solely on the side of art. Finally there is an intermediary schema that pacifies the struggle: the *classical schema*. Broadly connected to Aristotle, the classical schema says that art has no relation to truth and that it fulfils a therapeutic function. Today all three schemas are saturated: didacticism because of the 'state-bound and historical exercise of art in the service of the people', romanticism 'by the element of pure promise', and 'Classicism, finally, is saturated by the self-consciousness conferred upon it by the complete deployment of a theory of desire' (2005c: 7). The saturation is an effect of the twentieth century, during which the avant-gardes failed in their attempt to establish a new schema that would have combined didacticism and romanticism. Badiou situates the avant-gardes, then, between the two antagonist schemas, which they try to

bridge: didactically, art has no truth in and of itself, but romanti-
cally it is nevertheless absolute in its procedures. This impossible
bridge, which the avant-gardes tried to build, prefigures once more
the disjunctive synthesis as the central figure of the century. In the
Handbook, Badiou remains critical of the avant-gardes, showing
that their Janus-headed configuration leads to a mutual suspension
of their intentions:

> Revolutionary didactics condemned them on the grounds of their
> romantic traits: the leftism of total destruction and of a self-con-
> sciousness fashioned ex nihilo, an incapacity for action on a grand
> scale, a fragmentation into small groups. Hermeneutic romanticism
> condemned them on the grounds of their didactic traits: an affinity for
> revolution, intellectualism, contempt for the state. (2005c: 8)

The avant-gardes are thus considered to have failed, so Badiou
proposes that a new schema be established that would grant to
art both 'immanence' – its truths are immanent to its procedures
– and 'singularity' – these truths belong only to the realm of art.
As Badiou sees it, in romanticism there is immanence but no
singularity, while in didacticism there is singularity but no immanence, and 'in classicism, we are dealing only with the constraint
that a truth exercises within the domain of the imaginary in the
guise of verisimilitude, of the "likely"' (2005c: 9). This is to say,
that the romanticist schema conceives of art as a process with an
immanently unfolded truth but there is no singularity. Rather it is
the general truth that is displayed in art, and philosophy becomes
a helping hand for its delivery. In the didactic schema, truth is
extrinsic and not immanently unfolded but there is a singularity of the relation of truth and art insofar as art and philosophy
fulfil different tasks and only art is capable of displaying truth as
a semblance.

Badiou himself does not open a clear reference to the avant-
gardes in relation to this new schema. But the new schema would
have to combine didacticism and romanticism in a parallel to the
avant-gardes: from didacticism it would be necessary to retain and
refine the singularity, and from romanticism, the conception of
immanence. Furthermore, it would be directed against the same
adversary: in a manner comparable to that which Badiou assigns
to the avant-gardes, Badiou's own schema could be understood as
being essentially anti-classicist. But besides the parallels, this new

schema would have to differ fundamentally from the avant-gardes' attempt insofar as it joined two schemas in a way that repeats the 'disjunctive synthesis', turning them thus into 'partisans of the absoluteness of creative destruction' (2005c: 18). The new schema would have to exceed this position.

However, one could go one step further here and add that the new schema amounts to a reversal of the romantic schema: because while for romanticism the infinite idea descends into the sensible, on Badiou's account art is the 'sensible creation of the Idea' (2009a: 19), and thus the aspect of immanence ascribed to art in the romanticist schema (truth is unfolded in art) is maintained, but the relation between art and truth is reversed: truth is not *exposed* in the sensible, rather truths are *produced* in it. Singularity is thus inscribed, because these truths are now the truths of art, and the truth is no longer one.

And what of the didactic schema? In the preface of *Logics of Worlds* Badiou refers to images as examples for the artistic truth procedure. And he contradicts Plato:

> This means that – as in the Platonic myth, but in reverse – to paint an animal on the wall of a cave is to flee the cave so as to ascend towards the light of the Idea. This is what Plato feigns not to see: the image, here, is the opposite of the shadow. It attests the Idea in the varied invariance of its pictorial sign. Far from being the descent of the Idea into the sensible, it is the sensible creation of the Idea. (2009a: 19)

So here the new schema turns out to be also a reversal of the didactic schema: the aspect of singularity is maintained (art has a unique relation to truth), but the truths of art are coextensive with the material procedure and no longer extrinsic. Thus, by inscribing immanence, the singularity of the relation is redefined: there are specific artistic truths.

Finally, Badiou's anti-classicism could also be taken as a reversal of classicism. The fourth schema he proposes seeks to establish a concept of art in which art develops itself as a truth procedure, materialising the idea not as a representation but immanently constructing it in a material sense by presenting singular truths. In the terms of *Logics of Worlds* this is about bringing an appearance from inexistence to existence. Thus, if the classicist approach – and its classical medium of *catharsis* – consists in reducing art to a purely 'therapeutic' means, an ethical tool, and in referring art to the Imaginary, anti-classicism does not simply do away with ethics, or with the question of the image, but rather reverses their sense. The quote from *Logics of Worlds* shows that, for Badiou, the animal on the wall is more a pictorial sign than it is an image. It could perhaps even be understood as a pictorial formula. This formula can in a certain sense be read as the reversal of the image, that is, if we anticipate that Badiou's take on art is strongly oriented against the representational function of the image, an aspect that has more recently come to be a cornerstone of his critique of the contemporary situation. It is here that the origin of Badiou's theory of the cinema could be located: in the 'false' picture of the cave, which truly understood is a formula rather than a representation. The cinema reassigns this quality of non-representationality to the image, and is therefore a good medium for the passage of the 'impure' idea (Badiou 2005c: 83).

Then again, the reversal of the romantic schema opens the path for an ethics of infinity, against the expression of the infinite in the realm of the finite, as it is maintained by romanticism. The new schema would rather understand art as the process of producing real infinities, and any ethics would have to revolve around these infinities, instead of subjecting art to some sort of servicing of goods. Thus, the negation of the classical schema consists of the doubled reversal of the didactic and of the romantic schema, combining the formula and the production of the infinite.

Here, we can come back to the question of the avant-gardes and their production of the present. If the twenty-first century can be understood as the Century after the failure of the avant-gardes, the task of the present – the invention of a new schema – then takes on a more complicated structure. For the task of the present is related to the failed attempt of the avant-gardes in two important respects: 1) it needs to come to terms with the notion of contemporaneity implied by the avant-gardes; and 2) it will have to build a stronger anti-classicist bridge between didacticism and romanticism than the avant-gardes were able to do. However, the combination of art and truth under the paradigms of immanence and singularity has also 3) to take up the question of education, which Badiou understands as the 'third term of this link' between art and philosophy (2005c: 5). Education is a floating theme that is completely destitute with the succession and saturation of the schemas.

In starting with the notion of contemporaneity, let us turn again to *The Century* in which Badiou further examines the avant-gardes' relation to their concept of the present. The notion is in fact one that proves to be essentially split. Though the avant-gardes were concentrated on the 'pure present' and 'revolved around the act rather than the work' (Badiou 2007: 136), tending thus to get lost in the spiral of an always repeated beginning, they simultaneously had to counterbalance the intensity of a beginning which is the end in a *'formula'* (2007: 137). This formula could be a theory, a manifesto, a declaration or a commentary. Badiou emphasises here that what the manifesto 'bears witness to is a violent tension that seeks to subject to the real all the powers of form and semblance' (2007: 137). It is not without interest that Badiou has written two manifestos for philosophy himself (in the *The Century* he even refers to his own *Manifesto for Philosophy*, written in 1989), and a *Manifesto of Affirmationism*, which, as we will see, can be read as a direct theoretical consequence of the analyses of the avant-gardes.

For Badiou, the manifesto opens a dialectic between the real of the artistic intervention in the present, the act and the future of this act. Through their programmatic character, manifestos work to extend the act into the future. But this is an inessential, fictional extension: the manifestos invent a future for the real of a presence they cannot name. A declaration, a manifesto, a programme 'is a rhetorical device whose relation to what really takes place is only ever one of envelopment and protection', a 'linguistic shelter': the avant-gardes 'produced the envelopment of a real present in a fictive future' (2007: 139). The manifesto in this sense has to be understood as a material support of the fugitive act in the present. This recalls the Lacanian dictum according to which the truth has the structure of a fiction – one that Badiou often refers to and that further indicates that the rhetorical moment displayed by the avant-gardes is actually a structural moment in any truth procedure: the structure of declaration may be the declaration 'I love you' under the condition of love, in politics it may be a slogan, in science the provision of the results for everyone. It is a common structure, a common split.

In the context of the avant-gardes the manifesto works especially to link a specific notion of art to politics. For in politics, precisely, the concept of the party can be understood as the programmatic of the emancipatory event; it is its shelter from being swamped by the ordinary situation.[4] In both politics and art, however, there is a decisive difference between the act on the one side and its necessary rhetorical envelope on the other.[5] The programme does not express the intentions or the real of the act. It is rather the act's necessary counterpart, without which the weak act would be stripped of its purity. The act is the pure rupture, the pure beginning, and thus it is as threatened in its existence as it is pure: it cannot show itself to be a rupture, a beginning, of its own accord, because it would no longer be a pure rupture, but already be giving a reference to the situation in which it appears. For this reason it needs a declaration to come from the outside. The rupture cannot be without a declaration, and the declaration cannot be without the rupture, which it declares.[6] A declaration is thus not a speech-act, because it declares a point in the real, which it itself cannot be. Both sides – the point in the real and its declaration – belong together, but neither finds its own identity in itself.

Even if it is only a rupture that has not happened yet and maybe will not happen, it exists via the declaration. Act and declaration comprise the parts of the production of the present. But politics and art are not only linked via the declaration, but also via the importance of the rupture: art defined as interrupting the rules of the ordinary is always, *per definitionem*, more than art (as ordinarily defined) and politics is not only the name of a determined, concrete politics but also the (generic) concept of politics, which is a part of art, and – in common – of concrete politics. Politics thus becomes, as Badiou puts it in his lectures, 'the generic name of beginning'.[7] Through the rupture, politics and art are linked in the fabrication of the present: 'Only the recognition of the fabrication of a present can rally people to the politics of emancipation or to a contemporary art' (Badiou 2007: 140).

To summarise: the avant-gardes emphasise the notion of the present with the intention of producing a new beginning, a new present via the interruption of the given situation. The purity of this beginning can only be upheld by splitting it into an act and its provisional shelter. They are thus closely linked to the political ideas of the Century and so politics can be understood as the name for this conception of a radical new beginning – or perhaps 'avant-garde' itself as a structural moment that is common to art and politics in the Century. It is important to underline that this intersection does not identify art and politics: it is rather a paradox of the situation that both of them exceed themselves in their definition.

It is precisely at this point – the excessive intention to fabricate a new present – that Badiou shifts his argument to a consideration of our present, which he characterises as a lack of any 'real present' (2007: 140). We are, he argues, living through a sort of deactivated classicism, one in which no new beginning is possible and every dreaming of the future useless. For this reason, after their notion of the present, what needs to be reconsidered is precisely the avant-gardes' anti-classicism.

3

Nearly imperceptibly, Badiou's reflections on the avant-gardes are thus set into a different perspective. This perspective is directed towards the situation of the present, in the aftermath of the avant-gardes and the artistical-political knot they presented. From within the notion of the present as conceived by the avant-gardes, we now turn to the question of the missing present in our situation after the Century.

It is a perspective that Badiou adopts in the *Manifesto of Affirmationism*, several drafts of which have been published.[8] In it, Badiou declares our present time to have become swamped in a mixture of expressionism and self-important stylistics. After the end of the avant-gardes, in the desert following the twentieth century, not even any failing avant-gardes remain to have a struggle with. Instead, there reigns a

> domination in all the arts by figures of egoistic and communitarian expressiveness, which is only a degraded didactico-romanticism, a kind of avant-garde without the avant-garde. In a certain way, this is of a pair with the renascent pompierism. Pompierism today proffers violent technologized affects and a grandiose decorative style . . .
> (Badiou 2006b: 136)

Postmodernity is only capable of a weak anti-classicism,[9] Badiou continues, and as an expression of an anti-classical, subjective form it nevertheless refers to the category of form and thereby reveals itself to be romanticist in its structure. Today's scene boils down to the seeming alternative between 'circus games' in the form of sports and the culture industry on the one side and a 'meagre sophistication' on the other (Badiou 2006b: 138). The latter, which takes the form of a sophisticated art of bodily expression, can be understood as mirroring (or expressing) the circulation of images in the form of commerce. Art, then, in its dominant understanding, is today closely related to the culture industry. Badiou characterises the predominant concept of art in the present as a 'romantic formalism': romantic in its clinging to the body, and formalist in its belief that a single form could separate itself out from from the general commerce of forms (2006b: 138). Both parts form a couple: romantic formalism seeks to oppose obscene pompierism, but all its propositions rest on escapism, and by the attempt to escape the market and its circus games it concurrently sustains them. The commercial culture industry, the art of 'pompierism', can also be understood as a neo-classicism, as Badiou makes clear in a short remark in *Conditions* (2008e: 4). Thus, neo-classicism and romantic formalism form the contemporary two, the image of the present. On the one hand, there are the games of the empire, in which 'the Killer, the *serial Killer* torturer . . . the perverse gladiator' is the hero; on the other hand there is 'the *mise-en-scène* of supposedly sublimely singular ethnic and egoistical particularities' (Badiou 2006b: 139).

In a parallel to the classicist schema, one could extend this account and understand the neo-classicism of pompierism as one that refers art (as culture) to the realm of the Imaginary and subjugates it to the field of ethics. All that apparently remains are 'bodies and languages' (Badiou 2009a: 1), and all we can do is adapt to the given situation. It is in order to interrupt this situation that Badiou proposes a philosophical gesture that could be called an affirmative intervention:[10] a return to the avant-gardes and reaffirmation of the affirmative gesture they undertook. What he proposes is to affirm the affirmationism of twentieth-century art. This reversal of the avant-gardes would have to fulfil two aims: first, to open a new anti-(neo)-classicist front; and second, to oppose 'the degraded didactico-romanticism'. It could thus be said that the anti-classicism of the new schema consists in an affirmative reversal of the avant-gardes, one that takes a different ideological position to that of the reversal of the avant-gardes into pompierism. This affirmative intervention splits the avant-gardes into a progressive and a regressive part, its regressive part being the contemporary paradigm of the arts, and its progressive part being threatened with disappearance. This splitting of the avant-gardes of course simultaneously reactualises their inner principle, namely the strategy of upholding weak points threatened with disappearance. Thus it is also a split produced between image and formula:

> We want to make visible the genealogy of an axiomatic. An axiomatic that posits this: at the dawn of the century, we should recreate artistic desire in its incorporeal rigour, in its anti-romantic coldness, in the subtractive operations by which it holds most tightly to the imageless real, which is the only cause of art. (Badiou 2006b: 142)

Badiou unfolds a list of artists that are part of the 'affirmative constellation', among whom are Brecht, Pessoa, Picasso, Schönberg: 'These often isolated artists slowly composed configurations that have become legible only today' (2006b: 140). That they have become legible only today is the decisive marker of the shift of perspective. Badiou's titling his small text a *Manifesto* should be understood similarly to the way in which the manifestos worked for the avant-gardes. It is a rhetorical, that is, fictional shelter for a point in the real, which in its fragility is threatened with disappearance. It is therefore linked to a future. This link is also implied in the manifesto's grammatical form as a statement of imperatives, in its character of a declaration. Badiou's manifesto cannot be read as an explanation of something that has ever actually taken place; it does not have a representative function. But the ex-post-legibility also unfolds another of the manifesto's strengths, namely that of a rhetorical shelter that retroactively claims a point in the real. Far from being simply invented, the point in the real needs its declaration, which is already one of its consequences. Thus, the manifesto not only opens a future for this weak point, but also realises a point *in* the past *as* a missing point in the present. The declaration of its absence is both its affirmation in the present and its retroactive stabilisation. In a paradoxical statement it could be said that the future of the avant-gardes lies in a past that they will have had. Not *the* past, *the* future or *the* present: but instead *a* present of *a* past that opens on to *a* future. The reversal of the avant-gardes consists in their being split, and via the split temporality is differentiated.

The decisive difference can be found in the position of the floating theme of education. In an indirect manner, it can be concluded that the theme of education is the decisive moment when the reversal (as the ideological opposite to the 'degraded didactico-romanticism') is raised to another level. In Badiou's conception of a philosophical understanding of art, the educative function is taken over from the didactic schema:

> Art is pedagogical for the simple reason that it produces truths and because 'education' (save in its oppressive or perverted expressions) has never meant anything but this: to arrange the forms of knowledge in such a way that some truth may come to pierce a hole in them. What art educates us for is therefore nothing apart from its own existence. The only question is that of *encountering* this existence, that is, of thinking through a form of thought [*penser une pensée*]. (2005c: 9)

Following on from the discussion of the avant-gardes, it might be assumed that art has a special educative function in relation to politics insofar as its task is to create new forms in the sensible.[11]

In a talk given in New York City in 2010, Badiou provided further elaborations on his conception of art that help us to construct a preliminary answer to this point (Badiou 2010d). In it, he draws a distinction between a *militant* and an *official* conception of art: official art is art that is created in an inner relation to the state, one that is on the side of power. Militant art, by contrast, is on the side of resistance. Official art, Badiou contends, is an art of 'victory', of the 'glory of what exists', of the 'result' of a process, and is inscribed in an 'objective apparatus' – like the Party or the state – while militant art is 'the subjective expression not of what exists but of what becomes', an 'art of choice and not an art of victory' (2010d). In other words, we might say that militant art resists objectivation by insisting on the as-yet undecided moment of a process.

The common point of both conceptions of art for Badiou is ideology, which means 'a subjective conviction which is exposed in the language with a universal destination' (2010d). Here Badiou is clearly speaking of revolutionary ideology as it existed in the twentieth century. But the point is precisely that in each of these conceptions ideology takes a different place. In militant art it is on the side of contradiction, while in official art it is on the side of the artwork, or of the result. Official art tends to be conservative, to celebrate the new via old means, and this is also why it tends to be neo-classicist. Clearly, from this perspective, militant art is structurally assigned a certain weakness, one for which it has to create new forms. An important feature in Badiou's construction is that both conceptions of art may take place under the same subjective frame; the contradiction is one within ideology rather than one between ideologies. And it is a contradiction between a contradictory side and a side that identifies itself with the result; militant art not only contradicts the glorification of the results, but also is itself contradictory, in its 'contradiction between the affirmative nature of principles and the dubious result of struggles' (2010d).

The point, then, is that the presupposition of a strong ideology that would frame this dialectical process is no longer given today. Militant art, having lost its dialectical opponent, becomes indistinguishable, Badiou continues, from experimental art. But because art can no longer be inscribed in a progressive context, there is a 'temptation' to consider artistic novelty as political in and of itself. 'But this temptation', as Badiou puts it, 'is a temptation of avant-garde as such, or maybe the temptation to identify, purely and simply, artistic avant-garde and political avant-garde' (2010d). If this temptation is refused – as it should be – this does not involve refusing all relations between art and politics, but means only rejecting the notion that artistic novelty could by itself constitute a political effect. As such, the problem of today is precisely 'the weakness of the relationship between art and politics' (2010d).

Badiou then adds four 'provisional rules' for a possible militant art today. The first is to stay in touch with concrete political experiences. This rule works towards the recreation of a common space, one lost following the disappearance of a strong ideology. The second rule involves preparing for the return of an idea; that is, it is a sort of philosophical imperative oriented towards the overcoming of the weakness. And the third is to create new forms of presentation that are no longer representative, but that present the weakness. Finally, the fourth point is a synthesis of the first three:

> So to propose a work of art which is really in relationship to . . . local action, local transformation, which is intellectually ambitious, and not poor, and which is formally avant-garde – avant-garde in the classical sense of substitution of presentation for the fundamental vision of representation. (2010d)

Militant art is thus close to a concept of politics: not in its being political, but in its educational, preparative role of working on new forms of the sensible. 'Art', Badiou states, 'can be a preparation, a subjective preparation for the reception of a political event, because art is really an effective subjective process, the transformation of subjectivity' (2010d). The discontinuation of the avant-gardes means taking up their attempt to oppose classicism, but doing it in such a way as to position the link of education anew between the sides of art and politics: not to confuse art and politics as being one and the same process, but to reconsider strategies of art in developing new forms of existence. Art is not itself political but it might be of paradigmatic character in a time when the precise task is to invent a new present. To reverse and uphold avant-gardism is to be 'formally avant-garde', as a paradigm for a new politics. To invent the new against the neo-classicists is to be the point of conjunction between art and politics, with education as an intermediary between the two, which are not-one.

Or as Rimbaud famously and formally put it: one must be absolutely modern.

Notes

1. In the following, I will speak of the 'Century' with a capital 'C' to indicate its quality as a name given to a disposition of subjective processes, rather than an objective process. I would like to thank Steven Corcoran for his most helpful comments and suggestions on the text.
2. For the notion of compossibility, see Badiou 1999a: 37–9.
3. Badiou explains this further in his lectures on *The Century*. The unauthorised transcript is available at http://www.entretemps.asso. fr/Badiou/98–99.htm (accessed 18 July 2013).
4. See Badiou's lectures on *The Century* (2) (unauthorised transcript) http://www.entretemps.asso.fr/Badiou/99–00.1.htm (accessed 18 July 2013).
5. This is the term Badiou uses in the lectures. For the concept of the envelope see also Badiou 2009a: 128–31.
6. See Badiou's lectures on *The Century* (2), http://www.entretemps. asso.fr/Badiou/99–00.1.htm.
7. Badiou, lectures on *The Century* (2): 'politique devient le nom générique du commencement', http://www.entretemps.asso.fr/ Badiou/99–00.1.htm.
8. In the following, I will mainly refer to Alain Badiou, 'Third Sketch of a Manifesto of Affirmationist Art' (2006b: 133–48). An earlier version appeared in 2002, Alain Badiou, 'Esquisse pour un premier manifeste de l'affirmationisme', in Ciro Giordano Bruno (ed.), *Utopia 3, La question de l'art au 3e millénaire* (Sammeron: Germs,

2002), pp. 13–32. Yet another version that might be considered is Alain Badiou, 'Fifteen Theses on Contemporary Art', in Tobias Huber and Marcus Steinweg (eds), *Inästhetik*, Nr. 0 (Zürich-Berlin: Diaphanes, 2008), pp. 11–26. A talk Badiou gave in Berlin in 2008 under the title 'Art + Politics' could be considered a further version. To my knowledge this talk is only available as a recording on the internet: http://www.youtube.com/watch?v=C-viUxnlbQ4 (accessed 18 July 2013).

9. The passage I am referring to has found different forms in different translations, which is why at this point I would refer to the early 'Esquisse' (2002: 18).

10. In the above-quoted text from *Conditions* – itself a sort of a manifesto – entitled the '(Re)turn of Philosophy', Badiou argues for a break with the general opinion that philosophy is stuck between its own historicity and the anticipation of some mysterious advent. Instead of trying to legitimate itself in its history, philosophy should act and think immanently and judge its own history instead of being judged by it. See Badiou 2008e: 4–5.

11. In probably one of the best articles on the question of inaesthetics, Elie During makes a point comparable to mine: '"Inaesthetics" translates less a theoretical contradiction or tangle (as Rancière suggests) than a concern for the ethical and political efficacy of art. What is at stake is the educational potential of art. Badiou makes the wager, not only that art is capable of producing immanent truths, but that art *teaches* truth ... Despite all its "latent aesthetic", inaesthetics is not just another aesthetics: it's a slogan' (During 2005). I fully share this point, but try to extend it here so that that art's ability to teach truths can have a special impact in the absence of, or in times of the weakness of, political procedures, and that for the reopening of this capacity the reversal of the avant-gardes is the decisive point.

7

Badiou on Inaesthetics and Transitory Ontology: The Case of Political Song

Christopher Norris

I

In this essay I propose to take some themes and concepts from a number of texts by Alain Badiou and see what kinds of help they might offer in thinking about political song in terms of its status as a generic, aesthetic or ontological category. This proposal is likely to conjure puzzlement, scepticism or downright disbelief among a good many readers. Why should anyone propose so curious a topic or bunch of topics – ontology, aesthetics, politics and song – which could surely be conjoined only through some perverse taste for improbable hybrid couplings? If ontological considerations have any place in the discussion of music then that place needs to be earned by some hard argument since music is, of all the arts, the hardest to pin down, define or characterise in terms of its ontological status. As regards particular musical works this has to do chiefly with their distinctive and perduring mode of existence quite apart from their more or less extensive history of variant performances or interpretations.[1] Such problems become all the more daunting when politics enters the picture with its effect of creating a highly localised or context-specific link between 'work' (if that concept has any purchase here), performance history and particular socially mediated instances of production/reception.

Such is at any rate likely to be the reaction even among those who would in principle acknowledge the case for addressing the ontology of art, of music and (however grudgingly) of song. Still, they might say, does there not come a point on the scale of diminishing returns where the domain in question is so markedly bereft of distinguishing ontological features – so much a product of circumstance, occasion, context, impulse, passing inspiration, adaptive ingenuity, etc. – that the term 'ontological' seems

164

utterly out of place? After all, philosophers have difficulty enough with the ontology of musical works on account of their inhabiting an indistinct zone between this or that performance, history of performances, ideal performance, work *qua* score, work *qua* composer's intent, and (maybe) a realm of Platonic forms that is somehow accessed by all musical works or at any rate those that achieve classic status (see Sharpe 1995). The range of possibilities is such that every attempt at a solution in line with any of these alternatives seems to generate insoluble problems.

These problems are multiplied and deepened when the genre in question is that of song with its typical brevity, economy of utterance, lack of (at any rate long-range or formally imposing) structural markers and – most often – extreme reliance on subtleties and nuances of performance as well as closeness of rapport between singer and other musicians. All the more must this apply in the case of political song where these context-dependent features are yet further relativised by their insertion into a socio-cultural context or a highly specific situation which – it might be thought – removes any possible justification for affording them the dubious honour of a place in the ontological scheme of things. Such a claim is misconceived by reason of its failure to respect the proper scope of ontology as a highly developed discipline of thought yet one that has certain limits of proper or legitimate applicability. It also goes wrong by erroneously seeking to dignify a genre such as political song by subjecting it to just the kind of discriminative process – the application of high-art-derived and philosophically elaborated concepts and categories – which are wholly off the point in a context like this. Moreover, so the argument goes, it is liable to have just the opposite of its intended effect in so far as it risks devaluing that genre by holding it accountable to alien standards or criteria.

Such objections are apt to press pretty hard in a nominalist or anti-essentialist direction and deploy some version of the argument that political song is really not a 'genre' in any reputable sense of that term. This is because – on a certain understanding of musical ontology or ontology in general – it fails to meet the baseline generic requirement of possessing at least certain specifiable features, traits or distinctive marks that are not wholly or exhaustively context-relative. That is, it falls short of full-fledged generic belonging precisely in so far as its defining characteristic is that which marks it as a product of the strictly contingent or generically non-subsumable encounter between some particular set of socio-cultural/political circumstances and some particular, politically inspired or ethically motivated musical response. Yet this is nonetheless a generic description and one that has a fair claim to capture what is distinctive – even generically salient – about political song as performed in the kinds of situation (for instance on picket-lines, at protest meetings, or in response to state-sponsored injustice or violence) that most aptly qualify for that description. Here we are on familiar ground for anyone who has read Jacques Derrida's essays, such as 'The Law of Genre' (1980) and 'Before the Law' (1992), concerning the curious twists of logic – the paradoxes of inclusion and non-inclusion – that tend to crop up as soon as one asks what it means for a work to belong to some existing genre, or what properly counts as a mark of generic membership. At their least challenging these paradoxes have to do with the point made by T. S. Eliot (1964), with the metaphysical poets in mind: namely, that our reading of past writers must be very different from any reading that they might themselves have produced quite simply because our awareness of them includes many things that they could not have known, including (crucially) the subsequent impact or reception history of their own work. More tellingly, the paradoxes take us into regions of logic, mathematics or meta-mathematics where thinking comes up against Russell's famous problem about self-predication, that is, 'the set of all sets that are not members of themselves', or 'the barber who shaves everyone in town except those who shave themselves' (in which case who shaves the barber?) (see Russell 1930; Potter 2004).

This is not the place for a lengthy exposition of that problem or its various attempted solutions, among them Russell's stopgap remedy – his so-called Theory of Types – vetoing any formula that mixed first-order (object-language) expressions with second-order (meta-linguistic) levels of analysis, and so on up through the hierarchy of levels with a similar injunction at every stage so as to prevent such problems from arising in the first place. Suffice to say – with an eye to our present topic – that although its home-ground is in logic, mathematics and the formal sciences, this issue has a significant bearing on that of generic membership or affiliation as raised by Derrida's deconstructive quizzing of the boundaries between work and world, text and context, or art and its socio-politico-cultural-material environment. Thus any issue concerning the 'law of genre' and its constant liability to raids and incursions from across the generic border is closely bound up with the issue of aesthetic autonomy. Both questions are raised with peculiar force by works, performances or events – such as political songs – which would seem to be tokens maximally open to change or transformation from one context to the next, and hence minimally open to subsumption under this or that context-transcendent generic type. That is, they are peculiarly ill suited to treatment under the usual range of descriptive, prescriptive or evaluative predicates based on the presumptive autonomy of the musical work as a self-sufficient type with the ontological wherewithal to hold its identity-conditions firm across manifold shifting contexts of performance.

Hence, according to autonomists, comes the need to distinguish that work from the various factors – historical, political, socio-cultural, psycho-biographical and so forth – that make up its background history.[2] These latter kinds of circumstance may well have played some role in the music's genesis and perhaps in its reception history but cannot – or should not, to this way of thinking – be allowed to affect our 'purely' musical response, itself arrived at through a cultivated grasp of all and only those formal structures intrinsic to the work itself. Nothing could be further from the mode of existence enjoyed by most political songs, composed as they are very often on the hoof, under threat, against the clock, or out of some urgent communicative need and therefore with little regard to such high-cultural notions of musical autonomy. Indeed it is very clearly a part of their purpose – almost a defining feature of political song – to invite the kind of *engagé* (or *enragé*) listener-response that has no truck with that aestheticist creed or that appeal to timeless values beyond the time-bound contexts of production and reception. Such an auditor hears in the punctual coupling of words, music and event a call to action all the more effective for involving precisely those 'extraneous' elements that the formalist seeks to preclude.

Still there is a question as to whether such songs, or the best of them, may be said to possess that galvanising power not only by virtue of their timeliness and their happening to ride some wave of popular discontent but also on account of certain musical attributes – melodic, harmonic, rhythmic, structural –that place them in a class apart, or define them as veritable classics of the genre. The problem for anyone who makes this claim is that the notion of 'the classic' comes laden with a weight of inherited ideas concerning the markers of canonical status – of literary or musical greatness – and their timeless, transcendent character. It is this way of thinking that political song most pointedly calls into question since its very existence as a popular alternative to high-cultural art forms is premised on its audibly not going along with the various ideologies (of genius, transcendence, organic form, structural complexity, etc.) promoted by the guardians of musical good taste. Yet there are other, less ideologically compromised ways of thinking about 'the classic' – among them Frank Kermode's marvellously subtle and nuanced reflections on the topic – that entail no such commitment.[3] For Kermode, the classic is most typically a work 'patient of interpretation', or apt to reveal new possibilities of meaning in response to shifting historical-cultural circumstances. On his account it is still a work – not just a 'text' dissolved into its context or reception history – but a work whose very capacity to survive those changes should be taken as evidence of its openness to a range of alternative readings.

2

All the same it might be said that political song very pointedly challenges any such idea by calling into question the autonomy of musical form, its transcendence of the merely contingent or temporal, and the inviolable unity of words and music as a touchstone of aesthetic worth. Moreover, those values are further contested by the very existence of a genre (or anti-genre) that so conspicuously flouts the Kantian veto on artworks that have some palpable design on the listener/viewer/reader – some purpose to persuade, arouse or convert – and which therefore conspicuously fail to meet Kant's requirement of aesthetic disinterest (Kant 1978). After all it seems pretty much self-evident that any item of purported political song that did manage to satisfy this criterion would *ipso facto* be a bad or ineffectual instance of the kind, since incapable of stirring anyone to action or decisively changing their minds. Besides, such pieces are destined – if they succeed in 'catching on' – to undergo a history of changing contexts and varied applications which may result in their becoming very largely detached from any meaning or motive plausibly imputed to the original writer, singer or group of performers. And this despite the equally crucial point that they manage to conserve, as what amounts to a generic identity-condition, at least enough of that original purpose or motivating force still to count as political songs and, moreover, as this or that particular and utterly specific instance of the kind. That Badiou offers us some useful ideas with which to think through the seeming paradoxes involved – to 'turn paradox into concept', as he puts it with regard to advances in the history of set theory and various related contexts – is the claim that I shall develop in Section 3 of this essay.

Certainly there is no suggestion here that in switching focus from 'classical' song (i.e., concert-hall *Lieder* of whatever period or style) to instances of political street-song we are lowering our sights in musical-evaluative terms or electing to consider a sub-genre with no pretensions to high artistic, cultural or aesthetic worth. Hanns Eisler's songs, in particular his settings of Brecht, are equal to the finest of the twentieth or any century if heard without prejudice regarding their strongly marked didactic intent and with an ear to those features typically prized by devotees of the high *Lieder* tradition. Thus they are no less accomplished – dramatically powerful, melodically striking, harmonically resourceful and structurally complex – for the fact of their overt political content or, on occasion, their activist concern to discourage the listener from taking refuge in a purely aesthetic or contemplative mode of response. All the same their very success in so doing comes about through their constant supply of reminders, musical and verbal, that there is a world beyond the concert hall and that events in that world – like those that befell the twice-over *émigré* Eisler, driven out first by the Nazis and then by the watchdogs of US anti-communism – cannot be kept at bay by any amount of artistic creativity or degree of formal inventiveness. Indeed it is one of the most distinctive things about Eisler's music, not only his songs but also his larger-scale choral and orchestral works, that it maintains this perpetual sense of a nervous sensitivity to 'outside' events or the impact of 'extra-musical' promptings. This is probably why he seems most at ease, even in large-scale compositions such as his epic yet intensely personal *Deutsche Sinfonie*, when writing in a long-breathed melodic style with song-like contours and a strong sense that only by such means can he combine the pressure of subjective feelings with an adequate response to the pressure of (mostly dire) historical or political occurrences.

Political song is the genre that most effectively unites these otherwise conflicting imperatives and that makes it possible for music to express both the passionate force of individual commitment, and the historical or socio-political context within which it finds a larger significance. Ontologically speaking, it is that which (in certain cases) has the capacity to maintain its distinctive character while undergoing sometimes drastic changes of context, motivating purpose or performative intent. Songs that started life as protests against British government policy during the miners' strike of 1983 have since done service in a great many other campaigns, sometimes very largely unaltered (except insofar as the shift of context changed their perceived character), and sometimes with verbal modification so as to update their content or enhance their specific relevance. On a larger time-scale, songs that had their origin in the suffering or revolt of black slaves in the American Deep South are nowadays revived – not just recycled – in the name of anti-poverty campaigns, anti-war protests and calls for the rescheduling or outright cancellation of Third-World debt. What gives the songs in question this remarkable staying power – beyond some vague appeal to 'the test of time' – is a complex amalgam of musical and verbal features that is likely to elude the best efforts of formal analysis, but that is recognisable to anyone who has sung them and registered their continuing impact when performed on any such politically charged occasion. Here again, one might aptly recall what Derrida has to say about that minimal trait of 'iterability' that enables speech-acts to function, that is, to retain a certain recognisable (ethically and socially requisite) performative force despite their occurring across a potentially limitless range of contexts and their involving the ever-present possibility of deviant (or devious) motives on the utterer's part (Derrida 1977a; 1977b; see also Searle 1977). Just as this 'iterable' property of speech-acts is such as to resist any systematic formalisation of the kind attempted by theorists such as Searle, so likewise the 'classic' quality of certain political songs – those that have retained their radical force – is nonetheless real for its holding out against methods and techniques of analysis trained up on masterworks of the mainstream classical repertoire.

If I placed some queasy scare-quotes around the word 'classic' in that last sentence then it is no doubt a sign of my unease about dragging these songs into the orbit of a high-cultural or academic discourse where they are likely to suffer a gross misprision of their musical, verbal and political character. All the same, as Terry Eagleton (1990) has argued, it is just as mistaken for leftist cultural theorists to let go the whole kit and caboodle of 'bourgeois' aesthetics – especially its talk of arch-bourgeois values such as beauty, sublimity or aesthetic disinterest – on account of its being so deeply bound up with the hegemonic interests of a once dominant though now declining cultural and socio-political class. The fact that those values have largely been monopolised by that particular power bloc does not mean that they cannot or should not be recovered – won back through a concerted effort – by those among the marginalised and dispossessed who have most to gain from their redefinition in left-activist terms. This is why the label 'classic' may justifiably be used to describe those songs that have shown a special capacity to renew their impact from one situation to the next and have thus come to manifest a singular strength of jointly musical, political and socio-cultural appeal. Indeed, as Kermode very deftly brings out, if there is one perennial feature of the classic then it is the absence of just those reference-fixing indices that would otherwise place certain clearly marked limits on the range of options for anyone seeking authenticity or wishing to remain true to the song's original context and motivation.

Of course 'authenticity' is a notion widely challenged among leftist cultural theorists – often taking their lead from Adorno – since it is thought to harbour an appeal to supposedly 'timeless' or 'transcendent' values such as those invested in the high tradition of accredited musical or literary masterworks (Adorno 1973; Goehr 2007; McClary 2001). However, so it is argued, values of this kind, even when adduced as the upshot of a lengthy and detailed formal analysis, always have a local habitation in the time and place (that is to say, the formative ideological conditions) of their particular socio-politico-cultural setting. Such criticism of the Western musical and literary canons has been carried to a high point of technical refinement by various schools of thought – New Musicologists, New Historicists, deconstructionists, cultural materialists, feminists, the more analytically minded postmodernists – well practised in revealing the various sleights of hand by which promoters of a high formalist doctrine manage to occlude what is in fact a highly specific set of class-based or gender-related ideological commitments (see, e.g., Bergeron and Bohlman 1992; Cook and Everist 1999; Kerman 1980; 1983; 1985; Korsyn 1993; Kramer 1995; Solie 1993). From their point of view, Kermode could only be selling out when he argues for a stance of mitigated scepticism vis-à-vis the classic, that is, an approach that would balance the claims of intrinsic literary (or musical) worth against the claims of an anti-canonical case for regarding 'the classic' as one of those ideas that have served as a useful means of upholding the cultural and socio-political status quo. If anyone thought to extend Kermode's argument to the case of political song, then they would surely invite the charge of misrepresenting what is by its very nature a context-specific, historically located, resolutely non-transcendent mode of expression. That is to say, they would be seen as deludedly seeking to boost its status by hooking it up to an aesthetic ideology that no longer possesses the least credibility even when applied to works in the mainstream classical repertoire (see, e.g., de Man 1996; Lacoue-Labarthe and Nancy 1988; Norris 1988).

Such is at any rate the sort of claim nowadays put forward by zealous deconstructors of the Western musical canon. This project they pursue partly by engaging with those works in a heterodox or counter-canonical way and partly by challenging the discourse of post-Schenkerian music analysis with its deep attachment to (supposedly) conservative notions such as organic form, thematic development, harmonic complexity, structural integration, progressive tonality, voice-leading, long-range reconciliation of conflicting key-centres and so forth.[4] To think (and to listen) in accordance with these notions is to signal one's complicity – so the argument goes – with a formalist mystique of the unified artwork which mistakes the culturally constructed character of all such aesthetic notions for natural properties somehow inherent in 'the work itself', or else in the musical language (most often that of the high Austro-German line of descent from Bach to Brahms or Wagner) that made such achievements possible. And if this line of thought has a certain plausibility with regard to the dominant values of 'high' musical culture and their modes of propagation through the arcane discourse of academic musicology, then it seems even nearer the mark when applied to any claim for this or that political song as a veritable 'classic' of its kind. After all, what could be plainer as a matter of straightforward response to words and music alike than the fact that such 'works' constitute a standing affront to that whole classical-romantic aesthetic of timeless, transcendent, ahistorical and hence apolitical values?

3

Again it is Kermode, in his book *History and Value* (1988), who has given us by far the most subtle and perceptive treatment of this issue by examining the mainly left-wing English poetry and fiction of the 1930s and tracing the complex patterns of relation-ship between value as a matter of historical-political 'relevance' and value as a matter of critical esteem or canonical status. What emerges from Kermode's scrupulously nuanced yet far from apo-litical reflections is the sheer impossibility of imposing any such divorce, or coming up with a plausible account of literary value that would somehow exclude any reference to the way that literary (or musical) works have fared under certain specific yet histori-cally changing conditions.

It is here – at the elusive point of intersection between aesthetic, hermeneutic and socio-political modes of response – that Kermode locates his idea of 'the classic' and along with it his answer, albeit couched in suitably qualified and tentative terms, to the ancient question of just what enables some, and not other, works to enjoy a long, culturally varied and sometimes unpredictable afterlife. This is an approach that, on the one hand, keeps its distance from old-style notions of the artwork as possessed of a timeless and altogether context-transcendent value, while on the other hand rejecting the opposite (reactive) tendency to find nothing more in literature or music than an ideological sounding-board or a means of imposing this or that set of hegemonic beliefs. It is also, I would argue, a conception well suited to explain why it is that political songs – a few of them – have precisely this phoenix-like capacity to renew their force or to acquire new dimensions of relevance and motivational power from one protest movement to the next. That is to say, their longevity is not so much a matter of some deep-laid, essential or intrinsic quality of words and music that preserves them intact against the ravages of time and chance, but rather a matter of their exceptional adaptability to changes of social and political circumstance.

It is perhaps now time to recapitulate the main points of my argument so far in order to firm up the basis for what I have to say (with – at last – specific reference to Badiou) in the rest of this essay. Thus: 1) if the term 'ontology' makes any kind of sense as applied to works of art, then it had better be applicable to musical works, in which case; 2) it had better be applicable to those works falling under the generic description 'song'; and moreover 3) it had best apply convincingly to political song as a litmus-test since this places the maximal strain on received notions of generic character or identity. Hence the particular problem it poses for any formal

ontology of art based on the presumed existence of certain distinctive traits whereby to recognise and specify what counts as a
genuine instance of the kind. After all, 'political song' is a pretty
elastic label and one that is apt to find itself stretched around
some dubious candidate items if taken to denote any relatively
short and self-contained vocal work with a text that makes either
overt or covert reference to certain themes of a political character.
Thus the British national anthem would have to qualify under
this definition although there seems good reason to withhold the
title on account of its patently belonging to a genre that endorses
rather than challenges the institutional status quo, and whose
stolid combination of flag-waving words and foursquare music
is very much deployed to that end. Yet there are other national
anthems – most strikingly 'Amhrán na bhFiann' (Irish Republic)
or 'Nkosi Sikelel' iAfrika' (post-apartheid South Africa, originally
ANC) – which, although in very different ways, continue to communicate something of the oppositional spirit or of the strength of
concerted popular resistance that went into their making and the
often strife-torn history of their early performances. Indeed the
very fact of this (so to speak) stress-induced and to that extent historically indexed character has a lot to do with their staying power
as classics of the genre.

    This helps to explain why a classic of the 1983 British miners'
strike, 'We Are Women, We Are Strong', should thereafter have
turned up as a highly effective rallying call at numerous sites and
in numerous seemingly disparate socio-political contexts over the
past quarter-century of popular anti-government protest.[5] It can
best be put down to that song's having so perfectly captured the
quiet determination, resilience and un-self-conscious heroism not
only of the miners' wives and partners but of a great many others
whose livelihoods and lives were under threat from government
economic and social policy. The case is rather different with those
hardy perennials like 'We Shall Not be Moved', where the sentiments expressed, like the melody and harmonies, are so broadly
generic – so capable of being adapted to just about any political
context – as to offer a kind of Rorschach-blot for those in search
of all-purpose emotional uplift. It seems to me that, in order to
count as a genuine classic of political song, the piece in question
must exhibit something more than this smoothly accommodating
power to absorb a great range of otherwise diverse feelings, values,
beliefs and commitments. This 'something more' can I think best

be specified in ontological terms, even though the terms involved are sure to be somewhat fugitive given that political songs exist very largely in and through their reception history and thus exhibit a peculiar degree of dependence on contextual cues and the vagaries of historically situated listener response. All the same, as I have said, it would be wrong to conclude from this that they fall short of classic status insofar as they fail to meet to certain formal standards – at any rate certain widely agreed-upon and clearly specifiable criteria – that alone make it possible for judgement to transcend the shifting tides of social change or cultural fashion.

One might take a lead in thinking about this question from the title of Badiou's essay *Briefings on Existence: A Short Treatise on Transitory Ontology*, as indeed from his entire project to date. That project has to do with the relationship between being and event, or the way that certain unpredictable and yet (as it turns out) epochal or world-changing events – certain breakthrough discoveries whether in mathematics, science, the arts or politics – can lead to a radical transformation in our powers of ontological grasp and hence to a shift in the relationship between currently existing knowledge and objective (recognition-transcendent) truth (see especially Badiou 2005a; also Badiou 2003a; 2004a). What is most remarkable about Badiou's work is its emphasis on truth as always exceeding our utmost powers of cognitive, epistemic or rational grasp, and yet as that which constantly exerts a truth-conducive pressure through its absence – its way of creating problems, lacunae, unresolved dilemmas – in our present-best state of understanding. This is not the place for a detailed exposition of Badiou's masterwork *Being and Event*.[6] It is sufficient to say that he makes this case not only in relation to mathematics (very much Badiou's disciplinary home-ground) but also to the physical sciences, politics and art. More specifically: in each case it is a matter of truths that are opened up for discovery at a certain stage in the process of knowledge-acquisition or cultural-political advance, yet which may require a more or less extended process of further working out at the hands of those faithful exponents – 'militants of truth' – whose office it is to explore their as yet obscure or unrecognisable implications.

However, the main point I wish to make for present purposes is that Badiou offers a distinctive, and distinctly promising, line of enquiry for anyone pondering the ontology of political song and its status vis-à-vis conceptions of art or aesthetic value on the one hand and conceptions of politics or political engagement on the other. Thus on his account there is no choice to be made, as orthodox (e.g., Kantian) approaches would have it, between the value-sphere of artistic creativity or inventiveness and the action-oriented practical sphere of incentives to political change. In each case it is a matter of truth-claims – whether claims in respect of an as yet unachieved state of political justice or claims for the integrity of certain as yet unrecognised artistic practices – that exert a potentially transformative pressure on current ideas but which cannot be realised (carried into practice or brought to the point of adequate conceptualisation) under presently existing conditions. Moreover, it is with respect to ontology – to the question 'What exists?' as distinct from 'What counts as existing within some given mathematical, scientific, artistic, or political conception?' – that those conditions are brought into question or subject to standards of truth that transcend the criteria of presently existing knowledge. Above all, this enables an extension of truth-values beyond the realms of mathematics, science and the factual (e.g., historical) disciplines to other areas – such as politics and art – where they have rarely if ever been invoked in so emphatic and rigorously argued a manner.

Thus it is worth thinking some more about Badiou's seemingly oxymoronic, or at any rate odd, conjunction of terms in the phrase 'transitory ontology'. What it signifies – in short – is a conception of ontological enquiry as nonetheless objective, rigorous or truth-oriented for the fact that its scope and limits are subject to a constant process of transformation through advances in the range of available forms, techniques, investigative methods, hypotheses, theorems or proof-procedures. Badiou's paradigm case is that of mathematics and, more specifically, post-Cantorian set theory, since it is here that thinking can be seen to engage with an order of truths that always necessarily exceeds or transcends any given state of knowledge.[7] It is in consequence of the 'count-as-one' – that is to say, through some schema or selective device for including certain multiples and excluding certain others – that thought is enabled to establish a range of operational concepts and categories within the otherwise featureless domain of 'inconsistent multiplicity'. Most important is Cantor's famous demonstration that there exist manifold 'sizes' or orders of infinity, such as those of the integers and the even numbers, and moreover – contrary to the verdict of most philosophers and many mathematicians from the ancient

Greeks down – that thought is quite capable of working produc-
tively (framing hypotheses for proof or refutation) in this para-
dox-prone region of transfinite set theory.[8] Indeed, it is through
the process of 'turning paradox into concept' – a process most
strikingly exemplified by Cantor's conceptual breakthrough – that
intellectual advances typically come about, whether in mathematics, the physical sciences, politics or art. Hence the main thesis of
Badiou's work: that in each case the truth of any given situation
(scientific paradigm, political order, artistic stage of advance) will
exceed any current state of knowledge even among specialists or
expert practitioners, and yet be contained within that situation in
the form of so far unrecognised problems, dilemmas, paradoxes or
elements (multiples) that lack any means of representation in the
currently accredited count-as-one.

Politically speaking, this claim works out in a strikingly literal
way since it applies to those marginal, stateless or disenfranchised
minorities – prototypically, for Badiou, the *sans-papiers* or migrant
workers of mainly North African origin – who find themselves
excluded from the count-as-one since their lack of official docu-
mentation effectively deprives them of civic status or acknowledged social identity (see, e.g., Badiou 2005b; 2006b; 2007). All
the same, the very fact of their occluded existence on the fringes
of a *soi-disant* 'democratic' social order is such as potentially to
call that order into question or to constitute a challenge to the
self-image projected by its state-sponsored apologists. At certain
times – during periods of crisis or rising communal tension – those
minorities may well turn out to occupy an 'evental site' which
then becomes the focus of wider social unrest and potentially the
flash-point for some larger-scale challenge to the dominant structures of socio-political power. In the physical sciences, revolutions
come about most often at a stage of conceptual crisis in this or
that particular region when the anomalies, failed predictions or
conflicts of evidence with theory have become simply unignorable
and when something – some crucial load-bearing part of the old
paradigm – collapses under the strain. In the arts likewise such
transformations typically occur at times of imminent breakdown:
in music, say, with the stretching of resources and extreme inten-
sification of affect that overtook the tonal system in the late nineteenth century, or in literature with the advent of modernist poetic
and fictional genres that signalled a decisive rupture with previous
(realist or naturalistic) modes of representation.

4

Clearly there is much more needed by way of introduction to Badiou's work if the reader is to be in any strong position to assess these claims. However, my purpose here is to suggest that his thinking offers some useful guidance for our enquiry into the ontology of political song. More specifically, it may bring us closer to defining the mode of existence of songs whose comparative longevity and power to energise protest across a great range of political movements and causes is such as to merit their being accorded 'classic' status even though – for reasons that I have essayed above – that term seems rather out of place in this context. Badiou's idea of 'transitory ontology' best catches what I have in mind, namely the elusive combination of extreme adaptability or context-sensitivity with the singular power to retain a distinctive musical and verbal-ideational character throughout those (seemingly) protean guises. On his account the marks of a genuine event, as distinct from an episode falsely so deemed, are first that it make room for the discovery of a truth beyond any present-best state of knowledge, and second that it henceforth demand the allegiance – the intellectual, scientific or political fidelity – of those committed to its working out or the following through of its implications. False claimants may fill up the history books and make the headlines on a regular basis but are nonetheless false for that, since their occurrence, although unforeseen at the time, is retrospectively explainable as the outcome of various anterior happenings and in-place or ongoing developments (see, e.g., Badiou 2005b; 2006b; 2007). Genuine events may pass largely unnoticed at the time or, like abortive revolutions, go down only in the annals of failure and yet linger on in the memories of those attuned to their so far unrealised potential and thereby hold in reserve the potential to spark some future transformation.

Badiou offers many such examples, chief among them the Paris Commune of 1871 and Cantor's radical rethinking of mathematics on the basis of set theory as applied to the multiple orders of infinity (see Badiou 2003a; 2004a: 1–93, 95–160; 2005a: 21–77). Thus, despite the strong resistance to Cantor's ideas put up by many well-placed mathematicians at the time, and despite the Commune's having been suppressed in the most brutal and (apparently) decisive way, both can now be seen as events of the first order since set theory went on to revolutionise mathematical thought, while the Commune continues to inspire and motivate successive generations of political activists. This is why I have made the case – an improbable case, so it might be thought – for understanding the ontology of political song in light of Badiou's writings on mathematics and his extension of set-theoretical concepts to other, seemingly remote contexts of discussion. That case rests partly on the way that he establishes a more-than-analogical relation, *via* set theory, between the three principal areas – politics, music and poetry – which must enter into any adequate account of what makes a classic instance of the kind. Also it helps to explain how one can speak in ontological terms of an art form – again, if that is the right term – that depends so much on its contexts or occasions of performance and which therefore seems to elude all the terms and conditions typically proposed by critics and philosophers seeking to define what constitutes a veritable classic. Thus a really effective political song is one that catches the counter-hegemonic spirit of its time and succeeds in communicating that force of resistance to activists in later, politically changed circumstances. By the same token it is one that not only responds to the potential for some future transformative event – whether in the short or the long term – but can itself be heard to constitute such an event on account of its power to express and articulate those pressures of unrest in response to forms of economic, political and social injustice that are building towards a structural crisis point. It is here that Badiou's radical rethinking of the relationship between art, politics and truth (in his own heterodox yet clearly defined sense of that term) has the greatest power to illuminate our present enquiry into the ontology of political song. At any rate it goes some way towards explaining the anomalous status of a genre that somehow combines an extreme responsiveness to changes in its historically emergent contexts and conditions of existence with a striking capacity to retain its political as well as its musical-expressive charge despite and across those changes.

The issue is broached most directly in Badiou's *Handbook of Inaesthetics* where he examines the various kinds of relationship that have characterised art in its dealing with philosophy and politics. Among them may be counted its Brechtian 'didactic' role as a more or less compliant vehicle for conveying some preconceived political content (even if with the aid of certain formal innovations), its 'classical' role as a well-crafted product that satisfies purely aesthetic criteria and lays no claim to any truth beyond that of its own artifactual contriving, and the romantic role in which it aspires to a creative autonomy or self-sufficient power of world-transformative vision that would free art from all such prosaic or quotidian ties. As scarcely needs saying, Badiou has little sympathy with the latter conception, denying as it does his cardinal thesis that philosophy has its own special role in providing a more perspicuous account – a conceptual articulation – of truths that must remain implicit in the artwork. That is, they exist in the 'subtractive' mode of that which cannot find direct expression but can nonetheless be shown to haunt the work as a structural absence or symptomatic silence and thereby to indicate the future possibility of some as yet unknown further stage of advance. Romanticism, with its Shelleyan idea of the artist as unacknowledged legislator, effectively sells art short by ignoring its kinship with the likewise subtractive procedures through which mathematicians 'turn paradox into concept', or physics undergoes periodic revolutions through coming up against recalcitrant data, or political transformations are seen – albeit after the event – to have been brought about through the existence of 'uncounted' or unrecognised multiples at evental sites on the margins of the instituted body politic. Classicism fails yet more grievously since it makes a full-scale aesthetic creed of severing any link between art and truth, or any pretension on the artist's part to express, convey or communicate truths beyond the technical aspects of their craft.

Then there is the fourth, distinctively modernist conception of art, whereby it breaks with all three of those previous modes – didactic, classic and romantic – and devotes itself instead to a self-reflexive dealing with issues of language, discourse or representation that constantly call its own status into question. It is clear from his writings on (for instance) Mallarmé and Beckett that Badiou is strongly drawn to many works of this kind since for him they constitute one of the ways in which art can create or discover its equivalent to the breakthrough achievements of a formal discipline such as set theory. However, he also has strong reservations about the tendency of other such works to become overly hermetic, self-absorbed or preoccupied with linguistic or formal-technical devices and developments at the cost of renouncing any involvement with 'extraneous', that is, political or socio-historical conditions. After all, this brings them within close range of the turn towards various language-based schools of thought – Wittgensteinian, hermeneutic, post-structuralist or neo-pragmatist – that Badiou regards as a betrayal of philosophy and, moreover, as lending support to the status quo by reducing all issues of reason and truth to the question of what makes sense by the lights of this or that discourse, language-game, signifying system or horizon of intelligibility (Badiou 1999a). Thus art, like philosophy, had best avoid being too closely linked – 'sutured', in the idiom that Badiou derives from Lacanian psychoanalysis – to any of those conditions (politics among them, but also prevailing ideas of aesthetic value or form) whose function is artistically ena- bling up to a point but whose effect if taken beyond that point is to deprive art of its particular role as an oblique though potentially powerful means of access to truth.

This is one sense of the term 'inaesthetics' as deployed in the title of Badiou's book: the capacity of certain (rather rare and often under-recognised) artistic practices to question or challenge accepted notions of what properly constitutes art, or what counts as aesthetically valid. Another is the sense in which it denotes a strong and principled opposition to any idea that art should occupy a realm of distinctively aesthetic experience removed from all commerce with 'extra-artistic' interests or imperatives. Badiou's great aim is to specify how art can express or give form to truths that 'inexist' – that lack as yet any adequate means of conceptual articulation – yet which may nonetheless be signified obliquely by those gaps, anomalies or absences of formal closure that art is best able to reveal through its inventive capacity for testing the limits of established (e.g. realist, figurative or conventional) languages and genres.[9] To this extent art has a purchase on truth that may require the mediating offices of philosophy to spell out its implica- tions, but that could not possibly have been achieved except by means of its artistic presentation. I have argued here that political song is a test-case for this thesis since it is a genre (or anti-genre) that confronts the existing political order with a downright chal- lenge to all those political, social, ethical and musical values that serve to maintain the preferential self-image of a stable and prop- erly functioning liberal democracy.

The starting point of set-theoretical reasoning is the null set – in Badiou's terminology the 'void' – which, despite its foundational character, eludes any ascription of properties or determinate mem- bership conditions. That is to say, it is included in every multiple as a constituent part or strictly indispensable element yet cannot be reckoned as properly belonging to the count-as-one by any of the usual admission criteria. So it is, by far from fanciful analogy, that socially excluded or victimised minorities continue to exist at the margins of the body politic and, through the very fact of this marginal status, to exert a potentially transformative pressure on the forms of state-administered surveillance and control. Nor are the arts by any means excluded from this critical role, since they also have the capacity to function as reminders of that which cannot be expressed or represented in any language, form or genre available to artists working within the dominant socio-cultural conditions of their own time and place. If the phrase 'ontology of political song' makes any kind of sense – if is not just a bad case of semantic inflation applied to a wholly inappropriate, since temporally fleeting and insubstantial (quasi-)artistic, cultural phenomenon – then the best means of defending its entitlement to treatment on these terms is by conjoining Badiou's idea of 'inaesthetics' with his notion of 'transitory ontology'. What we are enabled to think without conceptual embarrassment is the standing possibility of artworks (nothing less) that are very much products of their own historical and cultural-political context yet that also have the power to live on – like the 'classic' in other, more elevated terms of address – and renew their inspirational charge across a wide range of historical, geographical and socio-political situations.

This is mainly by virtue of Badiou's deploying a 'subtractive' conception of truth whereby, as in the history of set-theoretical advances, progress comes about through locating those absences, lacunae, stress-points, anomalies, dilemmas, paradoxes and so forth that signal the need for some as yet unknown but obscurely prefigured advance. In set theory there is a known method by which such advances can best be explained, that is, how it is that mathematical truth can run ahead of present-best mathematical knowledge and yet exert a knowledge-transformative power on those who are still operating with the old concepts but who find themselves uneasily responsive to that which finds no place in current understanding. Such is the procedure of 'forcing', devised (or discovered) by the mathematician Paul Cohen who managed to explain its operative conditions in formal, that is, set-theoretical terms (Cohen 1966). This has been the topic of some highly pertinent commentary by Badiou who takes it to have decisive implications for our grasp of how epochal changes come about in disciplines, fields or histories of thought far afield from mathematics, at least on the commonplace understanding of what mathematics is or does. Whenever there occurs the kind of major transformation that is loosely described, after Kuhn, as a whole-sale 'paradigm-shift', then this is sure to involve another instance of the process whereby thought becomes alert to the existence of certain hitherto unrecognised problems, paradoxes or truth-value gaps.

At these points it is only by way of a 'generic' procedure, in Cohen's mathematically defined sense of that term, that knowledge is enabled to transcend its previous limits and achieve a new stage of conceptual advance. Then it becomes possible to explain – always after the truth-event – how and why those limits had remained in place despite their having always *potentially* been subject to the forcing effect of such unresolved issues at (or beyond) the margins of intelligibility. My main point here has been to argue that political song occupies that same, intrinsically hard-to-specify since at present not fully realised or recognised ontological domain. That is to say, it gives verbal-musical voice to the standing possibility of a mismatch between that which we are able to know or cognise under currently existing historical, political or socio-cultural conditions and that which may nonetheless be prefigured – obliquely expressed or latently contained – within those very conditions. Just as knowledge always falls short of truth in mathematics or the physical sciences, so likewise our grasp of what can be achieved in the way of political progress falls short of what *might* counterfactually be achieved if only thought were able to grasp the possibilities for radical change held out by the failings (e.g., the democratic deficit) that characterise some given social order. Or again, for those who come later and keep faith with the inaugural truth-event, these may be possibilities that they are able to imagine or conceive yet unable to realise – fully comprehend and carry into practice – by any means presently at their disposal.

If I were writing primarily for a readership of musicologists then I should feel obliged to press further towards an account of just what it is – what specific combination of features melodic, harmonic, rhythmic and of course conjointly musical-verbal – that constitutes the classic status or character of some political songs. My own best guess is one that I would advance with a measure of confidence after having sung in a socialist street-choir for many years and in support of many political causes from the 1983 miners' strike and the anti-apartheid campaign to protests in connection with sundry events in Northern Ireland, Chile, Colombia,

Guatemala, Nicaragua, Iraq and (most recently) Libya. It has to do with a certain quality, analogous to 'forcing' in the set-theoretical domain, whereby such songs are able to communicate – 'connote' would be too weak a term – the idea of an as yet unachieved but achievable state of justice that finds voice in their words and their music, and that thereby exerts a potentially transformative pressure on existing (conventionally inculcated) notions of the social good. Musically speaking, this involves certain distinctive melodic, harmonic and rhythmic patterns that manage to combine a vigorous sense of shared opposition to regnant structures of authority and power with a contrasting sense of the forces currently ranged against them and the outside chance of those structures giving way in response to any such challenge. I say 'contrasting' rather than 'countervailing' because protest songs draw much of their expressive and performative power from this readiness to face the possibility or likelihood of imminent defeat, but also this strong intimation of a will to hold out for the long term despite the current odds. Indeed, I would suggest that the crucial difference between 'political song' in the authentic sense of that phrase and 'political song' in the broader, non-qualitative sense that would include, say, 'Rule Britannia' or 'God Save the Queen' has precisely to do with whether or not some particular song is able to express so complex a range of highly charged and powerfully motivating sentiments.

5

To explain in detail how these feelings are combined in the best, most potent and moving political songs is no doubt a task for literary criticism and music analysis rather than for someone, like myself, making forays into that region where aesthetics overlaps with politics and where both intersect with the elusive domain of musical ontology. We can take a lead from Badiou's conception of being and event as forever bound up in an asymptotic process of discovery – an open-ended dialectic of 'infinite truth' and approximative states of knowledge – that is driven on from one landmark stage to the next by the powers of creative, inventive, paradigm-transformative or progressively oriented thought. This conception in its detailed working out by Badiou is one that very aptly captures the 'transitory ontology' of political song. It does so through a bringing together of art, politics and – improbably enough – those formal procedures that he finds most strongly represented in the history of set-theoretical advances from Cantor to the present day. What this enables us to think is a conception of art that would endorse none of those received ideas – least of all Kantian ideas about aesthetic disinterest or beauty as the product of an ideal harmony between the faculties in a state of perfect disengagement from all aesthetically extraneous matters – that have left such a deep imprint even on philosophies of art that expressly disavow them. On the other hand, Badiou can be seen to offer equally powerful arguments against the radically nominalist or conventionalist approach of a thinker such as Nelson Goodman (1976) who would press just as far in the opposite direction, that is, towards a wholesale dissolution of art into the various 'art'-constitutive languages or modes of representation that properly (that is, by agreed upon criteria) serve to define it. Nothing could be further from Badiou's passionate defence of the truth-telling power vested in art, along with his justified suspicion of those – especially followers of Kant – who consign artistic truth to a realm of autonomous or 'purely' aesthetic values wherein that power would languish unexercised. If any meaning attaches to the phrase 'ontology of political song', then Badiou's is the approach that can best accommodate so potent, resilient and endlessly renewable, and yet so protean or context-dependent a genre.

Of course this leaves room for the sceptic to respond by batting my claim right back and asserting that the phrase is indeed meaningless, since even granting that such talk makes sense when applied to objects falling under various regional ontologies – such as those of the physical sciences or Austin's 'medium-sized dry goods' – it doesn't when applied to the kind of ersatz or pseudo-entity in question here. However, if this argument goes through, then the sceptic's case would extend well beyond items such as political song to songs in general, musical works at large, art-works of whatever description (as distinct from their physical tokens or modes of instantiation), and beyond that to abstract entities such as those of mathematics and the formal sciences. The sceptic or the Quinean lover of austere desert landscapes may grasp this nettle without the least compunction and declare – albeit without Quine's blessing, since oddly enough he counted himself a Platonist in matters mathematical – that we are better off dumping all such commitments beyond the ontological-relativist idea that to be *just is* to be the value of a variable which in turn should be deemed nothing more than a matter of what happens to play a certain role in this or that going 'ontological scheme' (Quine 1961; 1969). Badiou's is an ontology which, when applied to political song, holds out against any such wholesale relativist slide, while nonetheless making allowance for the way that its identity-conditions change under shifts in some existing (dominant or emergent) set of socio-political circumstances. In this way it may help us to rethink the character of such works in relation to some of the more restrictive categories of high-cultural or canon-preserving aesthetic discourse. Moreover it offers a litmus-test for issues in musical aesthetics generally, since political song is the most extreme instance of that highly elusive ontological status that characterises all musical works.

Notes

1. See, for instance – from a range of positions – Dodd 2000; 2002; Kivy 1987; Levinson 1990; Norris 2006; Predelli 1995; 2001; Sharpe 1995.
2. See the works cited in note 1; also, for some marvellously deft and subtle meditations on this topic, see Hartman 1970.
3. See especially Kermode 1975; 1988. I discuss this and other aspects of his work in Norris 2011.
4. Schenker 1979. For some representative critiques and revaluations, see Blasius 1996; Narmour 1977; Siegel 1990; Treitler 1989: 67–78.
5. For some highly relevant (and in many ways heartening) social-historical-political background, see *We are women, we are strong . . .* (Sheffield: Sheffield Women Against Pit Closures, 1987).
6. For a detailed introduction, see Norris 2009.
7. See especially Badiou, 'Being: Multiple and Void. Plato/Cantor' and 'Theory of the Pure Multiple: Paradoxes and Critical Decision' (2005a: 21–77, 38–48); also 'Ontology is Mathematics' and 'The Subtraction of Truth' (2004a: 1–93, 95–160).
8. For a highly accessible introduction to these and other relevant chapters in the history of modern mathematics, see Badiou 2008a; also Potter 2004.
9. For a full-scale elaboration of these themes across a wide range of subject areas, see Badiou 2009a.

8

Love in the Time of the Communist Hypothesis

Norman Madarasz

In Alain Badiou's system, love and the political are both presented as discourses that condition philosophy insofar as the production of truths is concerned. As much as these discourses partake of a similar structure of truth production, the subjective forms that convey this production are distinct, autonomous and even compossible. Therefore, there is no metadiscourse from which to organise, foresee or anticipate the truths created in their local existence, that is, in their specific content. Badiou's configuration, though, does project the eventuality of supplements in the production of truths. Supplements are organised along an identical vector: radical reinvention. In love, this reinvention invokes the coupled subject, which turns lust into love and undermines pornography as an instance of shareholder sex. In politics, reinvention goes by the communist hypothesis, a discontinuous project incommensurable to any necessary association with the past disasters committed in its name. The aim of this chapter is to inquire as to how these two conditions merge within the philosophical claim for a communism of the multiple.

From the perspective of contemporary philosophy, juxtaposing love and communism leads without much delay to the work of Alain Badiou. It is true that Toni Negri and Michael Hardt consider a 'political act of love' possible. It is the spark of a future revolution, in which the combination of the opportunity of *kairos* and the insistency of desire enables the time of the multitude (Hardt and Negri 2004: 356–8). For Badiou, nothing destines love to twine with the political, although sex and politics are clearly a different story. Nothing destines love to bind with politics, even were we to consider love as well as politics as processes of thought. As the poet Fernando Pessoa's heteronym, Alberto Caeiro, utters, in a citation often repeated by Badiou, 'to love is to

187

think'.[1] Nonetheless, nothing destines love to force a union that is the incarnation of a thought insofar as it is novel. Nothing, that is, beyond a certain dynamic involved in the reinvention of self.

In this sense, Badiou asserts that there exists a fundamental distinction between sexual desire and love. As he puts it: 'Desire is immediately powerful but love also requires care and re-takes (*reprises*). Love knows all about the need for re-working' (Badiou 2012e: 84–5), in the sense that the poet Arthur Rimbaud would utter in *A Season in Hell*, 'As we know, love needs reinventing'.[2] Yet what is this love of which Rimbaud speaks? Wherefore art thou love? In Badiou's system, love as well as political invention are presented as discourses, indeed as discursive practices, that condition philosophy insofar as truth is produced in and through them. As much as the discourses present common aspects in the production of truths, the subjective forms that vehicle this production are distinct and autonomous, albeit compossible. Therefore there is no metadiscourse from which the truths produced would be organised, maintained or predicted. However, philosophy does intuit supplements to the discursive practices in the essential contingency of the entire process of production. This would be specific to the concept of generic truth.

The specific supplement appearing in the emancipatory ambition of organised politics is the concept of radical reinvention. This is the side of politics Badiou sees as conditioning philosophy: the right side, that is, that of the radical Left. Just as reinvention structurally points to the change that even power politics cannot afford to forget, so too does it prompt the inner dynamic of love. Love as a condition of philosophy is best understood as the experiential field in which the forms of the couple spin into variation and yield to an unfolding through which we get ousted on to an unrecognisable self. Such a description glosses Lacan on desire, of course, which we must distance from anything Badiou suggests about love. But prior to locating love in relation to the Other, which is an inclination when we consider the radical novelty Badiou seeks to emphasise in his reading of the subject of love, one also risks hastily positing what might ultimately be a category of the absolute. Instead what is required is a category of otherness.

Love is one of the conditions by which the new is triggered and the subjective process enabled. This also means that when Badiou speaks of love, he does not exactly describe the loving condition of the human animal. He leads us to an ontological love experience.

Though a culture of individualism might not easily lend credence to its ontological reality, this perspective on love is no less romantic than what comes to change our daily lives as persons. Whether this love, though, comes to fulfil ideals or dreams already crafted in childhood will have to be determined in due course. By definition, ontological love can only be more intense, regardless of the fact that Badiou's assertive rationality might induce some doubt about this claim. To that extent, not only is love thinking; it is also the essence of working.

The aim of the present inquiry is not merely to retrace Badiou's conception of love but to strike the definitive chord for the renewed depth of rationality and systematic thought he advocates as being part of the subjective process in the area of emancipatory politics. This means approaching the thought of radical politics through the experience of reinvented love.

Two essays, 'What is Love?' and 'The Scene of the Two', both of which were initially given as talks in the wake of *Being and Event*, show Badiou completing his systemic project of steering philosophical discourse towards an examination of the inner structure and subjective mode of each of the conditions, the aim being to demonstrate the soundness of his ontology of the multiple and concept of generic set. Following several commentaries and critiques, written primarily by women (see, e.g., Copjec 2005; MacCannell 2005; McNulty 2005; Jaques 1999), Badiou has returned to further articulate the import of love, locally and generally, for the phenomenology of truths. While the conference essays from the 1990s redesign the Lacanian dichotomy of desire and love, I argue that they ought to be recast in light of the communist hypothesis and the arguments presented in *In Praise of Love*. As such, while Badiou's insights give a new positive as well as critical perspective on philosophical thought about love, they are to be valued for what has been shown to be one of the structures, and not merely ethical principles, behind the new speculations on emancipation that the communist hypothesis posits.

I

Communism is more akin to a hammer than to love, Mao Zedong was once quoted as saying, since it is used to crush the enemy. Yet to disclaim the idea that revolutionary engagement, and furthermore engagement in building a communist society, stems from an act of love would misrepresent the difference between power politics and the political as a process of creating new truths. This amounts to preaching to the converted when voiced in a chapter of a book on the thought of Alain Badiou. It does not change the general fact that the political act is often exiled from the feeling of love.

That communism would leave personal amorous relations as we know them today intact seems to be an error in expectation and projection of what justice and egalitarianism entails for the human ethos, the human background in a truly emancipated setting. Is love a modality of the same and the immutable? Do its signs partake of gestures and acts that spread in a continuous curve from non-human animal experience to that of human? Love may not be constant, but when it does arise its ontology often suggests something of the same is at work. After all, how is it that we represent love as an invariable of the human condition? At times, love seems to possess an eternal subjective disposition, partly or entirely motivated by a genetic drive for self-preservation and auto-immunity. At others, it works as a matrix structured by the spatial and historical specificities of the language used to intensify the body's subjective expression. Either of these sightings seems to miss one of the main factors behind love's creative stimuli on any animal being caught in its thrall. The factor of surprise and utter transformation is part and parcel of general experience. A rare experience of self-modification comes about through a contingent encounter with some other being. Were this picture to sketch what love's first steps are about, an understanding of love would then have to focus on how it is enabled by such contingency.

In many of the experiences we take for granted, what is ordinary tends to occlude the manifestation of what might be universal in its implications. Love is certainly of that variety of experience, although it is also one to have accompanied human cultural evolution throughout its various twists and turns. Today we lie in an age of divorce. Deep doubts have destabilised the legal and religious orthodoxy surrounding the monogamous relationship. The main move to bolster a return to monogamous marriage seems to come from the gay and lesbian populations. A desire for marriage might ebb and flow, but love is what provides the steady tide. It is often put to banal uses, but its far-reaching value makes living worthwhile.

From a philosophical perspective, love is yet another human

experience that lifts individuals out of partiality, limitedness and normality. Love seems pointless if limited to the single person, the mirror reflection or the One. This is mainly why love is ontological, and why philosophy has given so much attention to its diverse expressions. To use one of Badiou's central concepts, love names a dimension of subjective experience enabled by an event. Love, then, is ontological to the extent that it harbours the creation of the new, the novel and the mutational drive needed for formal difference to be exerted (Badiou 2004b). Love also just happens to partake of a process of emancipation, emancipation from the misguided will to remain an individual identity.

Charles Sanders Peirce once observed that 'love is not directed to abstractions but to persons; not to persons we do not know, or to numbers of people, but to our own dear ones, our family and neighbours' (1992: 354). In his highly speculative essay from 1893, 'Evolutionary Love', Peirce nonetheless attempts to merge scientific reasoning with religious faith in an attempt to expand the horizon of what is 'dear' to us. By means of a theory of progressive love, Peirce is able to establish a fuller sense of the term 'evolution', which he deems is better understood as creative love, appropriately denominated *agapism*. Although Peirce steeps his reasoning as much in John's Gospel as in Hegel, the working definition he provides of agapism is striking in its materialist potential: 'In genuine agapism . . . advance takes place by virtue of a positive sympathy among the created springing from continuity of mind. This is the idea which tychasticism [i.e., evolution by fortuitous variation] knows not how to manage' (1992: 362).

The latter concept of tychasticism is plausible as a surface description of 'advance' in local fields with delimited parameters and patterns. Tychasticism underscores how a scientific perspective on focused change has to be prepared in order to give weight to the singularity of events, even if the latter shows an inclination to deviate from the linear course of what simulations and intuitive guesses inductively suggest as to what will most likely be its causal aftermath. As such, tychasticism is a bona fide event-based theory of subjective progression. Yet if it is insufficient to explain an affect such as 'sympathy', which Peirce describes as 'springing from continuity of mind', this follows from an overly rigid separation of structure and contingency, or what could be put in contemporary terms as the rift between structure and function.

We are living in a highly significant moment in the annals of political history. The structural rape of the commonwealth that had been acquired from decades of struggle and conquests has prompted a stern look back at two centuries of communist history. This is our opportunity. In that regard, it is remarkable to discover that one of the structural principles fostered by agapism has it that love, far from Peirce's conviction regarding its 'creative', that is, purposive force, also denotes its impact on the continuity of mind when the latter is applied to a broader project. Now, for Peirce, this broader project is continuity between 'man's mind and the Most High' (1992: 364). As seen through agapism, this is the phenomenon of what Peirce refers to as 'divination of genius', that is, of what 'may affect an individual, independently of his human affections, by virtue of an attraction it exercises upon his mind, even before he has comprehended it' (1992: 364). As conceived from Badiou's perspective, the concept of agapism acquires the subjective depth of an 'event', which its representation as tychasticism had kept at the margins. It describes the quadrangular relationship between the human animal, the event, subjective emergence and the event site.

A model that seeks to integrate the event as a principle goes beyond a doctrine of chance variations, like tychasticism, as it blends radical contingency with a subjective makeover. In this sense, though, there is nothing that destines continuity of mind to extend to a transcendent sphere, at least not until one of the major promises of political creativity has been exhausted as well. That promise suggests that continuity ought indeed to be seen as an abstraction, that is, the abstraction of an emerging, yet still formless, generic subject-figure irreducible both to the individual as well as to the 'Most High'. Despite Peirce's conviction, we have an abstraction here that is clearly a formative heartfelt experience. Love can both change, and be changed, by a political experience in which the novel subjective form unleashed by an event requires an egalitarian ethic to be its guiding principle, as well as its guideline for acquiring some formal manifestation.

2

Returning to the relationship between love and communism, revolution, contrary to Mao's view, ought to be tested through love's formative strengths. To fail to do so on principle would be to fall prey to a set of fallacies that has contributed so awkwardly to demonising a notion whose moral principle is by no means foreign to the other great love doctrine on which many of our societies were built: Christianity. As a moral principle, communism is an offspring of Christian moral thought and the Golden Rule. It is certainly much more so than the kill or be killed, or publish or perish mentality by which consumerist democracies function with respect to professional accomplishment. On what grounds does democratic idealism uphold its moral superiority over political systems other than by having capitalism submit to its ethics of solidarity, logic of care and sisterhood, and joining together for a common public purpose? When it comes to characterising political visions as idealist, liberal democracy supersedes communism only insofar as it believes it possible to tame the logic of capital as if it were a domestic pet. But as is well known, there is no shortcoming as evident as democracy's failure to do precisely that, both in economic practice and military logistics. There is no dearth of facts pointing to how democracy is ever prepared to undo itself so as to pledge subservience to plutocrat capitalists, whether the message is put in terms of the determinacy and inescapability of some human nature, or for the objective needs of 'trickle down' results of cutthroat competition and obsessive growth. We are still at a state in which democracy is a political slave.

It is trivial, for our philosophical purposes, to recall the socialist nature of early Christian community projects – although Badiou's particular interest, as far as late antiquity is concerned, would lie more in Spartacus than in Christ. In Spartacus' case, the fact of creating a fugitive society of equals is the phenomenological side to the ontological fact of its creation as an unprecedented collective body.[3] Throughout his work on love, Badiou emphasises what Joan Copjec has formulated as 'the difference between the community and the horde' (Copjec 2005: 120). According to Copjec, from Freud's Group Psychology and the Analysis of the Ego to Lacan's seminar on Antigone, the condition of presenting a doctrine on love in psychoanalysis has depended on making 'woman a positive force against the stultifying order of the horde or "group spirit" rather than a kind of unfortunate flaw, responsible for the crumbling of every community' (2005: 120–1). The question at the heart of Badiou's concept of love is how explicitly he, too, requires woman as a condition of the philosophical concept of subject.

Badiou's juxtaposition of love and politics as types of thought also depends on what lies in the further depths of the Freudian and

Lacanian texts cited. That is to say, his promotion of the hypothesis of a politics without parties is a structural push designed to establish a more radical democratic subject, but can this subject be portrayed as genderless? As if undercutting gender as an ontological necessity, Badiou tears down all logical relations between community members that allow a leader to prevail. In Badiou's critique of the political party in the third phase of the progression of the communist hypothesis, there is a latent critique of the leader figure. Whether a society can exist without a leader, can rise to transparency and become reality is something the hypothesis is very reluctant to assert without further historical analysis. The question of power is its unnamed dilemma.

Far from the state-controlled economies of the Soviet sphere of influence, the phase of communism in which parties are successfully shed would truly effectuate the withering away of the state apparatus. Yet it does allow for the permanence of a state, provided there are reasons to believe it can immunise civil society against its internal drive to accumulate and individualise power. How can one go about tilling and producing and enjoying internet and cellphone connections when threatened by armed groups of assassins, big or small, from machete-wielding thugs to joy-sticked drones, without a state providing protection and enforcing a conception of moral law? The condition according to which a state could be maintained as a functional apparatus is by guaranteeing not rights, but the moral norms that the novel subject installs collectively. In the communist hypothesis, there is no withering away of the state without the creation of a new collective structure. To examine this claim, take Liberation Theology as a living argument for the need to wither the state away, since its grassroots work in the base ecclesial communities was regularly undermined and threatened by state police and the Vatican's threat to excommunicate both practitioners and priests. Yet its organisational form and principles of moral governance sought to fill the vacuum produced by state structures turned terrorist, to which Vatican officials most often turned a cool, blind eye.

Even the most diehard of libertarians in the Pentecostal belts of the US, Ontario or Rio de Janeiro State call for the radical withdrawal or even disappearance of government from our daily lives. How is this fundamentally opposed to the Marxian ideal of the withering away of the state in order to achieve the ethical prescription of equality? In formal or generic terms, equality will have had to occur universally as a means of accomplishing truth as subjectively composed through structuration. Economic equality on the back of cognitive solidarity and civic sisterhood continues to be the means and ends of the revolutionary process – regardless of its projected 'idealism', and the arduous 'discipline' required to work towards it. The figure of the 'dictatorship of the proletariat' might, for more delicate Western sensibilities or psychopathic reactionaries, evoke childhood fears of bomb shelters and hungry wolf-like glares of conquest and destruction from Siberian soldiers. (Perhaps such images of the Red Russians are merely memorabilia, ever since blood-eyed, trance-induced Islamist 'fanatics' in Pakistan began to grace the front passages of *Newsweek* and Canada's *National Post*. Despite how difficult, indeed impossible, it is to accept the Islamists' anti-discourse of terrorism, it is fundamental to recognise that insofar as they symbolise something contrary to emancipation, it is not unlike our own societies' submission to bold technology prowess. As André Tosel puts it succinctly in Thesis 42 on 'Capitalist Globalization and a Possible Communism': 'Islamophobia is a crusade ideology that breeds upon Western theological-political populist furor while covering over the process of counter-emancipation in course [in our own society]' [2009: 16].) What state 'democracies' have shown in even clearer ways since the collapse of the Soviet zone is precisely how it is the state-governmental apparatus that holds the guarantees to acquiring or maintaining privileges, and not the market much-vaunted by neoliberal ideologues for its supposed rationality and independence. To guarantee reproduction of privilege, the state has to have recourse to the use of violence. Yet sovereignty as embodied by the state is an idea with a moral, or indeed, political origin, an acting idea, just as those posited by Badiou as partaking of the third historical sequence of communism.

The cycle of structural instability thus placates love by distorting its novel subjective experiences in the dead-end of fused bodies and souls. There is nothing astonishing in the fact that widespread depression is its logical outcome. What the reinvention of love can mean for philosophy is a liberation of a broader subjectivity that shapes a dual figure whose dynamic is to take up and assert again. Taking up, in this sense, is not merely repeating. The category of 'compulsion to repeat', to which psychoanalysis has stoically lent its gaze, reveals a part of this dynamic, but only, as Deleuze would say, as an eternal return of the same. The reinvention of love being advocated here incorporates, by contrast, the logic of radical difference as act. And this is exactly how Badiou situates the local logic of difference in his system – it is a mode of the generic set, which is what fundamentally legitimates difference in ontology.

3

John Protevi does well to point out that Deleuze presents his theory of love as a material actualisation of the virtual dimension of the body without organs. To accomplish this, Deleuze and Guattari set up, as part of the molecular revolution, a mechanism whereby the radically new is filtered twice, as it were, in order to rid it of capitalist-born sediment. As Protevi writes, 'revolutionary desire as sketched out in *Anti-Oedipus* is a desire for higher intensity in an encounter of multiple flows on a body without organs. Schizo love is only unleashed at the level of the multiple flows unhooked from a statistically dominant pattern' (Protevi 2003: 188).

This is why the body without organs can be so closely compared to the presentational plane in Badiou, the dynamism prior to any counting of the multiple. Badiou reads Deleuze (and Guattari) literally and considers his essential difference with Deleuze to be the latter's contextualising the body without organs in the quasi-assertiveness of the virtual. For Badiou, presentation as the real boundlessness of multiplicity is effective, real, albeit, by definition and principle, it cannot be represented. Trying to quantify the presentation plane introduces the count-for-one, an inescapable gesture since the possibility of thought is predicated upon it. The task, however, is to think multiplicity as also proving the need for an immanent strategy of thought whose perspective is receptive, even if momentarily and uncertainly, of the non-denumerable formlessness of the presentational plane.

The relentless questioning of the Deleuzean strategy thus bears out Badiou's recurrent claim that the real point of divergence with Deleuze is in their respective theories of subject. Deleuze's main focus is on processes of possible forms of subjectivation, regardless of whether they achieve some form of concrete existence. This is why Deleuze offers no theory of history beyond the narrative accounts of novel subjective experiences that are analysed almost exclusively for their creative component. Narratives such as Thomas de Quincey's *Revolt of the Tartars*, cited by Deleuze in *The Fold*, along with French psychiatrist G. G. Clérambault's descriptions of women erotically obsessed with the sensation of fabrics and the cry of silks, possess Deleuze because of what it is possible to achieve with a few arguments even by indirect inductive means: such narratives show the real continual process of the emergence of form from formless agitation. Few arguments, and perhaps no theories of history: the site of subjective emergence exists at a preformative affective level in Deleuze.

By contrast, Badiou rejects the virtual and accepts formative subjective processes only as strictly delimited by a real subject-structure. This formation has an ontological basis, argues Badiou, but only insofar as ontology is understood as inseparable from the simultaneously operating conditions and allows for an objective expansive component in set-theoretic terms, from which choice may proceed. Badiou's rejection of all transcendence from his ontology in favour of immanence is not merely an assertion: it is uttered from within the depths of the multiple configuration that makes the system operate.

This, in turn, points to the ontological destination of love and leads one to explore its perimeters according to Badiou's system. In this system, difference is not an ontological category per se, but instead is asserted specifically in experience and in worldly trials, according to two theses that are formed from within the love condition:

T1: There are two positions in experience: $M \perp W$.
T2: These two positions are totally disjointed:
$[(t \leq M) \text{ and } (t \leq W)] \rightarrow t = 0$. (Badiou 1992: 256–7)

Subject forms in the discourse of love do not reduce to the members of the couple. A stroke of genius might lead a spouse to grasp the truth of the couple, but Badiou here aims at structure and not luck. He defines the subject-couple as 'what, of love, is visible for a third party' (1992: 262). It follows that this visibility has no consistency within the subject. Given that the subject is unrecognisable in any total or positive manner from outside its zone of proximal development, as it were, 't' is indeed equal to zero.

Therefore, to catch the transformative importance of love in the time of the communist hypothesis, we need to analyse the singular position that Badiou attributes to love in the argument on the possibility of philosophy operating in a world of the *Two* as counted by a non-existent third: duplicity or radical difference in experience, disjunction between the two positions, as if it could be perceived from without. Hence, the need for symbolic equations. Radical reinvention of self is predicated upon immersion in a subjective structure with no conscious and embodied assertion of a renewed individuality.

Similarly, Badiou's aim to distinguish what he terms the subjective nature of the communist hypothesis is predicated upon a reworked concept of subject that, as of yet, has no bearing on its own truth. The hypothesis does not stem causally from the depleted forms of historically attempted projects of communist governance inspired by the Bolshevik Revolution, even if the latter did incorporate, at one point, a sexual revolution. At a purely historical level, one could easily argue that the disaster suffered by the Soviet Revolution in the Stalinist purges, the Nazi invasion and slaughter of some twenty-five million Soviet citizens in the Second World War, as well as the Soviet Union's exclusion from international post-war reconstruction policies, destroyed the ability of the administrative framework to be able to realise anything but the most instrumental implementation of an egalitarian society. As long ago as this was, there is apparent continuity in at least economic objectives. Causality in the communist idea may be observed, although it would be a mistake to ground the subjective structure in contingent conditions.

In this regard it may be asked, if there indeed was a sexual revolution involved in the political structure of the revolutionary subject, then what has become of love? Badiou observes that in love the external enemy does not exist. The hypothesis asserts that love would be transformed by the reconfigured subjective structure in a communist context. Paranoid and jealous fantasies are inevitable threats to a political subject that involve massive change to individual material possession. As such, it is self-interest that threatens the amorous subject – as it also does political, scientific and artistic subjects. In Badiou's argument on the ethic of truths, all self-interest that prompts a shift against the subject in formation also undermines the subjective mode by which the structure binds the new to the production of truths. Fidelity to the truth procedure is torn asunder by betrayal.

Thus, from T_1 and T_2, set within the subjective truth-producing structure, we get the following definition of love: 'love is both an exceptional infinity of existence, which creates the split within the One by the event and the energy of a meeting, and the ideal becoming of an ordinary emotion, of an anonymous seizing of this existence' (Badiou 2006e: 41). Insofar as truths are accomplished in the process a subject form acquires structural stability, which is quite opposite to the molecular revolutionary process as understood by Deleuze and Guattari.

It might seem odd in this characterisation that the productive forces precede the producer, and the encounter the acting-subject. Badiou's argument is that the event renders a previous subjective form indeterminate regarding choice and consciousness, and regarding its activity or passivity. The event prompts human animals to name or recognise it, prompts them to make a decision, regardless of whether it is immediate or not, or whether a specific human animal is part of a subjective form in truth procedure. Structurally speaking, Badiou's event is a concept that makes causal succession only as relevant as other secondary processes of prompting, influence or self-aware motivation. What counts is immanent, interruptive force.

The event entails a rupture with the general state of things, with the local state that might attempt to fix the event crisis situation according to the logic and protocol of identification in a representational system. This base situation is axiomatically postulated as comprising the unreflected coexistence of infinite multiples. In its interruptive force, the event represents the contingent surging forth of non-being, that is, that which in its unprecedented being precedes the possible in thought. As such, indexing the radical novelty of an event to the way of understanding it would constitute a contradiction to the defining principle of the situation. However, with respect to the state of the situation, the love encounter exceeds its law(s).

To see what Badiou means by the love event's extra-legal, or illegal, framework, it is appropriate to consider couplings between whites and African-Americans in the US, Jews and Palestinians in Israel or Gaza, Christian-orthodox Serbs and Bosnian Muslims during the siege of Sarajevo; or to recall the unforgettable games of betrayal and hate between the Montecchio and Capuleto families; or to fantasise about the locking embrace of two youths from heterogeneous and homo-affective worlds (but less perhaps about the hapless couple drunkenly sprawled kissing on a riot-torn street on Stanley Cup final night in Vancouver in 2011). Desire shifts to love if and only if the reason for an encounter turns a couple into a truth with respect to which the situation's law is recognised by everyone as being their own. Yet as opposed to an unconscious version of the categorical imperative, this recognition simultaneously refutes the legitimacy of the current configuration called world.

Insofar as truths are produced, what begins as a subjective formation or process is determined as subject merely in the form of bodies, works or sequences. To be sure, we are required to expand our understanding here of what truth ought to mean. Truth in the condition of love has little content to share with the truth created within politics, and even less to share with truth in the two other conditions, science and art, that are part of Badiou's system. In terms of love, it is again Rimbaud who can guide us in deciphering the acts of the subject, when in the conclusion to *A Season in Hell* he writes that happiness is a condition in which one is 'able now to possess the truth within one soul and one body'.[4] The poet's silence, however, should not be taken to double what could be perceived as a subject's necessary destiny: 'the real subject of a love is the becoming of the couple and not the mere satisfaction of the individuals that are its component parts' (Badiou 2012e: 90). In relational terms, we can say that lovers are nothing prior to the encounter that binds them together, though they may very well be breeders in the natural reproductive and sex-offender cycle.

Through these formal definitions of the love subject, the radical Two structuring any 'couple' t, it is possible to understand that Badiou's vision of love does not fail to be steeped in a deviant romanticism. As he writes, 'happiness in love is the proof that time can accommodate eternity' (2012e: 48). He asks himself how a radically new subject of love can protect itself in its unlimited happiness, when the energy of the encounter, of amorous passion, becomes subject to the claws of religions and states, when it is made vulnerable to state institutions that seek only to channel, limit and dominate its new shape and form.

It is precisely for this reason that we would be mistaken to believe that the concept of the Two as applied to a love-subject is a matter of monogamous conservatism in Badiou. I refer here to T2, now voiced from *within* the condition of love, according to which the definition grows in complexity: love produces a truth of the situation such that disjunction becomes a law for it. Just as the separation between philosophy and its amorous condition ensures one of the lines of transparency by which the new ontology is manifest as a science of multiplicity, so too is love never given in the immediate consciousness of the loving individualised subject, but instead in the distance separating the lovers as if in the inverted yoga of ontological Kama Sutra.

The real consequence is that, from the ontological perspective, the becoming of love as the Two can be mapped as a couple only as the subjectivation of a polarity, of a separation, albeit within a union. For Badiou, this plays out as the condition *sine qua non* without which the recognition of differences would fall short. By contrast, from the phenomenological perspective, subjectivity is not a merely formal distribution of positions, but ultimately an incorporation of polar energy. In the figure of love, fidelity is the process of maintaining the lovers in a logic of difference, under the figure of the Two, instead of one of identity and totalisation, which more accurately characterises the fusion of unified couples in a One. The latter represents a reversion, then, since it con-stitutes a return to transcendence, or, in Lacanian terminology, which is precisely what Badiou takes as his point of departure, to the phallic function. According to Lacan, the phallic function matches the description of the logocentric state of the situation insofar as the sexual pleasure triggered in it is the 'obstacle by which man falls short of feeling ... the sexual pleasure of the woman's body. And precisely because he comes to climax from the pleasure of the member ... he does not relate to the Other as such' (Lacan 1972–73: 15, 17–18). Clearly, the Two fails to function here as the sum of two units, but rather operates as an immanent figure of disjunction.

To the extent that the state of the situation is ruled by the logic of the One, love's potential remains a private affair, as it were. Badiou's thesis aims at a specificity of love that the realities of the world would force it to abandon. This is why 'Love cannot be reduced to any law. There is no law of love' (Badiou 2012e: 79). Lovers are fundamentally alone in this world, with no pro-tection in relation to society. Not even secularism (or its French version *laicité*) provides shelter to its blossoming form. From the ontological perspective, this solitude evokes the truth that '[lovers] alone possess that difference by which they experience the world' (Badiou 2012e: 79). The upshot of such immanence is that the Two of love is not a figure present to substantial transparency. The 'amorous relationship' demonstrates its singularity by not being a 'relation'. As a non-relation, the couple is a phenomenon held in pure difference so long as both bodies stand in unified separation.

The non-relation inscribes sexual difference insofar as Badiou strives to show that polarities are equivalent to the variations between the polar positions of Man and Woman.

However, in his thesis on sexuation, that is, sexual difference, Badiou asserts that, although a term of connection might exist between Man and Woman, the term of equality of positions as positions remains without due formulation and is indeterminate to any gendered bipolarity. The third term is said to be 'atomic' in relation to sexual difference. Atomism exhibits the particularity of Being prior to the One. Because it is located on the edge of the thinkable, this affirmation probably exceeds any single interpretation. This is why the third atomic term is not likely to be analysed positively as an attempt to conciliate between opposed interpretations. Contrary to Lacan's position, in which love is a supplement to sex, Badiou argues that love is what reaches towards the 'edge of Being' (1992: 256). Therein, as expressed by Rimbaud, love needs reinventing, every time, reinterpreting and reiterating, in a new understanding of its proximity to the enigma of Being and the event's lack of certainty.

In the phenomenology of truths in the logics of worlds, this projects as much to isolated couples as to lovers who mix love with lust. In the distribution of terms in the ethics, sex would belong to our condition as human animals prior to good and evil. Faced with a mouldable imaginary, the human animals that we are reach orgasm with mere scraps of desire. The reinforced consciousness of a sexed-up ego even goes as far as to allow Lacan's concept of the symbolic, to justify how sex is, after all, part of our spiritual, genetic and ontological makeup. Only in silence is its equivalence to death beheld. What love accomplishes instead, in Badiou's redistribution of the registers of the symbolic, is an inversion of pleasure into happiness, in as natural an Aristotelian sentiment as would go unnoticed were it not pronounced by a gesturing Platonist. An inversion of fidelity occurs here in which love becomes the truth of sex, because love is the subjectivation of a desire for sexual possession of a present or absent object, that is, the subjectivation of sexual pleasure itself in fulfilment.

4

We encounter in the condition of love, as in the other respective conditions, the criteria and terms grounding the thought of the

multiple irreducible to the One, here associated with phallogo-
centrism. The Two of love remains the structural separation of
the lovers who keep themselves tied in the relation that is not one:
neither an inclusive relation nor one of fusion. This is why Badiou
offers a second definition of love as a 'successful struggle against
separation' (2012e: 91). This is the condition to keep the couple
going, to guarantee its permanence by means of the vow to fidelity. Still, this is less the case of an empirical couple even within
separation than it is that of an organised singularity. The form of
the subject in which the couple is found can be universalised only
insofar as the bodies incarnate defined polarities in relation to the
Two of love, polarities that are definite and separated, like the
damning of Sodom and Gomorrah, in which each 'sex' stays on its
side until the end of civilisation (Badiou 1999b). The base of this
polarity is irreducible sexual difference.

In the essay, 'What is Love', from 1991, and the book *In Praise
of Love*, first published in 2009, we find examples of what the
amorous subject is in individuals. In *Saint Paul: The Foundation
of Universalism*, published in France in 1997, and the essay 'The
Scene of the Two', from 2000, Badiou presents figures of couples
comprising peoples, variables or masses. For example, in *Saint
Paul*, the universal figure of the Christian is not a fusion or a synthesis, but a separation in the plausible relationship between two
complementary positions. Adjoined, they convey a universal force,
one that holds distinct the positions of the Jew and Greek, or the
slave and freeman as in Gal. 3: 28. This logic of unified separation determines the figure of love in Badiou, as it also exceeds any
grounding in a typical Christian experience. The two polarities
appear equal, although not in relation to each other, but in relation to the third atomic term, even if the term is not expressed in
the form of a position. Hence, the third thesis Badiou presents in
his formula of the love-subject avoids submission to a transcendent figure:

> Thesis 3: There is no third position: $(\exists\ t)$ [not $(t \leq W)$ and not
> $(t \leq M)$].

In other words, to speak about love, to speak in accordance with
a mode to be included in its logic, there is a need for an event.
But an event does not represent an opening on to a transcendent
substance, or form, which could amount to merely justifying an

encounter. Instead, the encounter makes each component of the Two both active and passive: passive regarding the circumstances of the event, and active regarding the decision to recognise and perpetuate its truthfulness. As such, the event takes on the nature of an immanent exception to what already exists, which is what Badiou refers to as 'humanity':

> Thesis 4: There exists only one humanity. Humanity is the *historical* body of truths, and thus untotalisable: M ∪ W ≠ 1. (Badiou 1992: 257–8)

The demonstration of this thesis is asserted as follows: if a variable x, that is, the 'immanent exception', is active, or activated as subject in a generic procedure of the production of truths, then there exists also that which admits this variable x as an argument, that is, as included in the logic of the subject. That which admits a variable is defined as humanity, insofar as its condition is a base from which identity is a logical operator. But a variable is applicable since identity is but one operator, perhaps not even its main or initial operator. However, humanity accepts the existence of difference, even self-reflexively, as in any first order system. Yet difference is located mainly as an operator according to another logic. This is why, to supplement T1, according to which there are two positions in experience, an additional minor thesis is required to concretise separation:

> Thesis 4b: One position exists, as does another.

The scene of the Two of love thus shifts to the scene of humanity, which is a formal term that Badiou links to two sources: Marx's concept of species being and logician Paul Cohen's concept of a set whose elements and order is unknown, but whose extension is potentially universal. The true meeting between two subjects becomes the reaffirmation of humanity in its autonomy as faced with the unconscious and with the sexual connection expressed in Lacan's axiom 'the sexual relation does not exist'. It is precisely in order to compensate for this fundamental inexistence of the super-structural or illusory conception of the sexual relation in Lacan that Badiou activates the position of 'love is what comes to supplement (*supplée*) the impossibility of a sexual relation' (Lacan 1972–73: 44).

Insofar as there is supplementation in love, as we argued at the beginning of this essay, it is of the order of reinvention. The defining moment in the emergence of the amorous subject is the nomination of the encounter-event. For the most part, it goes by the expression 'I love you'. Fidelity to these words, to this demonstrative act, is manifested in daily strokes by the repeated decision to continue in the subjective configuration. Love fits into the dialectic of repetitions, variations and permutations of the words 'I love you', but the form taken by the subjective emergence is what ultimately checks whether the event has been consumed. That process of verification, then, is what is available from the perspective of an external non-existence, although not to any of the poles alone.

The equality of the two lovers faced with the third unattainable perspective is inscribed in the specific terms of an equality between extremes. In the project to resolve this difference with Lacan, Badiou names the poles with the terminology of sexuation: the masculine and feminine poles. However, he does admit in a talk given in 2008 that these denominations are made 'for the sake of convenience' (Badiou 2008f). To be sure, it is uncomfortable for duality to be evoked, biological names detected or even gender terminology enforced. The reduction of sexuation to hetero-affection in Badiou's work could be suspect. Yet the objectivity of formalism should make attempts to finally capture dogmatic instances in Badiou's system seem hasty.

Still, some would argue that just as his vision of the political 'generic' is essentially anti-democratic, so too there exists in his theory of love a unidirectional reading, that is, a perspective centred on the heterosexual, a heterologocentrism, despite this not being at any moment defined in Badiou's specific and written assertions.[5] Badiou's declarations stand against the temptation to exclude others. That extends to what 'humanity' designates and denotes. In humanity, one ought to include the land we tread upon whose exploitation we cannot allow without a fight. Agapism, for example, will be plausibly annulled if the current slaughter of bees around the world due to exploitational techniques of pollination, pesticide use and acarid infestation increase merely to satisfy human 'needs'. Nothing should exclude from the concept of 'humanity' an agent that is estimated to be indirectly responsible for roughly 33 per cent of our food consumption (Moore and Kosut 2012: 29). The work of bees in pollinating flowering crop plants of different varieties reveals the scope of the more expansive human reality in which the growth of the Two is stifled. Further still, Badiou argues forcefully for the need to balance the sexual paradigm in Greek antiquity, between homoerotic love and women's strategic withholding of heterosexual sex to preserve love for citizens, friend and family in the Polis, as Aristophanes portrays in the *Lysistrata* (Badiou 2006e: 37). We come full circle in a separation in union between erotic preference and the systemic needs of a philosophical endeavour.

To the extent that this might the case, we would nonetheless maintain that Badiou's system does not suffer from a subjectivist slant incurred as a result of his terminological choice to denominate the poles of the love-subject in accordance with the gendered heterosexual couple. Still, it is necessary to be radical here. It is critical for the success of the demonstration of the thesis of a universal ontology grounded by a formalism common to the four conditions 027of philosophy that the operations in love not be reduced to the figures of existing subjective forms: more specifically here, the biological man/woman, or male/female as gendered positions. Similarly, in the political condition, a dialectical logic might be introduced, though it would best be done in the phenomenology to avoid any associations with Marx's specific argument on the dialectical movement of history:

> **T2 modified:** $[(t \leq G_m) \text{ and } (t \leq G_w)] \rightarrow t \vee o$,
> where G is the generic multiple, indexed to a qualitative description of m: masculine, and f: feminine, and t: totality, with m and w being $<o, 1, 2, \ldots n>$.

Lacan attributed logical formulations to the symbolic power of the phallus, including the attempt to emphasise woman's singular position in the phallic logic in the definition of 'not-all', in the sense of her logic being 'not entirely' hers. The figure of that woman, inscribed within the logic of phallus, escapes from the mode of allowing the essential something of her position's participation in Being to be captured within that logic. In this sense, we shall keep, in the guise of an objection to Badiou's theory, the pure formal inscription of the two asymmetrical positions of love and the interiority that takes shape in relation to the Two: that is, one polarity recognises that the Two of love is everything and the One nothing, while the other polarity recognises merely the Two of love.

Yet the question of heterocentrism here may not even be the main issue or objection to Badiou's articulation in the 'Scene of the Two'. In the end, it is woman's very position in the formalism that is at risk in the deep split between sex and love. As Juliet Flower MacCannell has asserted 'Badiou has succeeded. He has formalised – to an unparalleled degree – the work of the object *a* in structuring the nonrelation of the sexes and opening the way to the relation that is in excess over them: the supplement called Love' (MacCannell 2005: 174). By attributing an ontological essence to love, he has separated love from the world of discourse, indeed, from the world of the law. In the same stroke, MacCannell emphasises that 'We will not find Women there' (2005: 176). Reading Badiou from his rebuttal of Lacan, especially through Badiou's rejection of Lacan's word-based hope for reconciliation of the non-relation of the sexes through a 'creationist sublimation' and logical reconstruction of the 'Woman-Thing' concept, that is, a concept that maintains woman's otherness free from the totalising structure of man's unconscious, MacCannell takes Badiou's rejection of the law as ontological as well as ontical.

In the final analysis, Badiou's conviction that love would find an innovative and richer expression as a subjective form juxtaposed with a new political subject makes no real distinction about love's corruption in the capitalist framework, in which ever more desire is created through the market's expansion of the commodity base. One of the key criteria for verifying a new configuration would be the inclusion of woman not only in the ontic, but also in the ontological sense, given that Being is expansive in Badiou's view. MacCannell warns that Lacan's interpretations of the Real involve a struggle against the death drive, whereas Badiou stridently believes that 'the Real-as-the-Impossible is precisely what must be compelled to become possible' (2005: 154). MacCannell does not play the conservative, moralist card here. For this, she ought to be commended. However, she leaves us with the preoccupation as to whether, from outside the law (of discourse and the signifier), in an ontology of the unconscious in which mathematics (or 'topology', in her words) expresses the multiple essence of Being, and hence the structure of new subjective forms, Badiou's matheme might not leave 'mad love and universal love to be coextensive' (2005: 174). Mad love in the context of a new communist subject could potentially also express a subjective tendency towards some fanaticism of the 'brotherhood', or disciples. Love would suffer through non-integration of woman in the fundamental structure of change. It would thus be at risk of reverting to mere sexual expression.

Nonetheless, MacCannell does tend to diminish an important aspect of the theory. For all of its situating mathematics or topology outside 'the law', Badiou's set-theoretic universe is one in which the truth receives firmer grounding than it does in poetry, or in religious revelation, or even hermeneutical symbolic interpretation. Truth is an outcome of the clarity and transparency of the deductive principles of bivalent logic and validity. In this regard, the risk of fanaticism is not a justified argument from within mathematics: the dexterity of fidelity is.

The main aspect of the reinvention of democracy in the sense of communism would thus be to accept that the 'big Other' does not exist. A leader can manipulate a subject to prize her liberty, but can never steer the new subject-form towards false promises of equality. Choice remains in the subjective configuration. Liberty is structurally enabled. What has to be conquered is equality. As Žižek goes on to stress in his own contribution to the communist hypothesis, one ought to learn to accept a form of democratic organisation that would be adequate to an awareness of the radical contingency in and through which we are living regarding the possibility for a new subject of emancipatory weight. As such, 'this, perhaps, is the lesson to be learned from the traumas of the twentieth century: to keep Knowledge and the function of the Master as far apart as possible' (Žižek 2009c: 152). The main variables of the hypothesis do not aim, at least not initially, at the question of power or hegemony. Therefore one does not encounter a Gramscian position that reduces the political question to ideological struggle. The name of Marx continues to be pertinent, beyond the culturalist turn of much of Marxist thought after 1968. Badiou contends, however, that at this point of differential repetition, or reinvention, 'making the communist Idea live is an ideological task (and by that fact, a philosophical one). It is not immediately a political task' (Badiou 2009g).

In the concluding sentences to his own analysis, Žižek points to how, of late, the history and memory of some of communism's accomplishments have prompted recent conversions. As this history is submitted to comparative analysis, the crimes committed in its name appear less specific to an allegedly morally corrupt essence in the struggle for more sweeping political change and real economic equality, than to the measures the capitalist colonial powers used to contain and undermine economic and social advance. One cannot merely extrapolate the covert counter-insurgency terrorism developed by the CIA in Latin America as an indication of the general policy the West displayed towards the USSR and the People's Republic of China, but it does give us an indication. The relentless destruction of the peasant and proletarian base of revolutionary movements throughout Latin America, and the arrest, torture and execution of intellectuals and activists involved in the movement, were not specific measures for dealing with local problems. They were part of a broad and sweeping war by capitalists and fascists alike against communism, intent on wreaking maximum havoc and damage.

The word conversion used by Žižek evokes an experience similar to Christian faith. Notwithstanding, Christianity has no monopoly on faith. In a blow against Schmittian arguments that merge secularism within a continuing history of Christianity, Žižek sees the communist hypothesis as evoking the history of a non-forgotten love: 'as with the old Christians, these late conversions [to the communist Idea] carry the same basic message: that we have spent our lives rebelling vainly against what, deep within us, we knew all the time to be the truth' (2009c: 157). Still, Marxism cannot be abandoned just because some of its arguments might reveal it as having a moral tenor in continuity with Christianity, or indeed as having arisen in and through the latter. That would be tantamount to betrayal for Liberation Theology, which emerged from Christianity, but was also expelled from it. If there is no splitting secularism from Christianity, then communism must break with secularism.

For Badiou, as for Marx, the question of the relation of ethics and revolutionary politics is one of the most intense and intrinsic fields of reflection. This is why, even in his book *Ethics: An Essay on the Understanding of Evil*, Badiou articulates a concept of the political subject as if he were betting on its structural benevolence. By contrast, a provisional morality is necessary to prove and dispute the unethical character of the current state of our situation. For Badiou, the most emblematic figure of the inhumane situation today is that of the foreign proletarian with no working papers in France, or in Brazil the landless peasant or 'roof-less' urban dweller: 'Asserting, against such a State apparatus, that any worker without working papers is of the same world as oneself, and drawing out its practical, egalitarian and militant consequences, is a typical example of provisional morality, a local orientation that is homogeneous to the communist hypothesis, in the global disorientation of which only its reinstallation can parry' (Badiou 2010b).

From the ontological perspective, then, love means the possibility of living as a new world is born. It is in this particular perspective of reinvention that love joins up ideally with the communist hypothesis, as act, gesture, thought and law. Peirce's agapism was an attempt to blend Hegel's speculative logical metaphysics with the idea that empirical science was an extension of practical reason. Peirce's task was to integrate the terms conceptually by which chance could be understood as existing absolutely in the universe. As Ian Hacking has written about Peirce, 'our ability for inquiry of an abstract sort is a product of evolution, but it is at best of indifferent value for our survival. We should think instead of mental abilities as evolving parallel to the evolution of the laws of the universe. We can discover the latter because they and our minds have evolved in the same way. Peirce called this "evolutionary love"' (Hacking 1990: 214). Agapism is thus a metaphysical supplement to practical reasoning, a concrete case of abduction. Evolutionary theory in Peirce's time was closer to the stage of principles and initial and general assumptions than it was to the reductive form in which we encounter it today in molecular biology and genetics. Still, Peirce's insight, which he left unexplored, is now grounded in an ontology, suggests the very reasons for which our political thinking must dare anew: ontology must embrace, in Peirce's vision, the 'whole community', that is, the new community being formed.

Badiou's praise of love is an ontological ode to the Two as the subjective structure of pragmatics itself. The phenomenological subjective mode of resurrection places in the domain of love a simultaneous power of renewal that shall go its own way, whether the social conditions allowing for its generalisation arise or not (Badiou 2006e: 57). This is another way of reiterating how fidelity, the key ethical designator in Badiou's thought, ought never to give up on asserting what the structure shows to be its subjective truth.

Notes

1. Badiou 1999b: 79. Alberto Caeiro, 'The Amorous Shepherd: 3/10/30', in *The Amorous Shepherd*, trans. Chris Daniels (New York: Shearman Books, 2007).

2. 'L'amour est à réinventer, on le sait'. A. Rimbaud, 'Une saison en enfer', in *Oeuvres complètes* (Paris: Éditions Gallimard, Bibliothèques de la Pléaide, 1972), p. 103.

3. Badiou employs the Spartacus event as one of the structural narrative motifs of *Logics of Worlds* (2009a), particularly in Book I 'Formal Theory of the Subject (Meta-Physics)'. Saint-Paul's achievements are even more important for Badiou, especially given the documented legacy he left.

4. 'Il me sera loisible de *posséder la vérité dans une âme et un corps*'. Rimbaud, 'Une saison en enfer', in *Oeuvres complètes*, p. 117.

5. Divergences in how to understand Badiou's formulas on this question have led some of his inner circle disciples to acts of auto-da-fé. The desire to occupy the position of disciple has been fraught with peril throughout the history of philosophy, and is iterated in narratives about Socrates, Alexander and Christ. The curious should consult the mail exchange between Fabien Tarby and Mehdi Belhaj Kacem regarding the book *Après Badiou* (Paris: Grasset/Figure, 2011), Fabien Tarby, 'Lettres ouvertes à Mehdi Belhaj Kacem', *Anabase*, 1, http://anabase-1.com/Files/f.t_l_affaire_apres_badiou.pdf (accessed on 5 July 2011).

9

The Politics of Comradeship: Philosophical Commitment and Construction in Alain Badiou and Slavoj Žižek

Sean Homer

Alain Badiou and Slavoj Žižek concluded a recent philosophical dialogue with a declaration of their solidarity and 'comradeship' (Badiou and Žižek 2009e: 104). Badiou, however, introduces a qualification: their dialogue centres on forms of philosophical commitment and their mutual agreement is all the greater for it, but if they were to broach the question of philosophical construction, then differences would certainly open up between them. Badiou highlights their respective notions of the event, the real, the function of the imaginary and, finally, politics as a decision or process (2009e: 101). Contrary to the tenor of our age, Badiou is a systematic thinker; philosophy, he argues, involves the organisation, the configuration, of concepts around the category of Truth. A Truth (with a capital T) 'is by itself *void*', it 'operates but presents nothing' (1999a: 124) and as such, as an operational void, it facilitates the gathering together, or compossibility, of local truths. Philosophy, therefore, does not produce truth but constructs procedures to 'seize truths' (1999a: 127). Philosophy in this sense is not the interpretation of experience, but the act of constructing truth or generic procedures that stand out from the cumulative fields of knowledge by their novelty, their eventful origin (1999a: 36). Žižek, by contrast, is known for his digressive, unsystematic and omnivorous style. If Badiou is precise in his definition of concepts and his construction of philosophy's four generic procedures (art, love, politics and science), then Žižek is often frustratingly loose in his deployment of concepts. He does, however, repeatedly return to the same philosophical and political debates with key interlocutors. In this chapter I will draw out the main threads of Žižek's critique of his longstanding friend and comrade Alain Badiou.

The dialogue between Žižek and Badiou has been rather one-sided as far as the published texts go. Since *The Ticklish Subject* (1999) each of Žižek's major publications has engaged with Badiou's work. In *The Ticklish Subject* Žižek argued that his primary difference with Badiou centred on their divergent understandings of the Lacanian real and the drive. For Žižek, every authentic political act is grounded upon an initial negative gesture, insofar as the act is a repetition of the subject's 'forced' entry into the symbolic order, and he contrasts this to Badiou's politics of affirmation and the 'pure event'. *The Parallax View* (2006) restates this critique, arguing that the death drive is the materialist support for Badiou's 'positive infinity'. *The Parallax View* also shifts the focus of Žižek's critique to political economy, arguing that this is the major weakness of Badiou's system and politics. *In Defense of Lost Causes* (2009a) provides Žižek's first sustained reading of Badiou's *Logics of Worlds: Being and Event II* (2009a) and once more he focuses on the function of the death drive and Badiou's concept of 'subtraction'. From Žižek's perspective the problem with the politics of subtraction – taking a distance from the state but not destroying it – is that it represents a negative gesture but not a 'determinate negation'. Underlying all of these exchanges are Badiou's and Žižek's respective understandings of the void, or gap, and its relation to the subject. Badiou argues that the subject is extremely rare, emerging only through a fidelity to the event, while for Žižek the subject is the void or gap, 'a Nothingness counted as Something' (1998: 256). In short, argues Žižek, are we to understand the relationship between void and subject in a properly dialectical, Hegelian manner or from a neo-Kantian perspective?

Badiou has hardly responded to Žižek's criticisms in print. In a rare comment on their relationship he describes it as 'a politburo of the two', the only question being who will shoot whom first, 'after having wrung from him a deeply felt self-criticism' (Badiou 2009a: 563). Bruno Bosteels has suggested that Badiou's silence in this respect may be a consequence of the blurring of exegesis and critique in Žižek's work. In his view, 'what presents itself as a straightforward summary of Badiou's philosophy is already heavily influenced and refracted by Žižek's own thought', while his counter-arguments are often faithful paraphrases of Badiou's ideas rewritten in Lacanese (Bosteels 2005: 225). This often makes it difficult to disentangle Žižek's critique, as his solutions to the aporias of Badiou's crypto-Kantianism frequently appear to be remarkably similar to Badiou's own position. Bosteels notes that Žižek's criticisms fall into three categories: psychoanalytic, philosophical and political. While it is impossible to separate these three areas of criticism, as each directly implicates the others, I will broadly follow these distinctions below.

Circumventing Psychoanalysis: Between Two Deaths

Žižek's first explication of Badiou's work appeared in *The South Atlantic Quarterly* (1998) as 'Psychoanalysis in Post-Marxism: The Case of Alain Badiou'.[1] Žižek elaborates a Lacanian critique of Badiou in relation to the real, the death drive and the subject that has remained constant. Badiou's circumvention of psychoanalysis, argues Žižek, derives from his homology between Christianity and Marxism and specifically his Pauline turn. Badiou inverts the usual opposition between the Law and Grace, whereby we are all subject to divine law and the elect are touched by grace. Furthermore, the law is particular and grace universal. Corresponding to the two lives (the finite biological life and the eternal life promised through grace) are two deaths (biological death and death through sin):

> The direct result of the intervention of the Law is thus to *divide* the subject, introducing a morbid confusion between life and death, between the (conscious) obedience of the law and the (unconscious) desire for its transgression that is *generated by the legal prohibition*. (Žižek 1998: 249, original emphasis)

The problem is how to break out of this vicious cycle of law and transgression, how to think transformation, and here Badiou introduces the cut of the event, the novelty of the resurrection as an 'absolute disjunction'. There is, however, an alternative to this separation of death and resurrection: Lacan's insight into the domain 'between two deaths', the domain of lamella.[2] In order to open oneself up to the true life of Eternity, writes Žižek, 'one's attachment to "this" life must be suspended for entry into the domain . . . between the two deaths, the domain of the "undead"' (1998: 247). The domain between the two deaths crystallises, argues Žižek, the gap that separates Badiou from Lacan and psychoanalysis in general.[3] The only kind of fidelity one has from a Lacanian point of view is not to compromise on one's desire.

There is no resolution or harmony to achieve but what Žižek calls a 'wiping the slate clean' (1998: 252). It is this negative gesture of wiping the slate clean that creates the space for the arrival of the new and precedes any positive gesture of identification with a cause. In this sense, argues Žižek, Lacan implicitly shifts the balance between death and resurrection towards death. Death stands for:

> [T]he 'night of the world', the self-withdrawal, the absolute contraction of subjectivity in which its very links with 'reality' are severed – *this* is 'wiping the slate clean', which opens up the domain of the symbolic New Beginning and enables the emergence of the 'New Harmony' sustained by a newly emerged Master-Signifier. (1998: 253)

In Lacanese every event remains a mere semblance, masking the prior void of the death drive. A 'Truth-Event', argues Žižek, operates against this background of a traumatic encounter with the domain of the undead, with the real. The conflation and capitalisation of truth and event by Žižek is precisely the blurring of exegesis and critique mentioned above. After presenting Badiou's theory in his own terms, Žižek then proceeds to critique a construct (the Truth-Event) that is not in the original. Truth and event, for Badiou, remain distinct but related concepts; an event is a moment of opening through which the new can emerge, while truth is a generic procedure which retrospectively nominates an event. Through thinking the nature of their relation Badiou renders the domain of truth. I will come back to this below; first, however, I will address the issue of the death drive.

The Death Drive: Repetition or Rupture?

The principlal difference between Žižek and Badiou regarding an authentic event turns on the death drive, or the primacy of negation for Žižek versus affirmation in Badiou. An event for Badiou emerges from a rupture in the order of being; it is an opening between one closure and another. Through a subject's fidelity to the truth of that moment of opening, the event is retrospectively constituted. The French Revolution constitutes such an event: on the one hand, it was merely the sequence of traces or facts that took place between 1789 and 1794; on the other, it retrospectively became the 'central term of the Revolution itself' (Badiou

2005a: 180). From Žižek's perspective, 'the New can only emerge through repetition' (2009a: 140). A revolution is exemplary of such a process, insofar as 'the October Revolution repeated the French Revolution, redeeming its failure, unearthing and repeating the same impulse' (2009a: 139). Badiou's rejection of repetition derives from a critique of Lacan's structural dialectic. Lacan did not push his insight into the real far enough and consider that which exceeds the repetition compulsion of the signifying chain. Everything that repeats, writes Badiou, is invariably unjust and inexact, whereas justice and rightness are novelties (2009b: 39). Žižek's failure to directly engage with Badiou's critique of Lacan is telling, as this critique of psychoanalysis underpins his later work.

For Žižek, it is the repetition of the death drive that accounts for the emergence of novelty. He rejects, however, the traditional reading of the Freudian drive that links it to human biology and an organism's tendency to return to an inorganic state:

> The paradox of the Freudian 'death drive' is therefore that it is Freud's name for its very opposite, for the way immortality appears within psychoanalysis, for an uncanny *excess* of life, for an 'undead' urge which persists beyond the (biological) cycle of life and death, of generation and corruption. The ultimate lesson of psychoanalysis is that human life is never 'just life': humans are not simply alive, they are possessed by the strange drive to enjoy life in excess, passionately attached to a surplus which sticks out and derails the ordinary run of things. (Žižek 2006: 62)

The death drive has nothing to do with a will to self-annihilation, but is the reason that this will is never realised and the subject gets 'stuck' on partial objects. If the metonymy of desire is the infinite pursuit of a lost object, then the drive designates how desire becomes 'fixated' or 'stuck' on a specific object, 'condemned to circulate around it forever' (Žižek 2006: 62).

It is the mute, repetitive, rotary motion of the drive, contends Žižek, that is primary and ultimately the groundless ground of human freedom (Žižek 1996: 32–5). The death drive is beyond human mortality; it is a 'vanishing mediator' between being and event, or the mortality of the individual and the immortality of the subject. As Adrian Johnston puts it, the death drive 'is a name for subjectivity qua the void of a radical negativity irreducible to any and every form of positive inscription or representation' (2009:

157). The death drive facilitates Žižek's distinction between the subject as void, as pure negativity, as nothing, and what he calls *subjectification* – in Badiou's sense of a subject-of-the-event – as secondary to this moment of pure negativity. The elementary act of freedom, then, is negation. It is saying 'No' to the big Other; it is breaking out of the closed repetitive circuit of the death drive and asserting a minimal distance, a parallax gap, between the real and the symbolic. The radicalism of the Freudian drive lies in this negativity behind all affirmation. The death drive is a self-sabotaging structure and the minimum prerequisite for subjective freedom. In this sense the death drive decentres the subject and opens up the minimal space for a subject to act.

Bruno Bosteels (2011a) has convincingly argued that in order to understand Badiou's affirmationism adequately we must situate it in relation to his formulation of destruction in *Theory of the Subject*. Lacan, famously, was unable to comprehend the revolutionary upheavals of May '68 and to see anything positive in the movement beyond the hysterical demand for a new Master (Lacan 1990: 126). For Badiou, the fundamental impasse of Lacanian psychoanalysis and its weakness in thinking political transformation lies with its conception of lack and the real. In order to move beyond the impasse of the lacking subject and confer a degree of consistency upon it that would allow us to think radical change as well as the emergence of novelty beyond the repetition of the past, we must think lack with destruction. Every subject, writes Badiou, 'stands at a crossing between a lack of being and a destruction, a repetition and an interruption, a placement and an excess' (2009b: 139). It is at this intersection of lack and destruction that something emerges, 'an other of the Other, from which it follows that what functioned as the first Other now appears as nothing more than an unenlightened mode of the Same' (2009b: 156). Badiou's notion of destruction beyond the law of lack 'consists precisely in the capacity to bring into being the nonrepeatable within repetition', to bring about the new (Bosteels 2011a: 101). In a self-critique of his 'misguided' use of the theme of destruction Badiou later restricts the concept to 'a supplementation by a truth'; destruction is of the order of knowledge but is not true (Badiou 2005a: 407–8). Badiou clarifies this in his discussion of the Paris Commune; the Commune-event did not set out to merely destroy the political elite – to wipe the slate clean in Žižek's terms – but to do something more radical: it sought the destruction of 'the political subordination of the workers and the people' (2009a: 379). The Commune destroyed 'the order of subjective incapacity', as the inexistence of the proletariat came into existence. Badiou's more measured appreciation of negation and destruction provides a useful antidote to the valorisation of negation and violence in Žižek. As the drive in Lacan is inextricably tied to the real, the debate between Žižek and Badiou essentially turns on their respective understanding and deployment of this concept.

Splitting the Real

Žižek has undoubtedly done more than any other contemporary theorist to reorient our understanding of Lacan around the concept of the real. In his early work he stressed the impossibility of the real, the real as an impenetrable kernel resisting symbolisation, and insisted on the necessity of maintaining the gap separating the real and the symbolic (Žižek 1989: 3). From this perspective *'the only point at which we approach this hard kernel of the Real is indeed the dream'* or symptom (Žižek 1989: 47, original emphasis). Over the years Žižek's deployment of the real has changed but, as with Lacan, he never completely abandons his prior formulations. In his debate with Judith Butler and Ernesto Laclau, Žižek identified the real with capital, insofar as the real marks the absolute limit to resignification. Moreover, he began suggesting the possibility of 'touching' the real, when the symbolic markers that distance us from it are suspended (Butler et al. 2000: 223). In *The Parallax View* Žižek distinguishes between the Lacanian real and the 'parallax real', as 'the disavowed X on account of which our vision of reality is anamorphically distorted; it is simultaneously the Thing to which direct access is not possible and the obstacle which prevents this direct access, the Thing which eludes our grasp and the distorting screen which makes us miss the Thing' (2006: 26). The parallax real is not the Lacanian real that 'always remains in its place' and neither is it the hard impenetrable kernel beyond the symbolic. The parallax real is the gap itself, the gap which renders two perspectives radically incommensurable (Žižek 2006: 281). The impossibility of the real is now conceptualised as 'the cause of the impossibility of ever attaining the "neutral" non perspectival view of the object'. In other words, the Lacanian real is not only the distorted object but the principle of distortion itself, and in this sense the real is *within* the symbolic (Žižek 2009a: 319, original emphasis). Today, Žižek argues that the real is not an abyss that forever eludes our grasp or an inaccessible Thing, but 'the *gap* which prevents our access to it' (2004: 168, original emphasis), and it is this real, he contends, that Badiou fails to grasp in his opposition of being and event:

> The ultimate difference between Badiou and Lacan thus concerns the relationship between the shattering encounter with the Real and the ensuing arduous work of transforming this explosion of negativity into a new order. For Badiou, this new order 'sublates' the exploding negativity into a new consistent truth, while for Lacan every Truth displays the structure of a (symbolic) fiction, i.e. no Truth is able to touch the Real. (2004: 177)

In order to forestall the charge of postmodern relativism Žižek invokes the notion of the real in all three of Lacan's orders – the imaginary, the symbolic, the real – and in a strictly homologous way he invokes three modalities of the real within the symbolic. 'Far from being reduced to the traumatic void of the Thing which resists symbolisation,' writes Žižek, 'the Lacanian Real thus designates also the senseless symbolic consistency (of the "matheme"), as well as the pure appearance irreducible to its causes ("the real of an illusion")' (2004: 177). The real appears to have become an infinitely malleable concept.

In a brief footnote to *Logics of Worlds* Badiou argues that Žižek's conception of the real is 'so ephemeral, so brutally punctual, that it is impossible to uphold its consequences'. He continues: 'The effects of this kind of frenzied upsurge, in which the real rules over the comedy of our symptoms, are ultimately indiscernible from skepticism' (2009a: 563). There are two notions of the real in Lacan, according to Badiou: first, the structural understanding of the real as a vanishing cause or the lack of being, and second, the late topological Lacan that gives a minimum of consistency to the real, as the being of lack (2009b: 132–9). Lacan's insight was the role of the real as antagonism, as that which always already fissures the social and means that it can never be rendered whole or complete. But if we think the real only in this way, then we remain caught within the totality of the structure itself and cannot think its potential transformation. Lacan's 'materialist' dialectic is only half the picture; we must not only think the real as impossible, unbearable trauma but also as something that, on rare occasions, becomes the site for a newly consistent truth, that is to say, the real as novelty:

> The line of demarcation between idealism and materialism in Lacan's thought must therefore be drawn through the very concept of the real, splitting its core in order to mark off those aspects that remain tied to a structural lack and those that point at a torsion, or destruction, of the structure itself. (Bosteels 2011a: 87)

In *Theory of the Subject*, Badiou develops this idea through the concept of forcing: it is not enough to merely expose the lack, the absent cause, we must also force or distort the real in order 'to give consistency to the real as a new generic truth' (Bosteels 2011a: 88). In other words, it is not enough merely to think the subject as lack; we must also think it as excess. The theory of the subject is complete only when 'it manages to think the structural law of the empty place as the punctual anchoring of the excess over the place' (Badiou 2009b: 261). In short, we have two opposing views of the subject: the subject as consistent repetition, in which the real ex-sists (Lacan), and the subject as destructive consistency, in which the real ex-ceeds (Badiou 2009b: 239). While this might not be strictly Lacanian, it does have the advantage of allowing us to think radical structural change in ways foreclosed by Lacan himself.

Philosophy: Mind the Gap

For Žižek, the central axis of Badiou's theoretical edifice is the gap between being and event, and it is this gap that he will repeatedly pry apart in his critique of Badiou's non-dialectical separation of being and event, subject and subjectivisation, truth and knowledge, representation and presentation, facilitating his final charge of Kantian formalism. From his initial explication of Badiou, Žižek has consistently presented an event as external, beyond, or in opposition to the order of being. In the proto-Kantian opposition between the positive order of being and the radical unconditional demand for a 'Truth-Event' lies Badiou's fatal weakness (Žižek 1998: 259). An authentic event, insists Žižek, is something that emerges *ex nihilo* and is the truth of a situation that makes visible what the official discourse has had to repress. Furthermore, it 'does not entail any ontological guarantee' but a decision of a committed, engaged subject (Žižek 1998: 240). In Lacanese, 'Event is *objet a*, while denomination is the new signifier that establishes ... the new readability of the situation on the basis of Decision' (Žižek 1998: 242). While the presentation of the event as 'creation *ex nihilo*' is crucial for Žižek's identification of an event with Lacan's act, it is not strictly speaking Badiou's formulation:

> [A]s far as its material is concerned, the event is not a miracle. What I mean is that what composes an event is always extracted from a situation, always related back to a singular multiplicity, to its state, to the language that is connected to it, etc. In fact, if we want to avoid lapsing into an obscurantist theory of creation *ex-nihilo*, we must accept that an event is nothing but a part of a given situation, nothing but a *fragment of being*. (Badiou 2004a: 98, original emphasis)

Commenting on this passage, Žižek reiterates that there is a fundamental ambiguity within Badiou's ontology, that is, 'how do Event and Being relate ontologically' (Žižek 2009b: 212). For Žižek, there is no beyond of being which inscribes itself into the order of being, there is just the order of being itself. The underlying philosophical choice, writes Žižek, is between Kantian transcendental finitude and Hegelian speculative infinity; 'if one asserts the non-All (ontological incompleteness) of reality', then 'an Event is irreducible to the order of Being (or to a situation with regard to which it is an Event) – *it is also in-itself NOT just a "fragment of being,"* not because it is grounded in some "higher" spiritual reality, but because it emerges out of the void in the order of being' (Žižek 2009b: 213, original emphasis). One problem with this Kantian antinomy between being and event is that it is not Badiou's. As Badiou writes, 'I would like to insist that, even in the title *Being and Event*, the "and" is fundamental'; he continues, it 'is not the opposition between the event and the situation that interests me first and foremost'; indeed 'the principal contribution of my work does not consist in opposing the situation to the event' but in posing the question 'what can we derive or infer from this from the point of view of the situation itself' (Badiou, qtd in Bosteels 2011a: 306). The event designates 'what-is-not-being-qua-being' (Badiou 2005a: 173–4) and is therefore not submitted to the operation of the count-as-one; as 'non-being' the event is supernumerary (2007: 178). Another term for this non-being of being is the void. The void 'is the unpresentable *point of being* of any presentation' (2005a: 77, original emphasis). The event is supernumerary but it is not beyond being; it emerges precisely out of the void of the order of being. Žižek's critique simply targets a straw figure here.

What is at stake here is the nature of the limit, whether it is an internal limit in the order of being itself, as Žižek asserts, or what he sees as an external limit between the order of being and the domain of the 'Truth-Event' in Badiou. We can see this most clearly in Žižek's distinction between subject and subjectivisation, as that which separates Lacan from post-Marxists, such as Badiou and Laclau.[4] Badiou's subject, the subject of truth, only emerges post-event through a truth procedure and thus, according to Žižek, fails to take into account the distinction between subject – as lack, gap, void, nothingness – and subjectivisation as a process of interpellation. Therefore, it is secondary to the subject as lack. For Lacan, the subject prior to subjectivisation 'is the pure negativity of the death drive prior to its reversal into identification with some new Master-Signifier' (Žižek 1998: 257). The subject is simultaneously the ontological gap in the symbolic order and that which comes to fill the gap:

> 'Subjectivity' is a name for this irreducible circularity, for a power which does not fight an external resisting force (say, the inertia of the given substantial order), but an obstacle that is absolutely inherent, which ultimately 'is' the subject itself. (Žižek 1999: 159, original emphasis)

The subject's endeavour retroactively to fill the gap sustains and generates the gap itself. Badiou refuses this identification of the subject with the gap and thus, according to Žižek, restricts the contingent act to a moment of decision, the moment of subjectivisation. From Žižek's perspective, the whole Kantian opposition within Badiou of the universal order of being and the contingent excess that punches a hole in this universal order is a false dichotomy; 'the subject is the contingent emergence/act that sustains the very universal order of Being', in other words, the subject is a paradox, the particular element that sustains the universal order (1999: 160).

Žižek, however, completely ignores Badiou's critique of the Lacanian subject, a critique that will later be reformulated but not completely abandoned. *Theory of the Subject*, Part V, is devoted to the dual processes of 'subjectivisation' and 'subjective process'. Both processes can be found in Lacan. The former obeys the logic of the signifier and the structural law of lack and it can be found in Lacan's work up to the mid-1960s. The latter is governed by the topological logic of the Borromean knot, the real as excess and consistency, and can be found in his work post-1968. Badiou diverges from Lacan in two respects: first, he insists that the real confers on the subject a degree of consistency; and second, that Lacan does not have a conception of *force*. The subject emerges out of the crossing of these two operations or temporalities; subjectivisation is an interruption of the state of things and is distinguished from the subjective process through the anticipation of its own certainty. The subjective process operates *après-coup* to confer consistency on the effects of subjectivisation: 'the subjective process amounts to the retroactive grounding of the subjectivisation in an element of certainty that the subjectivisation alone has made possible' (Badiou 2009b: 251). The subject is the product of this dialectical division of destruction and recomposition, of Lacan's structural law of lack, the empty place and the excess of the real which exceeds this place. As Badiou writes:

> The subject proceeds from a subjectivisation by forcing the empty place, which a new order grounds retrospectively *qua* place, by having occupied it . . . Any splace [the place of the subjective] is thus the after effect or *après-coup* of the destruction of another. Subjectivisation is the anticipation whose structure is the empty place; the subjective process, the retroaction that places the forcing. (2009b: 264)

The subject *is* the splace, which comes from what has been destroyed. As Bosteels puts it, the appearance of a new structure, in which a subject not only occupies but exceeds the empty place in the old structure, results in the first becoming obsolete (2011a: 75). Badiou, then, maintains a distinction between subject and subjectivisation. His subject is at once the empty place and that which comes to fill the place. What differentiates Badiou's subject, however, is that the real confers on the subject a degree of consistency that allows it to reconfigure the consequences of its initial act of destruction.

Politics: Wiping the Slate Clean

In the concluding paragraphs of 'The Politics of Truth' Žižek claims that Badiou's resistance to psychoanalysis is part and parcel of his hidden Kantianism. According to Žižek, Badiou's implicit Kantianism ultimately 'leads him to oppose the full revolutionary *passage à l'acte*', despite his explicit anti-Kantianism and radical leftist politics (1999: 166). For Žižek, we must ultimately reject the Kantian distinction between the order of a positive knowledge of being and a wholly different order of the Truth-Event and embrace the radical gesture of an authentic Lacanian act, an act as the real of an object preceding naming, the real as the unnamable that eludes our grasp. Žižek initially defines an 'authentic act' as that 'which reaches the utter limit of the primordial forced choice and repeats it in reverse, it is the only moment when we are effectively "free"' (1992: 77). An authentic act pushes beyond the limits of the social, realising what Lacan calls 'the pure and simple desire of death as such' (1992: 282). This definition raises a number of issues for a politics of the act, as it is an individual ethical gesture rather than a collective political response. Indeed, Žižek's two favoured examples of authentic acts are suicide and terror and his repeated examples are Antigone, Sethe from Toni Morrison's novel *Beloved* and Bartleby, that is to say, individuals who act alone in order to achieve a form of subjective destitution. In *The Ticklish Subject* Žižek argues that there is no authentic ethical act without the 'suspension of the Big Other', of the socio-symbolic network which guarantees the subject's identity. An act is an act of faith, it is a moment of self-authorisation. Furthermore, we must distinguish between those acts that are merely performative and reconfigure the symbolic and the 'much more radical *act*' that reconfigures the entire socio-symbolic field (Žižek 1999: 264). The act is now conceived in terms of Badiou's event and Žižek's examples shift accordingly from individual acts of subjective destitution to collective moments of revolutionary change such as the Paris Commune, the October Revolution and the Chinese Cultural Revolution, although, contra Badiou, he reads these events as manifestations of the death drive (2009a: 196).

In marked contrast to his later enthusiasm, Žižek's initial assessment of Badiou's politics was dismissive. In 'Psychoanalysis in Post-Marxism' he charges Badiou with using psychoanalysis as a 'justification of failure' and using it to explain why things go wrong politically. Žižek describes Badiou's politics as a 'hysterical provocation', to which he opposes 'the true revolutionary stance':

> [T]he heroic readiness to endure the subversive undermining of the existing System as it undergoes conversion into the principle of a new positive Order that can *give body* to this negativity – or, in Badiou's terms, the conversion of Truth into Being. (Žižek 1998: 259, original emphasis)

This view was tempered in *The Ticklish Subject*, where a more sympathetic picture of Badiou's politics was presented. The fundamental lesson of postmodern politics, argues Žižek, is that *'there is no Event*, that "nothing really happens"', and in this sense Badiou 'is fully justified in insisting that – to use the term with its full theological weight – *miracles do happen*' (1999: 135, original emphasis). Today, Žižek unequivocally endorses the slogans of Badiou's former *Organisation Politique* and has adopted many of his political positions (2009c: 118–19). There remain fundamental differences between them, however, especially with regard to questions of the party and the state, the function of negation and the place of the economy.

The major dilemma facing the Left today, argues Žižek, is confronting state power when the very thought of taking over the state is seen as a redundant old Left paradigm (2009a: 339). The academic Left today tends to conceive the primary political task as one of resisting state power by withdrawing from its scope, by 'subtracting oneself from it, [and] creating new spaces outside its control' (2009a: 339). Žižek's conceptualisation of the state, party and dictatorship of the proletariat, all filtered through Lacan's logic of 'not-all', is much closer to Badiou's *Theory of the Subject* than his later work, but as mentioned above he does not directly engage with this text. Badiou now rejects his earlier formulation of the subject of politics as the class party (2008c: 37), a sequence that has exhausted itself in the sterility of the party–state couple and state socialism. The subject of politics today is the militant, who maintains fidelity to the truth of the event. The collective character of the political event opens up the infinite character of situations and 'interrupts the subjective errancy of the power of the state' (Badiou 2005b: 145), forcing the state to reveal itself, its excess of power and repressive dimension. Contra Žižek, politics must take a distance from the state. The essence of politics 'is the prescription of a possibility in rupture with what exists' (Badiou 2005b: 24). Politics is a generic procedure, a 'collective action, organised by certain principles that aim to unfold the conse-quences of a new possibility which is currently repressed by the dominant order' (Badiou 2008c: 31).

Žižek draws rather different conclusions regarding the politics of subtraction, insofar as an act redefines the very horizon of what is politically imaginable, or 'redefines the very coordinates of what I cannot and must do' (2006: 49). Bartleby's gesture – 'I would prefer not to' – is exemplary of an impotent *passage à l'acte;* 'the necessary first step which . . . clears the ground, opens up the place for true activity, for an act that will actually change the coordi-nates of the constellation' (Žižek 2006: 342). Žižek sees in this gesture 'subtraction at its purest, the reduction of all qualitative differences to a purely formal minimal difference' (2006: 382). The political lesson to be drawn from Bartleby's gesture is that it 'is not merely the first, preparatory, stage for the second, more "constructive," work of forming a new alternative order, it is the very source and background of this order, its permanent founda-tion' (2006: 382). In other words, in a post-revolutionary situation the explosion of destructive rage is never abolished but the new situation gives body to this negativity. The problem with Badiou's politics of subtraction – taking a distance from the state but not destroying it – is that it is a negative gesture but not a negation of the negation. It is not a determinate negation in the sense that it seeks to destroy the state. From Žižek's perspective subtraction is a negative and destructive force that becomes constructive once it has undermined the very coordinates of the system it seeks to subvert. The true art of subtraction is when the whole edifice collapses (Žižek 2009a: 410). What we need today, according to Žižek, is a renewed Jacobinism, a form of egalitarian terror that combines egalitarian justice, terror, voluntarism and a trust in the people (2009a: 461).

Times of Riot and Rage

If we turn to recent events in Europe, North Africa and the Middle East, we can see how these differences between Badiou and Žižek concerning the state, negation and violence have important con-sequences for their respective analyses of the present conjuncture. Žižek's focus is primarily Eurocentric:

Recent events in Europe – student protests in Greece, for example – already mark the first step in this passage from "abstract" to "determinate" negation: while they are no longer just blind acting-outs, many observers have noted their *violent* character as a key feature. Not violent in the sense of killing people, but violent in the sense of disturbing public order and destroying symbolic objects of private and state property. (2009a: 482, original emphasis)[5]

For Žižek, the anti-austerity movements in Europe have the potential to become more than merely negative, reactive protests. The French and Dutch rejection of the European constitution in 2005, for example, can be seen as a positive choice and not simply a negative reaction. Although the French and Dutch 'No!' is not sustained by a coherent and detailed alternative vision, 'it at least *clears the space for it*, opening up a void which demands to be filled in with new projects – in contrast to the pro-Constitution stance which effectively *precludes thinking*, presenting us with an administrative–political fait accompli' (2009a: 276, original emphasis). Similarly, protests in Greece can be seen to mark 'the first step in this passage from "abstract" to "determinate" negation' and are not simply eruptions of blind acting-out (2009a: 482). What impresses Žižek about the Greek protests is that they represent a NO without content, without concrete demands, but as such they open up 'the space into which concrete demands and projects of change can inscribe themselves' (2009a: 482). The protests represent an excess of means over ends, an excess without end. What Žižek misses here, from my perspective, is the entirely ritualised form that violence takes in most Greek demonstrations. The confrontation between the 'Black Bloc' and riot police at the end of major demonstrations is entirely predictable and would appear to be a perfect illustration of what Žižek criticises elsewhere as 'pseudo-activity'.[6] As such, these acts only serve to legitimise state violence rather than challenge it.

Žižek's response to the 2005 Paris riots was rather more ambivalent. He characterised these riots as 'an implicit admission of impotence' (2008: 69), as a pseudo-activity which we should resist. At the same time, he saw in these riots a radical act, 'an impulsive movement to action which can't be translated into speech or thought and carries with it an intolerable weight of frustration' (2008: 65). The riots are at once an expression of impotence and of the protesters' inability to locate their experience in any meaningful sense. They were about visibility, an excluded group claiming the right to be recognised as citizens in the country in which they live. What remains unclear is how we are to distinguish between the two, between an abstract and a determinate negation, and how we move from the first to the second. Badiou offers us an alternative reading of these events through a distinction between immediate, latent and historical riots, which introduces some clarity into the situation. An immediate riot signals unrest among a section of the population, nearly always in response to an act of state violence, is led by the young, and takes place in a specific locality and its demands remain indistinct (Badiou 2012d: 22). Immediate riots, for Badiou, are not political or even pre-political, but can at best work to pave the way for a historical riot and at worst they merely reveal the state's inability to control certain spaces. The riots in Paris (2005) and Athens (2008 and 2010) are immediate riots in this sense. They were led by youth, localised and articulated no specific demands (2012d: 21).[7] Badiou also notes that the presence of organised crime, apparent in both the Athens riots of 2008 and 2010, are a sign of the riots' complicity with the state. Historical riots, on the other hand, 'indicate the possibility of a new situation in the history of politics, without for now being in a position to realise that possibility' (2012d: 27). These are the riots we see taking place across North Africa and the Middle East. They are historical riots in the sense that they represent a direct challenge to the state and articulate the demand for the recognition of the existence of the masses of people who have 'no existence'. In this sense, the historical riot has the potential to become a pre-political event insofar as an idea emerges that fidelity can be organised around. For this to happen a form of organisation – this is the work of the militant – needs to be created to produce the idea and universalise the demands of the riot. Badiou is adamant here; this organisation cannot take the form of the traditional party and must distance itself from all symbols of the state. It is too early to tell what will become of the struggles of the Middle East but, for Badiou, they have the potential for radical change that the riots across Europe currently lack.

The weakness of Badiou's politics, as Žižek sees it, is that he is a communist but not a Marxist and therefore has no critique of the political economy:

[W]hile he is aware that the anti-Statist revolutionary Party politics which aimed at taking over the State apparatus is exhausted, he refuses to explore the revolutionary potential of the 'economic' sphere (since, for him, this belongs to the order of Being, and does not contain potential 'evental sites'); for this reason, the only way left is that of a 'pure' political organisation, which operates outside the confines of the State and, basically, limits itself to the mobilisatory declarations ... the only way out of this deadlock is *to restore to the 'economic' domain the dignity of Truth*, the potential for Events. (2006: 328, original emphasis)

While it is certainly true to say that Badiou does not accord the economy the dignity of a truth procedure, he has discussed the factory as an evental site (Badiou 2006d). Furthermore, until recently Žižek has also avoided any sustained discussion of political economy; indeed his political commitments are largely limited to 'mobilisatory declarations'. In *The Rebirth of History* Badiou directly confronts those 'friends' – his reference here is to Toni Negri but the comments equally apply to Žižek – who call him a communist but not a Marxist. Badiou responds that he is perfectly aware of capitalist economics and does not need any lessons in Marxism. Contemporary capitalism retains all the features of classical capitalism and, in this sense, Marx's predictions have been fulfilled. If Marxism is reduced to the dominance of the economy, then everyone is a Marxist today; but Marxism is also about the realisation of an egalitarian society, communism, and our task today is to rethink the form of political organisation that can bring this about. For Badiou, this organisation must be 'outside time' and 'outside the party'. The era initiated by the Jacobins is over and we must rethink what form of political organisation can today articulate and preserve the generic Idea. Badiou's critique of the party–state form offers a counterbalance to Žižek's empty invocation of the party as that which formalises the revolution but does not in actual fact exist.

In Conclusion

Sarah Kay has observed that Žižek's long-running exchanges with interlocutors, such as Ernesto Laclau and Judith Butler, often served to facilitate the refining of concepts within his work (Kay 2003). I believe that as much can be said for Žižek's engagement with Badiou. Tracing Žižek's critique through the categories of psychoanalysis, philosophy and politics we can see how his central concepts, such as the real and the act, have subtly changed through this encounter. Žižek's Lacanian critique of Badiou's implicit Kantianism, however, fails to engage with Badiou's early critique of the Lacanian subject and the real and, more often than not, simply restates Badiou's philosophy in Lacanese. At the same time, there has been a distinct radicalisation of Žižek's politics and identification with the political positions of Badiou; but again, his recourse to the party and the dictatorship of the proletariat filtered through Lacan's logic of the 'not-all' fails to acknowledge Badiou's present self-critique of just such a position in *Theory of the Subject*. Žižek's engagement with Badiou has been one of the most productive, stimulating and frustrating in contemporary radical philosophy, and whatever their differences with regard to the function of repetition and negation, the real, or Kant versus Hegel, to paraphrase Badiou's remark in *Logics of Worlds*, the future is in their hands (Badiou 2009a: 563).

Notes

1. Žižek's first reference to Badiou in print can be found in *For They Know Not What They Do* (1991: 188).
2. Lacan introduces the 'myth of lamella' in seminar XI, where he describes it as 'something extra-flat, which moves like the amoeba . . . This lamella, this organ, whose characteristic is not to exist, but which is nevertheless an organ . . . It is the libido, *qua* pure life instinct, that is to say, immortal life, or irrepressible life, life that has need of no organ, simplified, indestructible life. It is precisely what is subtracted from the living being by virtue of the fact that it is subject to the cycle of sexed reproduction. And it is of this that all forms of the *objet a* that can be enumerated are the representatives, the equivalents. The *objet a* are merely its representatives, its figures' (1979: 197–8).
3. This is exactly the same criticism Žižek makes of Judith Butler's account of sexual difference and same sex identification (1999: 275).
4. This is an argument that Žižek repeatedly levels against his opponents, especially in relation to deconstruction and discourse theory. For an early critique of Laclau along these lines, see Žižek 1990.
5. Žižek has not, to my knowledge, reconsidered this statement in the light of the deaths of three young bank workers who died when their bank was firebombed in the general strike of 6 May 2010.
6. In *Living in the End Times* (2010: 390), Žižek identifies the violent demonstrations that followed the police shooting of Alexandros

Grigoropolous in December 2008 as exemplary of leftist violence against the state. These protests were more complex and contradictory than I can develop here, but in Thessaloniki they involved at least three distinct groupings: anarchists, students and immigrants, each with very different agendas. The fact that the state restrained the police from any direct confrontation with the protestors also facilitated the continuation of violence beyond the usual night. I can see little that distinguishes these protests from those in France in 2005, which Žižek characterised as impotent acting-out.

7. Badiou observes that the 2005 Paris riots were 'violent, anarchic and ultimately without enduring truth' (2012d: 21).

10

Not Solvable by Radicals: Lacan, Topology, Politics

A. J. Bartlett and Justin Clemens

In Abel's wake, Galois replies: 'Yes, we can decide. These equations are not solvable by radicals, the question is settled. And the point is held.' (Badiou 2009a: 472)

Man is a promising animal. (Nietzsche 1989: II, 16)

It is only by working out an organisation for the subjectivisable body that one can hope to 'live', and not merely try to. (Badiou 2009a: 470)

Alain Badiou's philosophy will remain entirely incomprehensible if its relation to psychoanalysis remains unclarified. Badiou's topics, concepts and methods develop out of a long, obstinate confrontation with the challenges that psychoanalysis poses to philosophy (see Bartlett and Clemens 2012; 2011). This chapter pinpoints one key aspect of this confrontation as it is articulated in *Logics of Worlds*: the question of the body. We propose to stage this confrontation through a close reading of the lesson devoted to Jacques Lacan in *Logics of Worlds*, to expose both the links and aporias of the relation between the two thinkers on this point. On the basis of a topological exposition we will flesh out what a truth requires to appear in a world as an exception to it. This exception manifests as a new body, which is not, for all that, natural.[1]

One of the key disarticulations that Lacan, following Freud, insists upon – one that philosophy allegedly cannot countenance and that politics also maintains in one way or another – is to sever the subject from consciousness and, by extension, also from nature or presence. As Badiou argues, this is essentially an anti-phenomenological claim on Lacan's part.[2] Badiou engages this position through a critique of Aristotelian logic, from Leibniz and

Kant up to Heidegger himself. An essential part of this demonstration depends upon phenomenology's having 'become commonplace'. In essence, the Aristotelian 'space of placements', to use the language from *Theory of the Subject*, ensures that any subject/body or 'physical being has a natural place'. Hence, the ontological correlation of being and place – to be is to have a proper place – is 'naturally' integrated with the question of the subject according to the determinations of *physis*.

For Badiou, this determination accorded to place is possible because of a covert priority of some kind already accorded to one or another figure of the One, inaccessible to thought or ineffable as such. The question of the subject, qua effect of a body, experiential, specular or cosmic, is therefore *a priori* predetermined insofar as place and possibility are correlated on the side of being or, alternatively, affective experience is held to be primary in any thought of what a subject can do. For Lacan, the discovery of the unconscious renders all such accords not only unthinkable, but stupid. The division of the subject requires a topological conceptualisation precisely because there is no originary bond between subject and place such that its existence is substantively guaranteed. There is now not only a third place to be thought – the place of the cut – but even a fourth, the trace. The key is mathematics: 'It is a fact that mathematics rectifies and that what it rectifies is the object itself. Hence my reduction of psychoanalysis to set theory' (Lacan 2013a: 7). The drives and 'objective' relations that inscribe the subject – both 'subjectivisation' (algebra) and the 'subjective process' (topology)[3] – make the step into (reactionary) relativism equally impossible: this is especially crucial insofar as it is precisely in terms of relations and objects that any world is known (transcendental). Lacan, in manifest contradistinction to every other thinker of his generation, simultaneously managed to sustain a fundamental commitment to 1) an antiphilosophical project; 2) a divided and desubstantialised subject; 3) mathematical formalisation; and 4) truth as in excess of knowledge.

Given that *Logics of Worlds*, under the ideological condition of the materialist dialectic, affirms at its core the existence of truths as an exception to 'democratic materialism', with its 'free' (natural and juridical) play of bodies and languages, and that it does so by conceiving these exceptions as bodily manifest and structurally distributed, it is imperative that Badiou has recourse to a discourse that de-situates the body *and* maintains the double form of the subject at the same time, and that also does not preclude that this subject has some necessary relation to truths. As the brief sketch of Lacan above should already make evident, it is Lacan – and he alone – who has provided all the necessary directions and provisions for such a step.

There is only one point at which Badiou departs from his master, but it is, as ever, a minimal point of difference that makes all the difference: Badiou is a philosopher. In this context, this effectively amounts to a thinking of the real of the subject, in such a way that it is the guarantee of consistency without the mediation of the imaginary (Badiou 2009b: 246). Hence the coherent, rigorous thought of the actual existence (as distinct from being) of that which is not reducible to the 'enjoyment' equation of individual and body or the juridical norms that confirm and sustain the force of this reduction and the typology of its pleasures (Badiou 2009a: 2).[4] In other words, what is at stake in this 'body', qua support of a subjective form, is the thinkable and practical existence of what is empirically unapparent – of what we 'postmoderns' cannot know as good democratic materialists (2009a: 2). For Badiou, truths, the impossible-real exception to bodies and languages, are established in a world point by point, not in the instance of what breaks with its norm. Their consistency is a topology, and therefore a recomposition of the Real, so to speak, and not, as Badiou says of Lacan – bringing him (on this point only) too close to the 'anti-Marxist war machine of contemporary times' (2009b: 246) – a fall back into the imaginary. 'A truth', Badiou contends, 'is what thought goes on presenting even when the regime of the thing is suspended (by doubt). A truth is thus what insists in exception to the forms of the "there is"' (2009a: 6).

Note that, of all the thinkers with whom Badiou engages in *Logics of Worlds*, there are several noteworthy peculiarities about the section on Lacan. First of all, it is placed right at the centre of Book VII, the final book of *Logics*, which deals with a question hitherto foreign to Badiou: 'What is a Body?' Indeed, it is 'Section 2' of this book that deals with Lacan. Since we are emphasising topology here, let us also mention how this relates to the structure of *Logics* as a whole: Section 2 of Book II is dedicated to Hegel; Section 2 of Book III is dedicated to Kant; Section 2 of Book IV is dedicated to Leibniz; Section 2 of Book V is dedicated to Deleuze; and Section 2 of Book VI is dedicated to Kierkegaard. Not only that: all these 'Section 2s' are the only parts of the divisions of the treatise that bear a single proper name. We begin to glimpse the absolutely crucial role that Badiou assigns to each of these sections with respect to his key interlocutors in regard to the thought of, respectively, the whole, the object, relation, the event, points and the body. We also begin to glimpse something of the extraordinary organisation of *Logics* as a whole. The relation between logic, conceptual discussion and history of philosophy within a single philosophical 'act' itself is at stake in such divisions, as is the problem of method more generally: note that these sections, then, are dedicated to forcing out a difference between Badiou and his interlocutors, where those interlocutors are the canonical references who have established the strongest and most extreme accounts of the concepts under discussion. From the point of view of a logic of worlds, it picks up on the division between philosophy and its conditions (the most fundamental division in Badiou's thought, and one regularly elided in the most stupefying fashion by commentary to date), in order to demonstrate how these four worlds (art, politics, science and love) are inscribed and inscribe themselves as the topology of appearances that are always material but not always perceptible.

Let us also note that whereas all the other thinkers mentioned above are notorious for the very concepts that Badiou discusses here (e.g., Hegel and the whole; Deleuze and the event), Lacan is not usually noted for his doctrine of bodies. On the contrary, Badiou himself begins by invoking the various ways in which Lacan's work may even seem to be directed against any primacy of bodies: Lacan argues for the signifier against the body; that science can only take place by 'forsaking perceptual information'; and that the body is constitutively secondary (Badiou 2009a: 477). Badiou's intervention here thus takes Lacan up on what may seem to be a paradigmatically un- or anti-Lacanian point.[5]

This, however, has the result that Badiou explicitly affirms Lacan's thinking about the body. Whereas the other sections upbraid Hegel or contest Kant, and so on, regarding the interpretation of key concepts, Badiou here proposes something rather odd: 'It appears that [with Lacan] we are as far as possible from the doctrine that we have been defending, which makes of the body an active composition' (2009a: 478), he states, before immediately adding: 'In truth, the distance is not so great' (2009a: 478). It is this odd remark – its motivations, justifications and consequences – that needs unpacking.

Lacan's thinking about the body, Badiou argues, issues in three key ways:

1) Lacan's relating the constitution of the subject to the signifier relegates the body to being, as it was for Plato, that which resists the subject. This is to say that the body, and not consciousness as such, is what pulls the subject back to its corporeal distress, 'resisting its division'.

2) Given that, for Lacan, scientific truth refuses the perceptual as the price of its success, a success both Lacan and Badiou affirm, then the body can only be that which a truth leaves behind. Given the tie of perception to a perceiving body qua its 'grip on nature', the body can only be a hindrance to truth – precisely to the truth of the subject. We could say then that the organs of the body, precisely that upon which phenomenology or even to an extent empiricism rely, are the conditions of the impossibility of any truth coming to be.

3) It is not at all the body that conditions the self-knowledge of the subject. That is to say, as Lacan does in Seminar XXIII, that no one says 'I am a body' but rather 'I have a body' – 'its belonging or the natural "sameness" of the self' – for the body is nothing but the 'receptacle for the impact of the other' (2009a: 477). This is paradigmatically the image of *le sac*, the body as body-bag, the body as place of habitation pure and simple, the place where the subject is 'constituted as exterior to itself'.

In sum, as Badiou quotes, 'the body comes second whether it is dead or alive'. Thus it is either 'inert mediation' or 'exposition' with regard to 'linguistic structure' for Lacan. A body is what it is for a subject; not as cause, but as effect. Certainly the biology of the subject is 'at stake' in analysis, but the body is itself not the cause of the subject effect. The body bears the brunt of the effect of structure or, more precisely, is 'affected by structure'. Badiou highlights affect as equivalent for Lacan with the body, such that structure effects it. Clearly the inertia of the body cannot effect the constitution of the subject of language qua the unconscious, as the 'animal that inhabits language' (2009a: 478). There is a place of speech, and it is 'in flesh and bone, that is with all our carnal and sympathetic complexity, that we inhabit this place' (2009a: 478). Subordinated to the signifier in this way, Badiou suggests that the body according to Lacan is far removed from 'the doctrine . . . which makes of the body an active composition, the support for the appearing of a subject-form, whose organs treat the world point by point' (2009a: 478). Yet, as Badiou contends, it is actually by way of this anti-phenomenological (and anti-vital) reduction of the body to the affect of structure and the subject separated from any effect of this affect – ostensibly through Lacan's delimitation of the subject vis-à-vis 'mathematical formalisation', for example, to topology[6] – that Badiou himself can come to re-purpose the phenomenon of the subject 'objectively', as a body of truth.[7]

Insofar as Lacan stands opposed to the phenomenological constitution of the body as the 'presence of consciousness to the world' (Badiou 2009a: 478), Badiou concurs with him. His citing Lacan here is of the order of an affirmation, one that has been inscribed in his philosophy for some time: 'By wanting to resolve itself into presence-through-the-body, phenomenology ... condemns itself both to transgressing its field and to making an experience that is foreign to it inaccessible' (2009a: 478). The motif of the 'construction' of the 'inaccessible' ('ineffable', 'unsayable', 'mystical', etc.) is one that Badiou opposes in all philosophies and is in fact for him a fundamental mark of antiphilosophy and sophistry alike: of the former, insofar as the vitality of subjective action reduces the question of truth to its active performance; of the latter, insofar as its motif is the reduction of appearing to being such that any attempt to think their in-separation supposes a Real by definition inaccessible to thought. Either way, the ineffable emerges as the limit of the subject, the death and dearth of its knowledge as such. Such phenomenological construction requires as the horizon of its possibility and the basis of its knowledge a subjective incapacity as the guarantee of any subject at all. Yet what Lacan means by 'an experience foreign to [the subject]' is essentially the unconscious and its 'structure'. In a tight formulation Badiou shows that, for Lacan, under the condition of the signifier the letters that effectively structure the subject's being – a being subject on the basis of its 'speaking' – are entirely at odds with phenomenology. For phenomenology, 'by separating the body from the letters that target it, institutes the presence-to-the-world of the body as the ontology of originary experience' (2009a: 478).

At this point there is a first explicit concord between Lacan, in the guise of his rejection of phenomenology, and Badiou in terms of what he can elicit from this rejection for his own 'minimally different', yet consequentially maximal, materialist concept of a body as a body of truth. Badiou notes that Lacan's ostensibly polemical thesis does not preclude the body being the name of the subject: 'We can also grant Lacan that the body is the place of the Other, since for us it is only the evental becoming-Other of the site which commands the possibility of a body of truth' (2009a: 479). Moreover, Lacan's thesis concerning the trace of the signifier as written in the body of the animal such that it constitutes the very materiality of the conditions of desire means that 'if we understand that these effects on the animal are also the effects in the world of the animal', we have 'a marked body whose fate would then lie on the side of the True' (2009a: 479). Yet the question of this oscil-lation (what Miller calls its 'duplicity' [2004: 43]) in the subject between the two poles of what effects it, that is to say, its marking as such – which is its existence – opens it to the 'precarious equi-librium' of resistance to both the obliterated and the vanished. Or, in other words, in the guise of the 'true' subject (incorporation), the animal body is always torn or tempted between assertions of its existence (dogmatism) or claims for its in-existence (obscurant-ism). This typology of the subject – which is laid out both figurally (faithful, reactionary, obscurantist) and destinally (production, denial, occultation and resurrection relative to the new form of the present) – is set out in the first sections of *Logics of Worlds*.[8]

As such, the subject in appearing depends, like anything else, on the regime of identities and differences organised by the tran-scendental of its world and, as such, on the intensities or degrees of its existence (between the minimum, m and the maximum, M) relative to and sustained by this transcendental order. Change, as Badiou points out, actually names the repetitions that reproduce this order as integral to it. Yet change in the transcendental itself is what this (re)production actively proscribes. Let us note this is not an act of ignorance but of knowledge itself. In effect, it cannot know as knowledge anything but its own repetition.

The key motif Badiou retains here from Lacan is that of the mark or the trace; in Badiou's sense, the trace in the world of a disappeared event – thus articulating the m, minimal degree of appearing of the site, with the transcendental, to M, maximum intensity for that world. The materiality of what forms on the basis of this immanent reversal of existential existences preserves, in its taking place, point by point, the trace of this occurring. Badiou remarks on the image Lacan himself uses of the 'shearing' effect the signifier has on the subject, an image that is formalised in and by Category Theory in terms of the theory of sheaves. In this case, it refers to the onto-logic of the passing of the subject into its negation or obscurity and thus as one possible effect of the intensity of its relation to the trace which marks it out. The trace is not, strictly speaking, a new notion in Badiou given that the subject in terms of its deployment of a name provided the disappeared event with its material trace, but here its function is better discerned, effectively marking the real of the subject insofar as its becoming is correlated to the event and its persistence to the consequences whose significance the trace effects.[9] The trace (of the event) marks the beginning of the body – composed of all the eventally incorporated elements of the site – and its orientation (Badiou 2009a: 480).

Following this line of thinking, Badiou concurs with Lacan over the necessity of the cut, of the uptake of the 'upsurge of the new': 'It is then necessary that the truthful grasp of a subject over the world manifest itself in the regime of the cut, of the upsurge of a new present, and not in that of productive continuity' (2009a: 480). For Lacan, the cut is that by which the speaking being presents itself to the world. This act of presentation, possible only on the basis of what happens in the world as exception to reproduction and repetition – 'punching a hole in knowledge' – thus demonstrates the non-whole or not-all of what insists as the knowledge or transcendental regime of a given world. What for Lacan is thought of as the subjective cut of truth that holes-out knowledge in its act is precisely what Badiou here calls 'incorporation'. For Badiou, Lacan has mistaken a contingent, creative operation for the mere consequence of a structure. Incorporation is the 'effect of truth' (2009a: 480).

As Badiou elaborates: 'Incorporation into what? Into this new body electrified by the impact of the trace' (2009a: 480). Affect becomes the name for the articulation of what we might call the body a subject divides as an effect of its relation to truth. In Badiou's words, 'it is indeed by its affect that the human animal recognizes that it participates, through its incorporated body, in some subject of truth' (2009a: 480). These affects register in the four conditional discourses of science, art, politics and love as joy, pleasure, enthusiasm and happiness respectively (2009a: 77). The key point is that these affects are of recognition and not constitution – there is no natural correlation at stake whatsoever. Instead, this 'correlation' can only be adequately thought according to a formal topological distribution. Against every vitalistic account, these affects do not register an experience of the world, or an emergence of any type of thing, but rather the mundane inscription of the idea:[10] the idea of what it is to live.

To live, in this sense – whether joyfully, happily, and so on, to be thinkable and thus be 'by truths' – is to be subject to a specific and formalisable orientation to one world in particular. For, if there are worlds at all for Badiou, they are worlds that are (logically ordered) localisations and consequences of the (ontologically emergent) conditions. In fact, strictly speaking, there are only four possible types of significant world for Badiou insofar as a truth is manifest therein – art, love, science and politics – and they are incommensurable. Philosophy is not a world, and nor is there any affect – except, perhaps, indifference – that is characteristic of it. There is no total world or universe, as Badiou demonstrates again and again, often by recourse to Russell's paradox. For any such total 'world' would be necessarily inconsistent, and therefore not a world at all. Just as inconsistent would be any philosophy that considered itself inherently political (or scientific or artistic or amorous): there is no such thing, except as obscurantist *flatus vocis*.[11]

But this entails that every world worthy of the name must itself be such that it admits of a point which is effectively that by which it is *this* world and not another. For Badiou, the regime of democratic materialism – to the extent that it is not simply inconsistent – effects as itself the drive towards pointlessness or what he calls atonicity:

> A world is said to be atonic when its transcendental is devoid of points ... in such worlds no faithful subjective formalism can serve as the agent of a truth, in the absence of the points that would make it possible for the efficacy of a body to confront such a truth. (2009a: 420)

A world without points is a world without truths, Badiou continues, a world of 'nothing but objects, nothing but bodies and languages'. This, he says, is the type of world or the 'happiness that the advocates of democratic materialism dream of' (2009a: 420). This conception of a world, such that it is of the very order of appearing, is the reverse of the Platonic conception, which sees in appearing perpetual change. Rather, as Badiou insists and conceptualises via the 'transcendental', the astonishing thing about democratic materialism is how constant it is, how stable its laws of appearing. Hence, the necessity of the event's contingency, and the take-up of its rupture with these laws as divergent consequences of the event. As Badiou remarks, in the order of appearing the pointed reverse – m's becoming M, that is, the inexistent minimum becoming the maximum – is what makes negation appear.[12]

We now need to elaborate the 'point' at which Badiou dissents, as always, from Lacan. The character of this dissent is nothing other than fidelity; which is to say, of taking the next step. It is not surprising, then, that Badiou finds or founds this point in the Other, in the ambiguity of the theory of the 'two bodies' as already mentioned above: 'In this aspect of his teaching, Lacan treats what I believe to be a sequence or a contingent becoming as a structure' (2009a: 480). This structure is language, which is what provides the human animal with its modicum of difference from the animal as such. Badiou cautions against the Heideggerian influence within this claim, which in turn suggests a residual Aristotelianism in Lacan (insofar as logic retains an ontological priority, thereby overreaching its capacities). If man is the political animal par excellence, distinct from all others insofar as it organises itself, language as structure – more primary than politics perhaps – still situates the 'what is not' in the first body in the second via what recurs, and not via what is exception. That is to say, it is as speaking being – man insofar as inhabited by language – that the division of bodies and the Other body is ensured, to which language effectively bars man access. As so often, it is a question of the recurrence of the One, even if not every approach to this One is the same.[13]

Badiou's reference here is to the opposition Lacan discusses in Seminar XXIII, manifest in speech between the body a man *has* as speaking being and that which he is, and *is* insofar as this body is 'used' by him. In a talk from around the same time, 'Lecture on the Body', Lacan asserts and extends this point and offers a paradoxical conceit:

> Between the body insofar as it is imagined and what binds it (namely, the fact of speaking), man imagines himself as thinking. He thinks in so far as he speaks. Speaking has effects on his body. Owing to the fact that he speaks, he is almost as clever as an animal. An animal gets by very well without speaking. (2013b: 8)

The body is split between its imaginary and the real, which are in turn, via a conceit inscribed in language itself – that of thinking –

bound insofar as the materiality of the latter supports the figural occurrence of the former. 'The real,' Lacan continues, 'is not the outside world; it is anatomy too, it involves the entire body' (2013b: 9). Hence the knotting-together of this body, upon which everything conceptually depends, requires what Lacan denominates as 'a geometry of the real'.[14] In effect, we have then an object body, a body one has (as is said in normal speech 'I have a body'), and an 'other' or symptomal body that nevertheless, Badiou notes, cannot be what the subject is in possession of and cannot be therefore 'the basis of a new subject'. Badiou, again:

> It follows from all this that the formal operations of incorporation into the place of the Other and of splitting of the subject constitute, under the name of Unconscious, the infrastructure of the human animal and not the occurrence – as rare as it may be – of the present-process of a truth which a subjectivated body treats point by point. (2009a: 481)

By turns, Lacan is too philosophical and then not philosophical enough: in determining the object of psychoanalysis to be what man lacks and not man himself, Lacan is in accord with philosophy, à la Badiou at any rate. For, insofar as it is what democratic materialism lacks – eternal truths and thus at least one decisive point – philosophy insists on the real of an *other* bodily incorporation *in* a given world. Yet, Badiou states, when Lacan de-absolutises *a priori* what such an incorporation entails, that is to say, when he inscribes a limit on the unfolding in a world of a truth, he 'takes a step too far in the direction of finitude'. Of course, Lacan is not interested in being a philosopher or (re)producing a philosophy whose 'inaugural mistake' is precisely to affirm the absolute against the 'breach of the subject' in order to 'bolt down truth' (Badiou 2009a: 481).

Badiou once described biology as 'a wild empiricism without a concept'. His dislike of Aristotle's 'bio-logic' is manifest. Thus it is with some trepidation that one reads Badiou's first claim against Lacan's situating of the essence of the subject as an effect of language. 'Inhabiting speech' does not suffice to 'situate the singularity of the human animal' nor, he continues, does its being linguistically marked suffice to account for its breaching of its animality per se. Badiou claims, in the first instance, that in fact 'animals with small brains' (and thus no speech) such as the 'water turtle' exhibit behaviours that demonstrate the divisibility of the body into 'mine' and its symptomal Other: 'As soon as it sees me [it] swims towards the glass of the aquarium, frenetically thrashing its feet, and looks at me with its shining yellow-green reptilian eyes, until, intimidated or culpable, I give it its ration of dried prawns' (2009a: 481).

Three aspects allay some of this trepidation: first, Badiou is directing his comments at Lacan's continuing regard for ethology and more specifically at the notion that the animal body articulates itself to the natural world outside it, to which it nonetheless remains internal. For Lacan this form of articulation between an *Umwelt* and an *Innenwelt* is not the way it works for the subject and thus this articulation cannot be good enough – hence the effort to provide a matheme not only for an existence which is otherwise inexpressible, but also for what cannot be expressed in a matheme. Thus Badiou's recourse to the turtle is not to say that the division of the subject is in nature – after all, we know that nature 'abhors a void' – but to mark that it is an ontological rather than a (bio)logical question.

It is not in fact topology that founds this division, given it is visible in animality. Topology does not 'construct holes', rather it localises in a world that by which some (non-w)'hole' may come to be thought (Miller 2004: 42). Thirdly, there is an intertextual issue: this biological example is related directly to Badiou's earlier figural sketch of the exhaustion of the subject. In his exposition of the renewed concept of the site, and using the failure of the Paris Commune as example, Badiou refers to a plaintive figure at the barricades handing out vouchers for dried herring; effectively, the symptom of a subject reduced to its linguistic effects and its bodily drives. 'It is only as a transhuman body that a subject takes hold of the divisible body of the human animal. The breach is then on the side of creation, not of the symptom' (or *sinthome*) (2009a: 481), Badiou argues: in the world following an event and not in the subject itself. This echoes his ontological refutations concerning the placement of the void in his essays on Lacan in *Conditions* and restated in 'The Formulas of *L'Etourdit*', wherein he demonstrates, via the formal apparatus of set theory, that Lacan situates this void on the side of the subject, whereas for Badiou it belongs, fundamentally in fact, on the side of being. Thus the subject is not itself divided, but is the effect of the immanent division between place and decision. Its real, so to speak, is marked by every point – itself the concentration of the nuances of the sets of relations that make up a locale – held through the unfolding of a truth in a world.

Apart from anything else we can take this reading of Badiou's as an instance of the compatibility (though irreducibility) of set and categorial thought, as he maintains: the category of the object being the hinge on which this 'fixion' (à la Lacan) of compatibility turns. Finally, then, it is what Lacan's body renders impossible to think concerning the body – that, as Badiou says, 'it is in vain that some, under the impulse of democratic materialism, wish to convince us, after the comedy of the soul, that our body is the proven place of the One' – that becomes Badiou's starting place – even if this lesson on Lacan is the second to last one on the body. This beginning is such that 'we observe the gap between, on one hand, the transcendental laws of appearing and, on the other, the present engendered by a subjectivisable body, a present that initiates an eternal truth. This is also the gap between the multiple-body of the human animal and its subjective incorporation' (2009a: 482).

As noted, the key claim is this: 'Lacan treats what I believe to be a sequence or a contingent becoming as a structure' (2009a: 480). This means that the subject is the effect of the One, ultimately, which is simply to say of language. To speak is to mark bodily this effect of structure – the subject's 'two bodies' – whereas, proceeding categorially and by means of his reconceptualisation of the 'object', Badiou is able to demonstrate literally (ontologically) distinct elements as categorially or logically the same (2006a: 147). Certainly where Lacan hesitates is in any claim to a full-blown ontology (see Badiou 2005a: 4). For Badiou, ultimately, what Lacan introduces is two things: first, that the subject and ontology are incompatible, which to the philosopher Badiou means that the topology of their non-relation will need to be found, established and formalised; and, second, that this arrangement of the subject as topologically conditioned is that which opens up the possible forms of the subject's appearing, even if what founds it is not itself topologically constituted and even if the latter must indeed itself inscribe, in its own logic, this non-constitution.

In *Being and Event* Badiou presents the fundamentals of a 'finally objectless subject': 'concerning such a subject, one can neither designate its correlate in presentation, nor suppose that it answers to any of thought's objectives' (Badiou 1988: 93). Badiou argues that, since Kant, the destitution of the subject has been conflated with that of the destitution of the object and hence the modern imperative that denies that any form of the object sustains any conception of truth results also in a similar denial with regard to the subject (1988: 93). De-objectifying the subject is the task Badiou undertakes in order to re-forge the link of subjects and truths: 'The "subject" thus ceases to be the inaugural or conditioning point of legitimate statements. He is no longer – and here we see the cancellation of the object, as objective this time – that *for which* there is truth, nor even the desirous eclipse of its surrection' (1988: 93, original emphasis).

In *Being and Event*, the subject 'de-idealised' insofar as it is 'woven out of truth' and neither precedes what it sustains nor remains without it and so the conception of an object or of objectivity as such has no recourse to the knowledge, experience or gaze of some subject. In *Logics of Worlds*, this concept of the subject is affirmed, but the axiomatic is reversed as Badiou presents the transcendental analytic '(order, minimum, conjunction, envelope)' and the axiomatic '(symmetry and triangular inequality for the conjunction)' of the subject-less object, or the coming to be of a being as being there (2009a: 238). In short, an object appears to a world, which is to say, a transcendental is the place of appearing for any elemental being and the being-there of this (ontologically demonstrable) element is as object. An object thereby is the *one* of elemental being and what it is for this element to be indexed by a transcendental, which, finally, is nothing but the spatial deposition of elements in terms of their relative degrees of identity and differences. It is an (onto)logic and not an effect of cognition, understanding, experience or emergence.

Yet this logic does not prescribe the being of the object, which *is* as element: '[T]he word "object" also designates a point of conjunction or reversibility between the ontological (belonging to a multiple) and the logical (transcendental indexing), between the invariance of the multiple and the variation of its worldly exposition' (Badiou 2009a: 250). Or, again: '[T]o borrow an image from Lacan . . . the One (the atom) is the quilting point of appearing within being' (2009a: 248). In other words, 'every atom is real' as Badiou's 'postulate of materialism' has it, such that 'real atoms [attest] to the appearance, in appearing, of the being of appearing' (2009a: 218). In a world, an element *becomes* an object. Or, an element is an object of a transcendental whose elemental being remains objectless. But as every world has a transcendental – being as being there – what appears has its objectival form. The world, insofar as it is *a* world and never *the* world – except perhaps for its inhabitants – is logically closed, in that its extension 'remains inaccessible to the operations that open up its multiple-being and allow it to radiate' and yet 'it unfolds it own infinity' (2009a: 309). The distinction between infinite, indefinite and unlimited recurs again, fracturing the whole:

> This impossibility is what assures that a world is closed, without it thereby being representable as a Whole from the interior of the scene of appearance that it constitutes. A world is closed for the operations that set out the being-qua-being of what appears within it: transitivity, dissemination, totalisation of parts. (Badiou 2009a: 309)

Category Theory, the abstract formalisation of the logic of *topoi* or possible worlds, is, as Badiou notes, a mathematised logic. Philosophically, a world qua transcendental qua its order is onto-logically given as a complete Heyting Algebra (Badiou 2004a: 531):

> [W]hat governs appearing is not the ontological composition of a par-ticular being (a multiple), but the relational evaluations that determine [*fixe*] the situation and localise it within it. (Badiou 2013: Book II)

The question that concerns us is that of the object body as the material incarnation of the truth of the subject. Thus the destruc-tion, via the logic of the reverse and the affirmation of at least one point, of atonality: what democratic materialism aims at (Badiou 2009a: 509). Hence we need to tie our elaboration of Badiou's conception of an objectless subject and a body of truth to the declaration Badiou aims at in this text: 'What is it to live?' Let us recall that in the preface he remarks on his effort to recast entirely the conception of the object and that this 'proud effort' takes up the greater part of the book. Yet

> radical as this project may be, and even though its complete logic is worked through in minute detail, it is not my real aim. In effect, I subordinate the logic of appearing, objects and worlds to the trans-worldly affirmation of subjects faithful to a truth. (2009a: 37)

To be faithful to a truth is for Badiou what it is to live with an Idea. As such, 'life is a subjective category' and 'a body is the materiality that life requires' (2009a 508) but the construction of a present, which is what is at stake in a fidelity – against the atonality of democratic materialism and its efforts to preserve what is as avatar of the past and object of the future (which it proceeds to under the name reform) – relies not on the proximity but rather the intensity of the relation of this body to the event. The body is the material support, the place in the world of a becoming truth only insofar as it incorporates to itself, and thus in the world for which it is a body, the trace of the event: 'To live is thus an incorporation into the present under the faithful form of a subject' (2009a: 508). This essentially takes the form of a 'recommencement' given that nothing happens other than as relative to a world.

The question of 'what is it to live' is certainly political but it is never only or uniquely political. For, contrary to the popular slogan, there are worlds besides the political. Even if it is the latter which prescribes the thought of collectives and hence that of its singular principle – justice – it is itself the very form of injustice itself to totalise worlds under its heading. The problem is, as we have seen, of a different order: 'Given that a subjectivisable body is a new body, this problem requires that one know what the "appearance" of a body means, and therefore, more generally, that one elucidate what appearing, and therefore objectivity, may be' (Badiou 2009a: 37). It is precisely this that Badiou accomplishes in *Logics of Worlds*, with an unprecedented vision and rigour, and with an explicitly topological approach.

As we have shown in this essay, it is the paradox of fidelity that permits Badiou to think this. He has done this above all by rethinking his way past Lacan – yet necessarily only through Lacan. Lacan, as we have seen, maintained throughout his career the instance of the subject against all comers, emphasised the necessity of mathematical formalisation as ideal, insisted on the primacy of topology in the thinking of the subject, held open the gap between truth and knowledge, and, perhaps above all, forced a rethinking of psychoanalysis as antiphilosophy insofar as analysis must locate itself at the impossible intersection of irreducible discourses – '"analysis of analysis" in Galois' words' (Badiou 2009a: 464). Yet in doing so, Lacan hit an aporia that he himself could not fathom: the disjunction between poiesis and matheme, creation and formalisation, ultimately and literally drove him to an act of dissolution. It is precisely at this point that Badiou picks up the challenge, to pass through the impasse. In doing so, Badiou maintains every decisive element of Lacan's *piste*, except for one: to be a philosopher, not an antiphilosopher. This entails a return to ontology, and thus a concomitant re-situation of the place of the void itself. In doing so, almost all the key determinations of Lacan's body are also sustained: division, affect, recreation. Moreover, the self-situation of philosophy as the act of compossibilising incommensurable practices to which it is itself irreducible (the conditions) remains definitive from the outset. What is not maintained is the limit-link between subject and object in Lacan (of void subject and evacuated object), and what Badiou has done in *Logics* is reconstruct the consequences for the philosophical formalisation of the subjective *body* of truth itself.

Out of our Socrates, Lacan, our Plato, Badiou.

Notes

1. Regarding Lacan's defence of the subject, Badiou reiterates: 'That is why traversing Lacan's antiphilosophy remains an obligatory exercise today for those who wish to wrest themselves away from the reactive convergences of religion and scientism' (2009a: 523).
2. In an interesting remark Jacques-Alain Miller notes that Sartre was a strong influence on Lacan particularly in the latter's development of the 'insubstantial subject' or 'sss' (*sujet-supposeé-savoir* or *sujet-sans-substance*) (Miller 2004: 38).
3. In *Theory of the Subject* Badiou cites this note from Lacan's *Ecrits* appended to the original text of 'The Purloined Letter' reproduced there: 'The introduction of a structural approach to the field in psychoanalytic theory through such exercises was, in fact, followed by important developments in my teaching. Concepts related to subjectivisation progressed hand in hand with a reference to *analysis situs* in which I claim to materialize the subjective process.' Badiou says: 'These concepts of subjectivisation and subjective process are crucial to me.' The first, algebraic, is a matter of the 'time of insurrection'; the second, topological, is a matter of 'recomposition' (2009b: 243–4).
4. 'It is essential to see that existence is not a category of being as such, but rather a category of appearing; or, more rigorously, that existence rises [*relève*] from the logic of being, and not from its ontological status. It is only according to its being-there, and not according to its multiple composition, that a being can be said to exist. And this is always, at the same time, a degree of existence, situated between

inexistence and absolute existence. Existence is at once a logical and an intensive concept' (Badiou 2013: n.p.).

5. Miller observes that given that the famous 'mirror stage' is not of the order of 'psychoanalytic experience' but that of 'observation', the body is effectively the 'first entry of an element foreign to analysis' (2004: 37). He says that in Lacan the 'Imaginary is the Body' and importantly for our discussion it falls under the structure of the signifier, which is to say it is the subject 'mortified' (2004: 38).

6. As Miller points out, topology has been integral to (or 'cannot be extracted from') Lacan since the Rome Discourse and so the earliest seminars of the 1950s. The key to it for Lacan, Miller says, is that it can serve to sustain a thing beyond its existence (2004: 29). Now, the distinction of being and existence is one Badiou will fully expound and in this he will concur with Lacan that topology formalises existence – or what it is to appear. But the 'science of appearing' or relation as such, remains for Badiou under condition of the mathematical science of being (2004a: 172–3).

7. It goes without saying that Badiou's efforts in *Theory of the Subject* are absolutely inspired by Lacan's deployment of topology, or by the fact that Lacanian psychoanalysis, insofar as it thinks structure, thinks topology. As Ragland and Milovanovic remark, 'Lacan called topology or RSI structure itself' (2004: xv). However, it is also necessary to realise that by the late 1970s Lacan had reached the point of impossibility of this trajectory, and the knot of the subject and its formalisation had become a suture. There was effectively no way that topology could still 'construct the holes' (Miller 2004: 42) necessary to think the continuation of the subject in analysis. Thus *Theory of the Subject*, vis-à-vis Lacan at any rate, is an attempt to have done with this suture and so recommence the thinking of the subject. It is also necessary to remark that *Theory of the Subject* fails. It is *Being and Event* alone that properly formalises being without existence (thus without relation or the dialectic – to the constant horror of some commentators) and thus solely what authorises the return to topology and the reformalisation of the subject and its material body in *Logics of Worlds*. Any effort to bypass *Being and Event*, no matter the rhetorical strategies invoked, no matter the conditions singly (thus erroneously) convoked, and thus to suture *Logics of Worlds* and *Theory of the Subject*, misunderstands the entire project and import of Badiou's philosophy. With Lacan, we must insist that 'mathematics' is 'not a metaphor'. On this, see Bartlett and Clemens forthcoming: ch. 1.

8. When 'crossed' with the four generic procedures and the affects that correspond to them there are, as Badiou notes, twenty concepts (2009a: 570) that make up the 'complex of the subject'. On this last notion, see Bartlett 2011: esp. ch. 4.

9. This point bears on the translation of the ontological-evental doctrines of *Being and Event* into the phenomenological-evental doctrines of *Logics of Worlds*. As we know from the first book, mathematics = ontology, whereas the poem = event. The event qua upsurge of a fragment of being suspends the axiom of foundation insofar as the event must precisely not be a 'well-founded multiple'. The poem is the paradigm of such a multiple, and one of its characteristics is therefore that of embodying the paradoxes of nomination or, in the latest vocabulary, trace. See Badiou 2005c, especially the chapters dedicated to poetry in particular.

10. 'I am outright opposed to the idea of a construction of truths as a process of an "emergent" type. I see there what has always been my capital philosophical adversary: Vitalism. Vitalism aims at making the "birth" protocols, that is, the result of an embryological formation, the paradigm of every kind of creation. Eternity is only a trace in the continuum of the non-temporal character of the eventor if you like, in the instantaneous caesura imposed onto worldly temporalities. The construction of a generic manifold is then a mix of continuity (the becoming of the subjectivizable body) and discontinuous (point-by-point construction). It is not the temporal emergence of a limit. It could not be, because it creates its own time' (Constantinou and Madarasz 2009: 788).

11. In François Laruelle's *Anti-Badiou* we see set against this conditional arrangement the positing of a quantum philosophy, one which, no less, makes of humanity as such the generic bulwark against all forms of 'philosophy'. In this case Badiou is the brilliant and paradigmatic – to use Laruelle's terms – form of it today. The subtitle tells the story: 'On the Introduction of Maoism into Philosophy'; hence a totalising and, as Laruelle says, 'pitiless' effort to subject humanity to the philosopher. See Laruelle 2013.

12. 'The fundamental consequence of an event, the crucial trace left by the disappearance of the strong singularity, which is its apparent-being, is the existential absolutization of the inexistent. The inexistent was transcendentally evaluated by the minimum; it is now, in its post-evental figure, evaluated by the maximum' (Badiou 2009a: 394).

13. Cf. *Being and Event*: 'It is not a question, however, of abandoning

the principle Lacan assigned to the symbolic; that there is Oneness. Everything turns on mastering the gap between the presupposition (that must be rejected) of a being of the one and the thesis of its "there is". What could there be, which is not? Strictly speaking, it is already too much to say "there is Oneness" because the "there", taken as an errant localization, concedes a point of being to the one' (Badiou 2005a: 3–4).

14. 'A slave is defined by the fact that someone has power over his or her body. Geometry is the same thing, it has a lot to do with bodies' (Lacan 2013b: 8).

Notes on Contributors

Alain Badiou teaches philosophy at the École normale supérieure and the Collège international de philosophie in Paris. In addition to major philosophical works, several novels and plays, he has also made a number of critical political interventions, including *Polemics*, *Metapolitics*, *The Meaning of Sarkozy* and *The Rebirth of History*.

A. J. Bartlett is an Adjunct Research Fellow at the Research Unit in European Philosophy at Monash University. He is the author of *Badiou and Plato: An Education by Truths*, translator with Alex Ling of *Badiou's Mathematics of the Transcendental* and with Justin Clemens and Jon Roffe author of *Lacan Deleuze Badiou*, forthcoming with EUP.

Justin Clemens teaches at the University of Melbourne. His recent books include *Psychoanalysis is an Antiphilosophy* (EUP, 2013). He is currently writing a monograph on Alain Badiou with A. J. Bartlett.

Born in Cyprus, still semi-occupied by Turkish troops, **Marios Constantinou** holds a PhD from the New School for Social Research. Until recently he held a post at the University of Cyprus from which he resigned in protest against corruption, censorship and the increasing NGOisation of academic life. His publications on and reviews of Badiou's work reclaim it in an anti-imperialist direction as the only available alternative to the postcolonial impasse of foreign dependence and local corruption. His forthcoming book is entitled *Empire and the Swerve of Politics*. Current publications on these issues have appeared in *Parallax*, *Third Text*, *Parrhēsia* and *The Year's Work in Critical and Cultural Theory*.

Dominiek Hoens teaches Philosophy and Psychology of Art at University Colleges in Ghent and Brussels. He is the author of articles and book chapters on Lacan, Badiou and Duras, on logical time, love and catastrophe. Together with Sigi Jöttkandt he edits the open access journal *S: Journal of the Jan van Eyck Circle for Lacanian Ideology Critique* (www.lineofbeauty.org)

Sean Homer is Associate Professor of Literature at the American University in Bulgaria. He is author of *Fredric Jameson: Marxism, Hermeneutics, Postmodernism* (1998) and *Jacques Lacan: Routledge Critical Thinkers* (2005). He is co-editor (with Douglas Kellner) of *Fredric Jameson: A Critical Reader* (2004) and (with Ruth Parkin-Gounelas and Yannis Stavrakakis) of *Objects: Material, Psychic, Aesthetic* (2006). His most recent publications have been on Balkan cinema and the position of Slavoj Žižek in Balkan politics and theory.

Canadian-born, **Norman Madarasz** earned his PhD at the University of Paris (Vincennes à Saint-Denis) under Alain Badiou's supervision. He is currently Associate Professor of Philosophy, in the areas of political philosophy and philosophical systems, at the Graduate School of the Pontifical Catholic University of Porto Alegre in Brazil (PUCRS). Author of *O Múltiplo sem Um: uma apresentação do sistema filosófico de Alain Badiou* (São Paulo: Ideias e Letras, 2011), he has published broadly on contemporary French philosophy, secularism and international political relations. At PUCRS, he co-directs the research group on Logics of Transformation.

Christopher Norris is Distinguished Research Professor in Philosophy at the University of Cardiff in Wales. He has written more than thirty books on various aspects of philosophy and critical theory, most recently *Derrida, Badiou and the Formal Imperative*. He has also published a volume of philosophical verse-essays entitled *The Cardinal's Dog* (2013) and many writings on music and music theory.

Ed Pluth is Professor and Chair of the Department of Philosophy at California State University, Chico. He is the author of *Signifiers and Acts* (SUNY Press, 2007) and *Badiou: A Philosophy of the*

254   Badiou and the Political Condition

New (Polity, 2010), as well as numerous articles on issues in the works of Badiou, Lacan and Žižek.

Frank Ruda is a Researcher at the Collaborative Research Center 626 at the Free University, Berlin, Visiting Lecturer at the Slovenian Academy of Arts and Sciences, Ljubljana, and Visiting Professor at the European College for the Liberal Arts (ECLA of Bard), Berlin. His most recent books are *Hegel's Rabble. An Investigation into Hegel's Philosophy of Right* (Continuum, 2011) and *For Badiou. Idealism without Idealism* (forthcoming with Northwestern University Press). Currently he is working on two books: *The Dash* (together with Rebecca Comay) and *Absolute Indifference. Descartes, Kant, Hegel and Plato*.

Jan Voelker is a researcher at the Collaborative Research Center 626 at the Free University, Berlin. He is the co-editor of the series *morale provisoire* at the Merve Verlag in Berlin and visiting lecturer at the Slovenian Academy of Arts and Sciences, Ljubljana. His publications include *Ästhetik der Lebendigkeit. Kants dritte Kritik [Aesthetics of Liveliness, Kant's third Critique]* (Fink, 2011) and *Neue Philosophien des Politischen zur Einführung. Laclau, Lefort, Nancy, Rancière, Badiou [Introduction to New Philosophies of the Political. Laclau, Lefort, Nancy, Rancière, Badiou]* (co-authored with Uwe Hebekus, Junius, 2012).

Bibliography

Works by Alain Badiou

Badiou, Alain (1975), *Théorie de la contradiction*, Paris: Maspero.

Badiou, Alain, and François Balmès (1976), *De l'idéologie*, Paris: Maspero.

Badiou, Alain (1985), *Peut-on penser la politique?*, Paris: Seuil.

Badiou, Alain (1988), 'On a Finally Objectless Subject', trans. Bruce Fink, *Topoi*, 7: 93–8.

Badiou, Alain (1991), 'On a Finally Objectless Subject', in Eduardo Cadava et al. (eds), *Who Comes After the Subject?*, New York and London: Routledge, 24–32.

Badiou, Alain (1992), 'Qu'est-ce que l'amour', in Badiou, *Conditions*, Paris: Seuil, 253–73.

Badiou, Alain (1999a), *Manifesto for Philosophy*, ed. and trans. Norman Madarasz, Albany: State University of New York Press.

Badiou, Alain (1999b), 'La Scène du deux', in *De l'amour*, ed. l'École de la Cause Freudienne, Paris: Champs Flammarion, 177–90.

Badiou, Alain (1999c), 'Politics and Philosophy', interview with Peter Hallward, *Angelaki: Journal for the Theoretical Humanities*, 3/3: 113–33.

Badiou, Alain (2001), *Ethics: An Essay on the Understanding of Evil*, trans. Peter Hallward, London and New York: Verso.

Badiou, Alain (2002), 'Esquisse pour un premier manifeste de l'affirmationisme', in Ciro Giordano Bruno (ed.), *Utopia 3, La question de l'art au 3e millénaire*, Sammeron: Germs, 13–32.

Badiou, Alain (2003a), *Infinite Thought: Truth and the Return to Philosophy*, trans. Oliver Feltham and Justin Clemens, London: Continuum.

Badiou, Alain (2003b), *Saint Paul. The Foundation of Universalism*, trans. Ray Brassier, Stanford: Stanford University Press.

Badiou, Alain (2004a), *Theoretical Writings*, ed. and trans. Ray Brassier and Alberto Toscano, London and New York: Continuum.

Badiou, Alain (2004b), 'Huit thèses sur l'universel', Centre international d'études sur la philosophie française contemporaine, http://www. ciepfc.fr/spip.php?article69Moore (accessed 8 August 2013).

Badiou, Alain (2005a), *Being and Event*, trans. Oliver Feltham, London and New York: Continuum.

Badiou, Alain (2005b), *Metapolitics*, trans. Jason Barker, London and New York: Continuum.

Badiou, Alain (2005c), *Handbook of Inaesthetics*, trans. Alberto Toscano, Stanford: Stanford University Press.

Badiou, Alain (2005d), *Politics: a Non-Expressive Dialectics*, London: Urbanomics.

Badiou, Alain (2006a), *Briefings on Existence: A Short Treatise on Transitory Ontology*, Albany: State University of New York Press.

Badiou, Alain (2006b), *Polemics*, trans. Steven Corcoran, London and New York: Verso.

Badiou, Alain (2006c), 'Plato, Our Dear Plato!', trans. Alberto Toscano, *Angelaki: Journal for the Theoretical Humanities*, 2/3: 39–41.

Badiou, Alain (2006d), 'The Factory as Event Site: Why Should the Worker Be a Reference in Our Vision of Politics?', *Prelom*, 8: 171–6.

Badiou, Alain (2006e), *Logiques des mondes. L'Être et l'évenement, 2*, Paris: Seuil.

Badiou, Alain (2007), *The Century*, trans. Alberto Toscano, Cambridge: Polity Press.

Badiou, Alain (2007–8), *Séminaire d'Alain Badiou sur: Pour aujourd'hui: Platon!*, http://www.entretemps.asso.fr/Badiou/07–08.htm (accessed 15 July 2013).

Badiou, Alain (2008a), *Number and Numbers*, trans. Robin MacKay, Cambridge: Polity Press.

Badiou, Alain (2008b), *The Meaning of Sarkozy*, trans. David Fernbach, London and New York: Verso.

Badiou, Alain (2008c), 'The Communist Hypothesis', *New Left Review*, II/49: 29–42.

Badiou, Alain (2008d), 'Fifteen Theses on Contemporary Art', in Tobias Huber and Marcus Steinweg (eds), *Inästhetik*, Nr. 0, Zürich and Berlin: Diaphanes, 11–26.

Badiou, Alain (2008e), *Conditions*, trans. Steven Corcoran, London and New York: Continuum.

Badiou, Alain (2008f), 'What is Love, Sexuality, Desire?', lecture given at the European Graduate School, http://www.egs.edu/faculty/alain-badiou/videos/what-is-love-sexuality-and-desire/ (accessed 15 July 2013).

Badiou, Alain (2008g), '"We Need a Popular Discipline": Contemporary Politics and the Crisis of the Negative', *Critical Inquiry*, 34.4: 645–59.

Badiou, Alain (2008h), 'Roads to Renegacy: Interview by Eric Hazan', *New Left Review*, 53 (September–October), http://newleftreview.org/II/53/alain-badiou-roads-to-renegacy (accessed 22 April 2013).

Badiou, Alain (2009a), *Logics of Worlds: Being and Event II*, trans. Alberto Toscano, London and New York: Continuum.

Badiou, Alain (2009b), *Theory of the Subject*, trans. Bruno Bosteels, London and New York: Continuum.

Badiou, Alain (2009c), 'Thinking the Event', in Alain Badiou and Slavoj Žižek, *Philosophy in the Present*, Cambridge and Malden, MA: Polity Press, 1–55.

Badiou, Alain (2009d), *Pocket Pantheon: Figures of Postwar Philosophy*, trans. David Macey, London and New York: Verso.

Badiou, Alain, and Slavoj Žižek (2009e), *Philosophy in the Present*, ed. Peter Engelmann, trans. Peter Thomas and Alberto Toscano, Cambridge and Malden, MA: Polity Press.

Badiou, Alain, with Nicolas Truang (2009f), *Éloge de l'amour*, Paris: Flammarion/Café Voltaire.

Badiou, Alain (2009g), 'L'hypothèse communiste – interview d'Alain Badiou par Pierre Gaultier', *Le Grand Soir*, 6 August, http://www.legrandsoir.info/L-hypothese-communiste-interview-d-Alain-Badiou-par-Pierre.html (accessed 23 October 2012).

Badiou, Alain (2010a), *The Communist Hypothesis*, London/New York: Verso.

Badiou, Alain (2010b), 'Le Courage du présent', *Le Monde*, 13 February, http://www.lemonde.fr/idees/article/2010/02/13/le-courage-du-present-par-alain-badiou_1305322_3232.html (accessed 15 July 2013). Eng. trans. 'The Courage of Obscurantism', *The Symptom*, 11 (Spring 2010), http://www.lacan.com/symptom11/?p=163 (accessed 15 July 2013).

Badiou, Alain (2010c), *Five Lessons on Wagner*, trans. Susan Spitzer, London and New York: Verso.

Badiou, Alain (2010d), 'Does the Notion of Activist Art Still Have a Meaning?', talk given at Miguel Abreu Gallery, New York, 13 October 2010, video and transcript available at http://www.lacan.com/thesymptom/?page_id=1580 (accessed 18 July 2013).

Badiou, Alain (2010–11), *Séminaire d'Alain Badiou sur: Que signifie*

in Gabriel Riera (ed.), *Alain Badiou: Philosophy and its Conditions*, Albany: State University of New York Press, 119–38.

Critchley, Simon (1999), *Ethics, Politics, Subjectivity: Essays on Derrida, Levinas and Contemporary French Thought*, London and New York: Verso.

Deleuze, Gilles (2006), *The Fold: Leibniz and the Baroque*, trans. Tom Conley, London and New York: Continuum.

de Man, Paul (1996), *Aesthetic Ideology*, ed. Andrzej Warminski, Minneapolis: University of Minnesota Press.

Derrida, Jacques (1976), *Of Grammatology*, trans. Gayatri Chakravorty Spivak, Baltimore and London: Johns Hopkins University Press.

Derrida, Jacques (1977a), 'Signature Event Context', *Glyph*, 1: 172–97.

Derrida, Jacques (1977b), 'Limited Inc. a b c', *Glyph*, 2: 162–254.

Derrida, Jacques (1978), *Writing and Difference*, trans. Alan Bass, Chicago: University of Chicago Press.

Derrida, Jacques (1980), 'The Law of Genre', trans. Avital Ronell, *Critical Inquiry*, 7 (Fall): 55–81.

Derrida, Jacques (1992), 'Before the Law', trans. Avital Ronell, in Derrida, *Acts of Literature*, ed. Derek Attridge, London: Routledge, 181–220.

Dodd, Julian (2000), 'Musical Works as Eternal Types', *British Journal of Aesthetics*, 40: 424–40.

Dodd, Julian (2002), 'Defending Musical Platonism', *The British Journal of Aesthetics*, 42: 380–402.

Donaldson, Peter S. (1988), *Machiavelli and Mystery of State*, Cambridge: Cambridge University Press.

During, Elie (2005), 'How Much Truth can Art Bear? On Badiou's "Inaesthetics"', trans. Laura Balladur, *Polygraph*, 17: 143–55, special issue 'The Philosophy of Alain Badiou', ed. Matthew Wilkens, http://www.ciepfc.fr/spip.php?article135 (accessed 18 July 2013).

Eagleton, Terry (1990), *The Ideology of the Aesthetic*, Oxford: Blackwell.

Eliot, T. S. (1964), 'Tradition and the Individual Talent', in *Selected Essays*, London: Faber and Faber, 3–11.

Elliott, Neil (1994), *Liberating Paul: The Justice of God and the Politics of the Apostle*, New York: Orbis Books.

Elliott, John H. (1996), 'Patronage and Clientage', in Richard L. Rohrbaugh (ed.), *The Social Sciences and New Testament Interpretation*, Peabody, MA: Hendrickson, 142–56.

Feltham, Oliver (2008), *Alain Badiou: Live Theory*, London and New York: Continuum.

Freud, Sigmund (1953), 'Three Essays on the Theory of Sexuality', in *The*

Standard Edition of the Complete Psychological Works of Sigmund Freud, trans. James Strachey, vol. 7, London: Hogarth Press and the Institute of Psycho-Analysis, 123–245.

Gallagher, Cormac (2001), 'What Does Lacan See in Blaise Pascal?', http://www.lacaninireland.com/web/wp-content/uploads/2010/06/ Aut_2001–WHAT-DOES-JACQUES-LACAN-SEE-IN-BLAISE-PASCAL-Cormac-Gallagher.pdf (accessed 28 February 2013).

Goehr, Lydia (2007), *The Imaginary Museum of Musical Works: An Essay in the Philosophy of Music*, rev. edn, Oxford: Oxford University Press.

Goodenough, E. R. (1962), *An Introduction to Philo Judaeus*, Oxford: Blackwell.

Goodman, Nelson (1976), *Languages of Art: An Approach to a Theory of Symbols*, Indianapolis: Hackett.

Graeber, David (2011), *Debt: The First 5000 Years*, New York: Melville House.

Hacking, Ian (1990), *The Taming of Chance*, London: Cambridge University Press.

Hallward, Peter (2002), 'Badiou's Politics: Equality and Justice', *Culture Machine*, 4, http://www.culturemachine.net/index.php/cm/article/ viewArticle/271/256 (accessed 15 July 2013).

Hartman, Geoffrey (1970), *Beyond Formalism: Literary Essays 1958–1970*, New Haven, CT: Yale University Press.

Hayek, F. A. (1988), *The Fatal Conceit: The Errors of Socialism*, ed. W. W. Bartley III, London: Routledge.

Hegel, G. W. F. (1956), *The Philosophy of History*, trans. J. Sibree, New York: Dover Publications.

Heidegger, Martin (1982), 'The Question Concerning Technology', in *The Question Concerning Technology and Other Essays*, New York: Harper Press, 3–35.

Heidegger, Martin (1991), *Nietzsche*, New York: Harper and Row.

Heidegger, Martin (1996), *Being and Time*, trans. Joan Stambaugh, Albany: State University of New York Press.

Heidegger, Martin (1998), 'Plato's Doctrine of Truth (1931/32, 1940)', in *Pathmarks*, Cambridge: Cambridge University Press, 155–82.

Heidegger, Martin (2008), *Being and Time*, New York: Harper and Row.

Herodotus (1925), *The Persian Wars*, Books VIII–IX, trans. A. D. Godley, Loeb Classical Library, Cambridge, MA: Harvard University Press.

Holy Bible (2007), New Revised Standard Version, Anglicized Edition, Cambridge: Cambridge University Press.

Horsley, Richard A. (1987), *Jesus and the Spiral of Violence: Popular Jewish Resistance in Roman Palestine*, San Francisco: Harper and Row.

Horsley, Richard A. (ed.) (1997), *Paul and Empire: Religion and Power in Roman Imperial Society*, Harrisburg, PA: Trinity Press International.

Horsley, Richard A. (ed.) (2000), *Paul and Politics: Ecclesia, Israel, Imperium, Interpretation*, Harrisburg, PA: Trinity Press International.

Huber, Carlo Ernst (1964), *Anamnesis bei Plato*, Munich: Hueber.

Jaques, Brigitte (1999), 'Corneille et l'amour', in Alain Badiou et al., *De l'amour*, Paris: Flammarion.

Johnston, Adrian (2009), *Badiou, Žižek and Political Transformations: The Cadence of Change*, Evanston: Northwestern University Press.

Josephus, Flavius (1997), *The Jewish War*, Vols II, III, IV, trans. H. St J. Thackeray, Loeb Classical Library, Cambridge, MA: Harvard University Press.

Kafka, Franz (1981), *Stories 1904–1924*, trans. J. A. Underwood, London: Abacus.

Kafka, Franz (2002), *The Great Wall of China and Other Short Works*, trans. and ed. Malcolm Pasley, Harmondsworth: Penguin.

Kant, Immanuel (1978), *Critique of Judgement*, trans. J. C. Meredith, Oxford: Clarendon Press.

Kay, Sarah (2003), *Žižek: A Critical Introduction*, Cambridge: Polity Press.

Kerman, Joseph (1980), 'How We Got into Analysis, and How to Get Out', *Critical Inquiry*, 7: 311–31

Kerman, Joseph (1983), 'A Few Canonic Variations', *Critical Inquiry*, 10: 107–25

Kerman, Joseph (1985), *Musicology*, London: Fontana.

Kermode, Frank (1975), *The Classic*, London: Faber and Faber.

Kermode, Frank (1988), *History and Value*, Oxford: Clarendon Press.

Kivy, Peter (1987), 'Platonism in Music: Another Kind of Defence', *American Philosophical Quarterly*, 24: 245–52.

Korsyn, Kevin (1993), 'Brahms Research and Aesthetic Ideology', *Music Analysis*, 12: 89–103.

Koyré, Alexandre (1968), *Discovering Plato*, New York: Columbia University Press.

Kramer, Lawrence (1995), *Classical Music and Postmodern Knowledge*, Berkeley and Los Angeles: University of California Press.

Lacan, Jacques (1972–73), *Le Séminaire. Livre XX: Encore*. Paris: Seuil.

Lacan, Jacques (1979), *The Four Fundamental Concepts of Psychoanalysis*, ed. J.-A. Miller, trans. A. Sheridan, Harmondsworth: Penguin.

Lacan, Jacques (1990), 'Impromptu at Vicennes', in *Television: A Challenge to the Psychoanalytic Establishment*, ed. J. Copjec, trans. D. Hollier, R. Krauss, A. Michelson and J. Mehlman, New York: W. W. Norton, 117–28.

Lacan, Jacques (1992), *The Ethics of Psychoanalysis, 1959–1960, The Seminar of Jacques Lacan: Book VII*, ed. J.-A. Miller, trans. D. Porter, London: Routledge.

Lacan, Jacques (1998), *Le Séminaire. Livre V: Les formations de l'inconscient*, ed. Jacques-Alain Miller, Paris: Seuil.

Lacan, Jacques (2001), *Le Séminaire. Livre VIII: Le transfert (1960–1961)*, ed. Jacques-Alain Miller, Paris: Seuil.

Lacan, Jacques (2004), *Le Séminaire. Livre X: L'angoisse (1962–1963)*, ed. Jacques-Alain Miller, Paris: Seuil.

Lacan, Jacques (2006a), 'Logical Time and the Assertion of Anticipated Certainty', in *Ecrits*, trans. Bruce Fink, New York and London: W. W. Norton, 161–75.

Lacan, Jacques (2006b), 'The Mirror Stage as Formative of the *I* Function as Revealed in Psychoanalytic Experience', in *Ecrits*, trans. Bruce Fink, New York and London: W. W. Norton, 75–81.

Lacan, Jacques (2006c), 'Le Séminaire. Livre XIII: L'objet de la psychanalyse (1965–1966)', ed. Michel Roussan. Unpublished.

Lacan, Jacques (2006d), *Le Séminaire. Livre XVI: D'un autre à l'autre (1968–1969)*, ed. Jacques-Alain Miller, Paris: Seuil.

Lacan, Jacques (2013a), 'Lacan is for Vincennes', trans. Adrian Price with Russell Grigg, in Marie-Hélène Brousse and Maire Jaanus (eds), *Culture/Clinic 1: 'We're All Mad Here'*, Minneapolis: University of Minnesota Press, 6–7.

Lacan, Jacques (2013b), 'Lecture on the Body', trans. Adrian Price with Russell Grigg, in Marie-Hélène Brousse and Maire Jaanus (eds), *Culture/Clinic 1: 'We're All Mad Here'*, Minneapolis: University of Minnesota Press, 8–11.

Lacoue-Labarthe, Philippe, and Jean-Luc Nancy (1988), *The Literary Absolute: The Theory of Literature in German Romanticism*, trans. Philip Barnard and Cheryl Lester, Albany: State University of New York Press.

Laruelle, Francois (2013), *Anti-Badiou*, trans. Robin Mackay, London: Bloomsbury.

Lavine, Shaughan (1998), *Understanding the Infinite*, Cambridge, MA: Harvard University Press.

Le Brun, Jacques (2002), *Le Pur Amour de Platon à Lacan*, Paris: Seuil.

Le Célibataire: Revue de psychanalyse (2006), 13, special issue, Lacan et Pascal.

Levinson, Jerrold (1990), *Music, Art and Metaphysics*, Ithaca, NY: Cornell University Press.

Losurdo, Domenico (2010), 'The Adventures of the Revolutionary Subject from the 19th to the 21st Century', *brumaria* 22: 87–99, special issue on 'Revolution & Subjectivity'.

Lyotard, Jean-François (1993), *The Inhuman: Reflections on Time*, trans. Geoffrey Bennington and Rachel Bowlby, Cambridge: Polity Press.

MacCannell, Juliet Flower (2005), 'Philosophical Outlaw', in Gabriel Riera (ed.), *Alain Badiou: Philosophy and its Conditions*, Albany: State University of New York Press, 137–84.

MacCannell, Juliet Flower (2009), 'Eternity or Infinity? Badiou's *Point*', *Environment and Planning D: Society and Space*, 27/5: 823–39.

Magee, Bryan (2000), *The Tristan Chord: Wagner and Philosophy*, New York: Metropolitan Books.

Mallarmé, Stéphane (1982), *Selected Poetry and Prose*, ed. Mary Ann Caws, New York: New Directions.

Mao Zedong (1926), 'Analysis of the Classes in Chinese Society', Marx/Engels Internet Archive, http://www.marxists.org/reference/archive/mao/selected-works/volume-1/mswv1_1.htm (accessed 15 July 2013).

McClary, Susan (2001), *The Content of Musical Form*, Berkeley and Los Angeles: University of California Press.

McNulty, Tracy (2005), 'Feminine Love and the Pauline Universal', in Gabriel Riera (ed.), *Alain Badiou. Philosophy and its Conditions*, Albany: State University of New York Press, 185–212.

Miller, J. A. (2004), 'Mathemes', in Ellie Ragland and Dragan Milovanovic (eds), *Lacan: Topologically Speaking*, New York: Other Press, 28–48.

Momigliano, Arnaldo (1971), *Alien Wisdom: The Limits of Hellenization*, Cambridge: Cambridge University Press.

Momigliano, Arnaldo (1994), *Essays on Ancient and Modern Judaism*, ed. Silvia Berti, trans. Maura Masella-Gayley, Chicago and London: University of Chicago Press.

Moore, Lisa Jane, and Mary Kosut (2012), 'Bees, Borders and Bombs: A Social Account of Theorizing Bees', in Ryan Hediger (ed.), *Animals and War: Studies of Europe and North America*, Leiden and Boston: Brill, 29–43.

Narmour, E. (1977), *Beyond Schenkerism: The Need for Alternatives in Music Analysis*, Chicago: University of Chicago Press.

Negri, Antonio, and Michael Hardt (2004), *Multitude: War and Democracy in the Age of Empire*, New York: Penguin Press.

Nietzsche, Friedrich (1968), *Twilight of the Idols* and *The Antichrist* [1895], trans. R. J. Hollingdale, Harmondsworth: Penguin.

Nietzsche, Friedrich (1989), *On the Genealogy of Morals and Ecce Homo*, trans. W. Kaufmann and R. J. Hollingdale, New York: Vintage.

Norris, Christopher (1988), *Paul de Man: Deconstruction and the Critique of Aesthetic Ideology*, New York: Routledge.

Norris, Christopher (2006), *Platonism, Music and the Listener's Share*, London: Continuum.

Norris, Christopher (2009), *Badiou's 'Being and Event': A Reader's Guide*, London: Continuum.

Norris, Christopher (2011), 'Remembering Frank Kermode', *Textual Practice*, 25/1: 1–13.

Parisot, Roger (2008), *La Doctrine du pur amour. Saint François de Sales, Pascal et Mme Guyon*, Paris: Pocket.

Pascal, Blaise (1654), 'Fermat and Pascal on Probability', http://www.socsci.uci.edu/~bskyrms/bio/readings/pascal_fermat.pdf (accessed 28 February 2013)

Pascal, Blaise (1966), *Pensées*, trans. A. J. Krailsheimer, Harmondsworth: Penguin.

Pascal, Blaise (2009), 'The Arithmetic Triangle', trans. R. Pulskamp, http://www.cs.xu.edu/math/Sources/Pascal/Sources/arith_triangle.pdf (accessed 28 February 2013).

Pasolini, Pier Paolo (2007), *Der heilige Paulus*, Marburg: Schueren.

Peirce, Charles S. (1992), *The Essential Peirce: Selected Philosophical Writings*, Vol. 1 *(1867–1893)*, ed. Nathan Houser and Christian Kloesel, Bloomington: Indianapolis University Press.

Penney, James (2006), *The World of Perversion: Psychoanalysis and the Impossible Absolute of Desire*, Albany: State University of New York Press.

Philo of Alexandria (1988), *De somniis II*, Vol. V, trans. F. H. Colson and G. H. Whitaker, Loeb Classical Library, Cambridge, MA: Harvard University Press.

Philo of Alexandria (1954), *De providentia*, Vol. IX, trans. F. H. Colson, Loeb Classical Library, Cambridge, MA: Harvard University Press.

Philo of Alexandria (1962), *The Embassy to Gaius*, Vol. X, trans. F. H. Colson, Loeb Classical Library, Cambridge, MA: Harvard University Press.

Plato (1937), *Republic*, Books 1–5, trans. Paul Shorey, Loeb Classical Library, Cambridge, MA: Harvard University Press.

Thucydides (1921), *History of the Peloponnesian War*, Books V–VI, trans. C. F. Smith, Loeb Classical Library, Cambridge, MA: Harvard University Press.

Tosel, André (2001), 'Devenirs du marxisme 1968–1995: La fin du Marxisme-Léninisme au mille marxismes', in *Dictionnaire Marx Contemporain*, ed. Jacques Bidet and Eustache Kovélakis, Paris: PUF, 57–78.

Tosel, André (2009), 'Cinquante thèses sur la mondialisation capitaliste et sur un communisme possible', http://www.marxau21.fr/index.php?option=com_content&view=article&id=150:a-tosel-cinquante-theses-sur-la-mondialisation-capitaliste-et-sur-un-communisme-possible&catid=49:tosel-andre&Itemid=68 (accessed 15 July 2013).

Treitler, Leo (1989), *Music and the Historical Imagination*, Cambridge, MA: Harvard University Press.

Weizman, Eyal (2006), 'Walking Through Walls: Soldiers as Architects in the Israeli-Palestinian Conflict', *Radical Philosophy* 136 (March/April): 8–22.

Xenophon (1914), *Cyropaedia*, Books I-IV, trans. Walter Miller, Loeb Classical Library, Cambridge, MA: Harvard University Press.

Xenophon (1998), *Anabasis*, trans. Carleton L. Brownson, rev. John Dillery, Loeb Classical Library, Cambridge, MA: Harvard University Press.

Žižek, Slavoj (1989), *The Sublime Object of Ideology*, London: Verso.

Žižek, Slavoj (1990), 'Beyond Discourse-Analysis', in Ernesto Laclau, *New Reflections on the Revolution of our Time*, London: Verso, 249–60.

Žižek, Slavoj (1991), *For They Know Not What They Do: Enjoyment as a Political Factor*, London: Verso.

Žižek, Slavoj (1992), *Enjoy Your Symptom: Jacques Lacan in Hollywood and Out*, London: Routledge.

Žižek, Slavoj (1996), *The Indivisible Remainder: An Essay on Schelling and Related Matters*, London: Verso.

Žižek, Slavoj (1998), 'Psychoanalysis in Post-Marxism: The Case of Alain Badiou', *The South Atlantic Quarterly*, 97/2: 235–61, special issue on 'Psycho-Marxism: Marxism and Psychoanalysis Late in the Twentieth Century', ed. Robert Miklitsch.

Žižek, Slavoj (1999), *The Ticklish Subject: The Absent Centre of Political Ontology*, London and New York: Verso.

Žižek, Slavoj (2003), *The Puppet and the Dwarf: The Perverse Core of Christianity*, Cambridge, MA, and London: MIT Press.

Žižek, Slavoj (2004), 'From Purification to Subtraction: Badiou and the

Real', in P. Hallward (ed.), *Think Again: Alain Badiou and the Future of Philosophy*, London: Continuum, 165–81.

Žižek, Slavoj (2006), *The Parallax View*, Cambridge, MA: MIT Press.

Žižek, Slavoj (2008), *Violence*, London: Profile Books.

Žižek, Slavoj (2009a), *In Defense of Lost Causes*, London: Verso.

Žižek, Slavoj (2009b), 'An Answer to Two Questions', in Adrian Johnston (ed.), *Badiou, Žižek and Political Transformation: The Cadence of Change*, Evanston: Northwestern University Press, 174–230.

Žižek, Slavoj (2009c), *First as Tragedy, Then as Farce*, London: Verso.

Žižek, Slavoj (2010), *Living in the End Times*, London: Verso.

Žižek, Slavoj (2012), *Less than Nothing: Hegel and the Spectre of Dialectical Materialism*, London: Verso.

Index